War Stories

Also by Jeremy Bowen

SIX DAYS: HOW THE 1967 WAR
SHAPED THE MIDDLE EAST

War Stories

JEREMY BOWEN

**SIMON &
SCHUSTER**

London · New York · Sydney · Toronto

A CBS COMPANY

First published in Great Britain by Simon & Schuster UK Ltd in 2006
A CBS COMPANY

3 5 7 9 10 8 6 4 2

Simon & Schuster UK Ltd
Africa House
64–78 Kingsway
London WC2B 6AH

www.simonsays.co.uk

Simon & Schuster Australia
Sydney

A CIP catalogue for this book is available
from the British Library.

Hardback ISBN 10: 0-7432-3094-9
ISBN 13: 978-0-7432-3094-0
Trade paperback ISBN 10: 1-8473-7018-7
ISBN 13: 978-1-8473-7018-1

PICTURE CREDITS
All pictures from the author's private collection except:
Reuters: 11, 27; Keith Tayman: 12, 14, 15, 17, 18, 19; VII Photo: 13

Typeset in Bembo by M Rules
Printed and bound in Great Britain by
CPI Bath

For

Abed Takkoush
Tihomir Tunuković
Rory Peck
Miguel Gil Moreno de Mora
Kurt Schork
Kerem Lawton
Julio Fuentes
Terry Lloyd
Gaby Rado
Kaveh Golestan
Paul Moran
Mazen Dana
Simon Cumbers
Paul Douglas
James Brolan

and all the others

Contents

Contents

Prologue

At seven o'clock on the morning that he was killed Abed Takkoush parked his Mercedes outside the Riviera hotel on the Corniche, the wide road that runs along the seafront in west Beirut. The Riviera has a fine view of the Mediterranean and its clients around the pool have a fine view of each other. Some people call it Silicone Beach because so many inflated breasts, pouting lips and lifted bottoms are on display around the pool, broiling steadily in the Levantine midday sun. But the sunbeds were still being laid out when Abed arrived to pick me up for the drive down to the south. The Israelis were ending an occupation of southern Lebanon that had lasted twenty-two years and Abed and I were going to wave them off. Once the BBC's cameraman Malek Kanaan had arrived, we set off down the coastal highway.

Abed was fifty-three. He had wiry black hair, going a bit grey in places, and lived with his wife and three sons in an apartment in Hamra in the centre of Beirut. He had dark, watchful eyes that could scowl or smile. Abed laughed a lot, and liked to boast about his driving. He said one of his other clients called him

ix

Schumacher. Yes, just like Michael Schumacher, he'd say, as he accelerated into a gap in the traffic, except Schumacher drives on empty roads. Let him try it in Lebanon! Other times Abed would drive silently, holding a cigarette with his yellow fingers, brooding. His sister was blown to pieces by a shell that exploded in a car park in west Beirut, during the so-called 'war of liberation' that the Christian politician and general, Michel Aoun, launched against the Syrians in 1989. They only found about half of her.

Abed's business card said he was a driver and producer. That meant he was the quintessential local fixer, the kind of person that foreign correspondents around the world need more than anyone else. He knew everyone, from the bearded and serious men at the offices of the Islamic resistance, Hezbollah, in the southern suburbs of the city, to the head waiters at the best fish restaurants. He was a taxi driver when the civil war started in 1975. The American television network NBC hired him, and because they shared a bureau with the BBC he started working with the British too, and never looked back. He used to carry a sheaf of old press identity cards in the glove box of his car, like campaign medals. In the photo on his first NBC card, he looked very young: not bad-looking, innocent about war. But he learned very fast, as everyone in Beirut had to do at that time, and his colleagues learned to trust him.

Malek, the cameraman, was a teenager when the Lebanese civil war started. He turned to television news after spending time as a gunman in one of the militias. He chose the Popular Front for the Liberation of Palestine, a strange decision for a Lebanese Shia Muslim. 'But it was the international section, Jeremy. The East German girls were beautiful . . .' Later on, his revolutionary credentials earned him a scholarship to study in East Berlin, where his lack of ideological purity got him into trouble with the authorities. And me, I was forty years old, in my fifth year as the BBC's Middle East Correspondent, and my twelfth war.

Abed loved action. We all did. On the day that he was going to die, we were expecting a small taste, though nothing too extreme. The plan was to follow the Israelis at a safe distance as they moved back towards their border wire. The day before, when it was becoming clear that the Israelis were pulling out a couple of months ahead of schedule, I had been down to the edge of what they called the security zone, actually a slab along the border of occupied Lebanese territory, with Malek and another driver called Mohammed Itani, who was Abed's nephew. The checkpoints were deserted, so we pushed a few hundred yards into what had been occupied territory only hours earlier, until someone fired at us – either the Israelis or their Lebanese mercenary force, the South Lebanon Army, who did a lot of Israel's dirty work in the south. The bullets hissed over our heads. They were probably warning shots, though you never know, and I felt only pleasure and excitement – even a sort of homecoming – that I was hearing bullets again and doing the sort of story that had given me some of the best moments of my life.

Back in Beirut, Abed, like everyone in Lebanon (except the turncoats in the SLA), was getting more and more excited that the Israelis were getting out and distraught that he had missed the beginning of it. So he pulled rank on Mohammed, ordering him to go to Tyre in the south to set up our base with my partner Julia Williams, who was running the BBC's Middle East operations, while he went with Malek and me to see the Israelis go. Abed, Malek and I thought we were the top news team in Lebanon that day. We probably were, but by the end of the day it didn't make any difference.

On the way south Abed steered with one hand while he fiddled with the car radio, listening to as many news bulletins as he could, talking loudly, enjoying every moment, telling his favourite stories about the Israeli invasion of 1982. Just south of Sidon, a 6,000-year-old town that is now a port full of hot, concrete streets, the road runs parallel to a long beach. It should be beautiful, but it is ruined by the road and the rubbish that has been dumped on it.

Abed hooted with laughter as he remembered the time in 1996 when we had raced along this beach road while it was being bombarded by an Israeli gunboat. ('Remember? We were under the shelling, under it!') We had stopped on a promontory just above the bay, watching the gunboat firing at every car going south. Cars going north were left alone, because the Israelis were trying to empty south Lebanon of as many civilians as possible in order to punish them for supporting Hezbollah and to put pressure on the government in Beirut. It also enabled Israel to declare that everyone moving south of Tyre, the last coastal town before the occupation zone, was potentially hostile and could therefore be destroyed.

Going down the road was dangerous, but not going down the road meant that we would not have had a story that day, and that was inconceivable. So we had put on our flak jackets, got back into the car and Abed had stepped on the accelerator. For the couple of minutes it took it was tense and silent in the ancient green Mercedes, which suddenly felt very slow. The springs and shock absorbers groaned and creaked as we bumped over the rubble on the road. The gunship had time to fire a couple of rounds as we trundled along the waterfront. We could see the flash from where the gun was mounted on the ship and then had a couple of seconds to wait before it exploded. The crash of the shell was the sound we needed, because it meant that it had missed us. When we hit the other end of the beach where the road went behind some buildings and we weren't dead, the tension broke into a million pieces when Abed raised a finger at the gunship and yelled, 'Fuck you, Shlomo!' Moments like that, of chasing stories, getting scared and then getting away with it, made the days sharp and bright. I could not find that feeling outside the war, any war, which was a small part of the reason why I kept going back. While Abed still had a few hours left to live, just talking about the day the Israelis didn't kill us put our little team in the right mood.

The Israelis were leaving because Hezbollah had made it impossible for them to continue their occupation of the south. Israel said it was occupying Lebanese land along the border to protect its northern towns. Originally it went into Lebanon to go after Palestinian fighters, who were finally cleared out by a full-scale invasion and attack on Beirut in 1982. After that Israel pulled back to the south and started a long occupation, which was the making of Hezbollah. It turned into a much stronger enemy than the Palestinians had ever been – formidable, well organised, with the backing of Syria and Iran. It was classic guerrilla warfare. Hezbollah would never have been able to beat Israel in a stand-up-and-knock-down fight. But once they realised there were better ways of fighting than yelling Islamic slogans and mounting frontal assaults, they matured into effective soldiers and killed enough Israelis to make the occupation deeply unpopular back home. The Israelis who couldn't take any more deaths, and were sick of sons following fathers into their concrete fortresses in south Lebanon, decided to pull out and were supposed to be going some time in the late summer. But to try to stop Hezbollah planning something special to see them off, they had brought the date forward by a couple of months, and now, on 23 May, they were getting out fast.

Julia and I were already in Beirut, planning how we would cover the Israeli withdrawal, when it started. It was the only piece of luck on that trip, a couple of days' start on the competition, but it meant we didn't have flak jackets, helmets or first-aid kits. I wasn't bothered – someone else was going to bring them in from Jerusalem – because I was not planning to get too close to the Israelis as they retreated. I was more interested in the thousands of Lebanese who were flooding back into the villages and hills of the south that had been closed to them for a generation.

By 2000 Abed had replaced the old green Merc with a newer one, so on the morning of the 23rd we drove fast down the coastal highway, past Sidon and Tyre and into the villages beyond. The only thing bothering me was that the sun was strong and I had lost the black cap, stained with sweat, that I had been wearing on hot days for the best part of ten years. Judging by the reports on Abed's car radio, the occupation was crumbling much faster than anyone had expected. It looked pretty clear that Israel had told its soldiers to cut their losses and to get out as soon as they could. While they retreated, Israel was relying on the South Lebanon Army to hold the line behind them. But as the SLA realised that their employers and protectors were leaving, they began to panic and melt away, concentrating on getting themselves and their families and their cars through the gate in the border wire before the last Israeli locked it. Without the SLA covering their rear, Israeli troops were dangerously exposed. The news kept coming out of the radio that more and more of the south was 'liberated' and Abed chuckled and drove faster and told more jokes. We crossed into Israel's 'security zone' that Hezbollah had made anything but secure, and poked about a base that had been abandoned the previous night. Israeli newspapers were scattered on the floor, mixed up with empty bottles of juice with labels in Hebrew, and pots of hummus, the chickpea and tahina paste that the Arabs and the Jews both claim they invented. They are so far apart that they can't even agree who made hummus first.

Prologue

Hezbollah fighters were everywhere. They were anything but a rag-tag army. As usual they looked very professional, wearing good quality, matching camouflage fatigues, proper boots and webbing belts that were hung with grenades and spare magazines. Their insurgency had defeated an occupation that for the fighters' whole lives had been Israel's main strategy for the defence of its northern border. They believed they had just inflicted Israel's worst ever defeat, and the people around them agreed. Boys were shinning up lamp-posts and telegraph poles, fixing on yellow Hezbollah flags. Women screamed and ululated and bombarded their heroes in uniform and anyone else who was passing with rice. Handfuls of it burst over the windscreen of Abed's Mercedes like hail and tinkled down over the bonnet. Lines of cars were coming in from Beirut and the north and they had the same treatment. It was liberation day for south Lebanon, and it was intoxicating for citizens who had suffered so much.

Abed smiled on the happy people and the stern fighters like a proud father. He had seen the beginning of the Israeli occupation and now he was seeing the end of it. He felt good, and we were getting a great story. I was relaxed, imagining our journalistic rivals still scrambling to get to Lebanon, while we were already on the job. We did all the right things, automatically, the way we had always worked. At each village we stopped to ask when they had last seen the Israelis and the SLA, and whether the road ahead was clear. Abed still had the car radio on, for the local news. Even though it was hot, we kept the windows open and the air conditioning off, so we could hear the sound of firing, or explosions. Then I decided to stop to do a piece to camera – a 'standupper' – at a place which overlooked the border wire and an Israeli kibbutz on the other side. It was quiet and it seemed peaceful. A burnt-out car blocked the road, but its ashes were cold and we assumed it had been destroyed the day before.

It was not like Abed to stay in the car when we were filming. He would usually get out to scout around, finding people to interview, checking out where the guns were, getting a feel for what was happening, working out what was safe and what was not. And he always said that parked cars were targets. But this time he stayed in his seat to call Mohammed, the eldest of his three sons, on his mobile phone. Journalists were arriving in Beirut, and they needed cars and drivers. Abed's extended family all worked in the news business, driving and guiding journalists, so there was money to be made. Malek and I left him talking, took the equipment from the boot and went off to get a few shots of the kibbutz on the other side of the wire. It looked down on us as we walked along the road. I waved both my arms in the air to show we were friendly. I felt a little foolish, because it seemed safe. I wondered if any of my friends from Jerusalem were there, and how weird it was that if I could get over the wire and into the kibbutz, not much more than half a mile away, I could drive home to Jerusalem in less than three hours. But since I couldn't cross the wire, the only way home would be to drive to Beirut, take a plane to Jordan, another car to the Allenby Bridge over the River Jordan to the West Bank, switch passports from the one with Arab stamps to the one with my Israeli resident's visa, deal with their security and then face another hour or so in a taxi back to Jerusalem. You could do it in a very long day.

As we walked down the road I was not worried because we were being so open. I was convinced that they were seeing us clearly and that it was obvious that we were unarmed newsmen. I was wearing a pink shirt and navy blue trousers, not exactly front-line clothes but when I packed I thought I was going to Beirut to see a few people, try out some restaurants and swim in the pool at the Riviera hotel. I didn't think that I would be covering a war. I was sure that we were in someone's camera lens. I had no idea we were in the sights of an Israeli tank, and that its crew were loading a shell.

Malek put the camera on the tripod as I tried to think of some words for a piece to camera. I spun round when I heard the explosion, a terrible thunderous crack. The grass on the bank that separated us from Abed's car was on fire. Automatically, I checked to see if Malek was filming. I hoped he had switched on in time to get the bang. It felt like a close call but for the first few fractions of a second I was pleased, because it meant we had some 'bang-bang', which helps make a piece from a war zone work. I felt a snatch of irritation that I wasn't doing my piece to camera when the explosion happened, because I probably would have kept going and it would have looked good. But then, beyond the burning grass, I saw that the Mercedes was blazing, pouring black smoke into the sky. Another second later, Abed somehow pushed himself through the window. His clothes were on fire. His body writhed as he forced his way out and fell head-first on to the road, where he was hidden by the slope of the hill.

Malek's camera was turning over, and I was dimly aware that I was in his shot. I turned away from the fire. I was reeling, trying to work out what had happened, talking, mainly to myself.

'It's Abed, he must be dead, he must be dead. The fuckers.'

I assumed it was a tank shell. Even though I had seen him twisting and kicking to get through the window I did not see how he could have survived. I wanted to run up to him. He was only about a hundred yards away and he was my friend. But I was scared of being killed. I remembered the instructor on a battlefield first-aid course I had taken with the British army. He kept saying that the first rule of first aid in combat was to avoid becoming a casualty. I told Malek we had to get up to him.

'No, Jeremy, don't do it. Abed is dead. Nobody could have survived that. Maybe he lived long enough to push himself out of the car. But he's dead now. If you go up there, the Israelis will kill you too.'

That was what I thought too, and I was relieved to hear it from someone else. I felt like a coward. I was scared of dying and I was scared of what I would find if I was brave or foolish enough to go up there, and I was neither. Many times I had seen corpses that had been burned and I did not want to see my friend turned into a piece of charred meat. We watched the flames around Abed's car fading away. After about ten minutes there had been no more shooting, so I walked out from behind the building where we had been sheltering and went a few yards up the road towards the wreck.

A heavy machine-gun opened up. Bullets that have just missed you sound like mad hissing insects. I heard them going past my head. I ran back behind the building, sure that the Israelis who killed Abed wanted to kill us too. Later, when I was back home in Jerusalem, Sam Kiley of *The Times*, who had been in the kibbutz at the moment that the tank fired, told me his driver had overheard a soldier saying that the tank had got one of the 'terrorists' but two had escaped. Another soldier told him not to worry, because the tank crew would get the other two with its machine-gun. When they opened up on us, I knew we had been right to stay put. But I still felt like a coward.

Malek and I sat in silence for most of the time we were trapped there, unable to get up to Abed's body and unable to retreat out of harm's way. I was thinking of Abed and his family. I was asking myself what I would say to his wife. And to his kids, his three teenage sons. What was I going to say to them? Every journalist who goes to war soon learns the fundamental equation that lies at the centre of the job. For us to have a good day, someone else has to have a bad day, or the last day of their lives. To get the story, we had to be near them, with the camera rolling, at their worst or last moments, when the people they loved were killed, when their lives were so smashed by war that they wished they had died too. It makes journalists sound like vultures but it is the only way to do it, the only way to show what war does to people. Moving in on someone when they are that vulnerable is very intrusive. They can be suggestible and easy to manipulate, especially if you show a little human sympathy. I believed that I always treated people decently, with dignity. But their privacy was the last thing I thought about, because with strong pictures of misery and suffering and killing, which after all are what war is all about, I could tell the world what was happening. For years, I had believed strongly that what we did was worthwhile, and necessary, and that I was a witness, not a ghoul. I would have preferred misery and killing not to happen. But since it was going on whether we were there or not, I wanted to be the one who showed it to the people back home. Abed, Malek and I made careers of reporting on other people's last days, or worst days. Now it was our turn: his last, our worst.

I thought of another day on a road in south Lebanon in the mid-1990s. We were following a UN convoy that was trying to get to some people who had been displaced by a fierce Israeli offensive. Suddenly, as the convoy was turning because rubble blocked the road, Israeli shells started exploding all around us. Some shells whooshed over our heads. Others exploded yards away and hot shrapnel fizzed in the air. I pulled off my helmet to do a piece to camera. It was not considered cool to appear on camera in a helmet, which was crazy with so much shrapnel spitting around. After I managed to get my words out, the crew I was working with leaped into a UN armoured personnel carrier and so did I. With the shells coming down I followed everyone else and piled into the back of it. Straight away, I knew it was the wrong thing to do. I didn't know what had happened to Abed.

I struggled to get out to find him but my legs were trapped under a couple of heavy cameramen who had come in after me. Someone was pulling the armoured doors closed and suddenly the APC was racing away. I felt sick with worry and shame. When the APC stopped in the nearest UN base a couple of miles away, I saw Abed immediately. He had been driving the green Merc in the lee of the armoured personnel carrier, using it to shield him from the shells. He sauntered over.

'What did you do, why did you get into the APC? You know I would never leave a crew. Don't you trust me?'

No, Abed, it wasn't that, I just panicked . . . I kept stammering apologies for about two days until he told me to shut up.

I kept thinking about his grin and his jokes as we watched his car burn. His body was just beyond the ridge and we could not see where it lay. I could not shake the thought that once again I had abandoned him. After an hour or so an ambulance from the Lebanese Civil Defence service arrived. They decided not to go up to the smouldering wreckage of the car either, in case the Israelis wanted to kill them too.

A few months later someone who knows these things told me how the overpressure created by the blast of a shell breaks open the internal organs of a human being. Abed would have lost consciousness and died almost immediately. But what if Abed lived for longer than a few minutes? I don't know, and that's the point. I shouted his name but he didn't answer. Maybe he was hoping that we would come to rescue him. If life was like a film I would have run up to him, bullets zinging off the gravel around me. I could have got to him and comforted him, and even if I had not saved his life he would not have had to die alone. But I decided I could not save him and that I had to save myself. The ending was not happy. Life is not a film.

1
Crazy

In Sarajevo, when the war was going on as if it was never going to stop, a cameraman called Robbie Wright cut some pictures to music. It was a pop video like the ones on MTV, only instead of being fantasy it was real. In lots of ways Robbie's video said more about the war and about the city than I had ever managed with words. He chose a song called 'Crazy', by Seal, and cut to it the best pictures he could find in the piles of tapes in his office that had come back from the mayhem and madness in the city. The images were what the rest of us in the Sarajevo news asylum called 'strong', because they showed people in a nightmare – babies covered in blood, a man walking along a winter street holding his grandson's hand tight, not breaking step and hardly looking as they pass a body in a pool of goo.

They were pictures of the war that was eating up a country and eating us up too; hateful pictures, but pictures I loved because I could not work without them. They contained the truth about a city that I could not do without. Not all Seal's lyrics were right for Sarajevo, but some were perfect. The chorus was the best part, about not surviving unless you get a little bit crazy. When I watch Robbie's cut even now, I can smell the city as it was during the war, and remember the kind of person I was back then. There is a picture of people sprinting across a road, taken from low down, which means that whoever shot it was running behind them, maybe ducking a bit and holding his camera so it was near the dust that they were kicking up. I can feel their fear that a sniper might want to shoot them in the head, and the relief of getting to the other side and back under cover. When I see the video I can still smell the damp ash in the charred buildings, and the fresh blood of the wounded, the wet earth in the cemeteries, and the bodies that rotted where they died. And there were people who looked like the war had made them crazy, old men yelling at the foreigners who were in the city and doing nothing to rescue them, pinched faces, doctors in an emergency room full of casualties with no water, children playing with home-made toy grenade-launchers, a baby grinning and gurgling with a stump for a leg. And there was a man standing on his window sill to throw a tiny beaker of water at the fire in the flat next door, which was more or less what the leaders of the big countries were doing to stop the war. Dr David Owen, a British foreign secretary in the 1970s, pops up, smiling like a wolf. He was the man brought in by the West to make a deal, early on, to end the fighting. This is what he is saying: 'Don't, don't, don't live under this dream that the West is going to come in to sort this problem out . . . Don't dream dreams . . .' In the end they changed their minds, and the West did come in to sort the problem out, but only after two hundred thousand people were dead. Sometimes I felt as if I had seen most of the bodies.

I am not crazy. But for a while I was, a little. I was crazy about news, and crazy for finding it in wars. I risked my life often, and that was crazy too, though I believed it was logical and unavoidable if I was going to cover wars properly. Many people have asked me why journalists bet their lives by going to wars. The answer is complicated, and different people have their own reasons, but this book is an attempt to explain mine, and trying to do so is not easy. I felt stretched, and full, in a war. For me it was the highest form of journalism. I hated the killing, but if it was going to happen I wanted it to be close to me and my television camera. In the end, after twelve wars, I realised that you cannot spend your time not just close to destruction but looking for it every day, and come out unscathed. And that makes you crazy too. The really mad thing is that I miss the thought of driving down a road towards the sound of gunfire and a horizon full of smoke, even though wars killed my friends and could easily have killed me. War reporting gave me some of my best moments, helped me build a career, made me a better journalist and most of all felt worthwhile. I was trying to shine a torch at the darkest places in the world; I thought it was a job that had to be done, and that I could do it better than anyone.

I went into journalism towards the end of the most violent century in human history, and the new one is already going bad. If I wanted to do the big stories, it was impossible not to go to wars, and compulsory to understand them. Some wars are necessary, vital, unavoidable. But they are all seducers. They must be, or humans would not make war, dread war, enjoy it, even love it in the way that they do. It can be sickening, exciting, affirming and terrifying. It brings out the best in people, and the worst, and it can do it all in a single day.

I know war is a seducer because it seduced me. This is the story of a love affair that went wrong. It still has its moments, but it will never be what it was when it started. It wasn't about a woman. I was in love with a job, passionate about reporting wars. It sounds a little sad, and in a way it was, though it was also compelling, addictive and fun, and it never felt like work. I had colleagues who became friends who had the same obsession. I know that the ones who were killed felt about the job the way that I did, and went about it the same way, and on their last mornings never dreamed that they would not live to file what they found out that day, and have dinner, and a drink, and call home.

I always wanted to be a journalist. And even before I knew properly what they did, I wanted to be a foreign correspondent. I thought I would get to travel and have an exciting life. I wasn't wrong.

My father, Gareth, is a journalist. I say 'is' not 'was', even though he is retired now, because being a journalist is as much an attitude of mind as a way of earning a living. He met my mother, Jennifer, who is a photographer, at the office Christmas party when she worked for the *Merthyr Express* and he was on the *South Wales Echo*. When I came along I used to go sometimes to Thomson House, the offices of the *Echo* and the *Western Mail*, across the road from the Arms Park in Cardiff. Just inside the side door of the building a man sat behind a counter and bent down to say hello, and guarded the way to the offices with typewriters and messy desks and interesting pots of paste where my father worked, and to the mysterious place at the other end of the building where machines roared every day to make the paper. Journalism was a noisy trade. Every week at home at night I fell asleep to the sound of my father hammering away downstairs at a manual typewriter in the dining room, finishing his column for the next day's paper. Some Saturdays my mother would go to work at Cardiff Arms Park, where she would be on the touch-line taking photographs of the rugby internationals. I tried to see if I could spot her sheepskin coat on our black and white television. When she was photographing my sporting heroes, like John Toshack and Gareth Edwards, she took me along, and I was so full of awe that I could not speak. Big bundles of newspapers – all the national titles and the Welsh ones – were delivered to our house tied up with hairy string, and the radio news was always on. I had a happy childhood, with two brothers, Nicholas and Matthew, and two sisters, Brigid and Charlotte, who came along later.

In the mid-1960s my father left newspapers to join the BBC. One day in 1966 he went to Aberfan, a village on the way to my great-aunt and uncle's house in Merthyr Tydfil. In those days almost every village in the valleys had a colliery. We used to see the wheels in the winding gear turning when we drove up to Merthyr from Cardiff. He seemed to be away a long time but it was probably only a couple of nights. When he came back his trousers were encrusted with the slurry that had slipped down from the coal tip that hung over Aberfan and swallowed part of the village and the local school and killed 116 children. Twenty-eight adults also died. My father slept when he got home, even though it was the middle of the day, and then went back to work. A long time afterwards I heard his reports for radio, which are in the BBC Sound Archives, on big long-playing records. They are still very powerful. He stood on the slurry that he called 'a jagged unexpected hill, lit by portable floodlights and lights from miners wearing helmets . . . men standing up to their knees in black water . . . They don't know why they're digging. They only know that they've got to dig . . . All over Wales men have been finishing work and coming straight down to Aberfan.' After that, when we drove to Merthyr, we could see a long line of white gravestones in the cemetery across the other side of the valley.

In 1970, when I was ten, a teacher asked the boys in my class what they wanted to be. Everyone else said footballer, soldier or astronaut (in those days the Americans were flying to the Moon).

I said foreign correspondent. I didn't really know what it meant. My mother, who had her doubts about life in the BBC because she saw that for most people it was a vocation not a job, told me not to be a journalist but if I really had to be one, to become a foreign correspondent. I had a vision of a fan turning in the ceiling of a hot, sweaty room in the east as I sat in a rattan chair. Maybe the picture came from *Point of Departure*, the book that James Cameron, who was one of the star reporters of the 1950s and '60s, wrote about his life, which I was trying to read. I was never very popular with the other boys in that class. Being good at football was the key to that, and I was useless. My strange declaration, about a job they'd never heard of, did not improve things.

At university in London I was not interested in student journalism. The student paper at UCL was too much like a club, and I was never much of a joiner. I always felt like an outsider, which I later discovered was the best way for a journalist to be. And, perhaps because I had seen the real thing when I was growing up, student journalism looked like play-acting, a game where people pretended to be editors, or reporters, or subs. I regretted being so stand-offish in the waiting room of the BBC appointments building in Portland Place one day early in 1983, when I was about to be interviewed for a place on one of the Corporation's graduate training schemes. Everyone else had a thick scrapbook of cuttings, and worst of all they all seemed to know each other. A few years later, when I had my first job as a reporter, one of the men who had been on the 'board', as job interviews are known in the BBC, told me that they did not expect me to get through. They had only given me an interview because they knew my father, who by then was editor of news at Radio Wales in Cardiff. But even though I had no cuttings to show them, I spoke well and I got the job. I had absorbed journalism and the BBC and its values around the family dining table, by untying the hairy string around the bundles of papers and reading them, because the programme my father edited, *Good Morning Wales*, was on the radio when we were having breakfast, and because of lunchtimes home from school listening to William Hardcastle on *The World at One*. Without realising it, my whole life was propelling me through the doors of Broadcasting House.

When I did the interview I was a student in Italy, doing the first year of a master's degree in international affairs at the Bologna Center of Johns Hopkins University School of Advanced International Studies, the best place in its field in the United States. I still had another year to do at its main campus in Washington DC, and there was just about time to finish the course before my job at the BBC started. I arrived in the United States at Newark airport in New Jersey, and took a bus to the Port Authority terminal in New York City. It was about six o'clock on an August afternoon and I had never been to America before. I came through the wide doors of the bus terminal on to the corner of Eighth Avenue and 42nd Street and the hot, heavy air slapped me in the face – even the exhaust fumes smelled different – and there were police sirens, and yellow cabs, like an episode of *Kojak*. I put my bag down on the pavement and stood and stared. I must have looked like the boy from the sticks, tasty bait for the creatures that were swimming down from Times Square, which in 1983 was untamed by zero-tolerance policing. A hooker with bright lipstick and not many clothes came up and ground her hip into me. 'How about it, big boy?' I stammered something, picked up my bag and hurried off to find my hotel, which was just down the street.

Large parts of Washington DC were not gentrified either. The city is cut into quadrants, and North-West was where the rich white people lived. I had never been to a city that was so divided by race. More than 60 per cent of the population were black, but you would not have known it in the rich parts of North-West.

Most of the students lived near Dupont Circle, which in those days was a few blocks away from easy streets to get mugged. The word among the students was that if you crossed 14th Street the chances of ending up with a gun in your mouth on your way to school went way up. I lived for free, far away from all that, in one of the poshest houses in Georgetown, in return for raking the leaves and serving drinks at parties a couple of times a month. I also had to take a poodle for a walk every morning until it crapped. The owner was the wealthy former wife of a top Washington lawyer, rich in her own right, I wasn't sure how. We disliked each other almost from the beginning, but she said I could stay because she was away a lot and she needed someone to be in the house. Pompously, she insisted on showing me how to mix 'a proper dry Martini'. I made them even drier by eliminating the Vermouth completely. Once, one of her friends, a woman whose face was so lifted it was taut, fell off her chair. I must have been an ungrateful little sod. The alcoholic cook, an elderly white lady from Virginia, was the other inhabitant of her vast house. She told me off when I went to put a dirty plate in the dishwasher, took it away from me and stuck it under a tap. Later I found out the dishwasher was where she kept her favourite tipple, a quart of domestic vodka. On my last day there I went into the kitchen, which was in the basement, to find her slumped comatose over the table. I felt sorry for her, so I pulled her, still on her chair, out of the kitchen and into the lift, which was an ornate cast-iron cage that Roosevelt had probably used. I reached inside, pushed the button and watched the cage disappear up into the house.

I asked the people at the BBC bureau in Washington if they wanted any help, and wisely they said no. But on the strength of my job offer from the BBC in London, and through a colleague of my father's, I was taken on as an unpaid intern across the road at National Public Radio, the nearest thing America had to Radio 4, on the weekend edition of their most popular programme, *All Things Considered*. They taught me how to edit recording tape with a razor blade, marking the point where to cut with a wax pencil, making sure that the right breaths were left in, taking out the coughs and splutters and fluffs. They let me write some intros for the tapes, which needed a lot of rewriting before they could be read out on the programme, and they even let me do some broadcasting. The first story I had on the air was about Thanksgiving, the holiday Americans have on the fourth Thursday of November, which I had kept asking about because I was new to the United States. They showed me how to use a tape recorder and sent me out with a list of questions about the Thanksgiving story, mainly about John Smith and Pocahontas, whose romance was supposed to have been an important part of it. I trawled the fern bars around 20th and M streets and spliced together the replies of people I accosted under the tiffany lamps and ficus trees. It was supposed to be a funny limey take on a great American festival. They helped me record it, and every time I sit in front of a microphone now, I remember how the first time I had been in a studio an American voice in my ear told me to sit straight, not to slouch, with both feet planted firmly on the floor, so that I could breathe and read clearly.

But I was not close to being a journalist, pretty useless, thinking and acting like a student, more interested in going out than working. On the morning of Sunday 23 October 1983 I woke up late, very late, because I had been at a party the night before. I was due at NPR, but thought I would sleep in instead until my head stopped hurting. I didn't bother to ring the office. Later, when I surfaced, I turned on the TV and saw that a building housing US Marines in Beirut had been blown up by a suicide bomber, killing 241 servicemen. I had no idea that this big news story might have made them busier than usual, and that it was a day when they would not have had to find things for me to do. I only dimly realised my mistake when I strolled in cheerfully, feeling much better, after lunch, to a row of dirty looks from producers who had been working without a break for hours.

My first proper attempt at reporting was a story for the *Western Mail* in Cardiff about Gary, a declining steel town in Indiana. Gary was dirty and desolate, freezing cold and covered in grey snow. Most of the shops on the main street were shuttered. In one that was open a man complained about the amount of crime and pulled up his shirt to show off the huge handgun he had stuck in the waistband of his trousers. It was chipped and the butt was covered with rubber bands. It gave me the start of my piece and it was the first lesson in the way that violence can make news stories more sexy. When I flew back to Britain to start work at the BBC my father met me at the airport and had the paper in the car to show me.

On 24 April 1984, my first day at the BBC, I caught the number 12 bus from Camberwell to Oxford Circus and walked along Upper Regent Street towards Portland Place and Broadcasting House. The BBC's headquarters had no sign then to indicate to the people who paid for it what it was. It just stood there, anonymously, the prow of a streamlined art deco liner moored next to All Soul's Church. If you didn't know what it was, you weren't supposed to be there, like the clubs in St James's, or (in those days) the government ministries in Whitehall. The British establishment didn't bother with name plates.

I pushed through the heavy bronze doors, reported to the reception desk and was ushered past the uniformed commissionaires and their medal ribbons, up some stone stairs to a room that followed the curve of the building which had long desks, manual typewriters, reel-to-reel tape players and seven other 'news trainees'. We were given two forms to sign. One was an elegantly printed green document that was our formal engagement with the BBC. It included the start date to our careers and, alarmingly, the end as well. My retirement day was neatly typed in, 5 February 2020, the day before my sixtieth birthday. Since I was only just twenty-four, it seemed so far off that they might as well have added that by then the BBC would have a bureau on the Moon and I would be its chief.

The other form laid out on a long table to sign was the Official Secrets Act. I hesitated for about half a second and then put my name to it. What the hell, I thought, I had signed it a few Christmases earlier when I worked at the Post Office, so what's the difference now? Everyone else was signing too, making a few jokes about it. We must have been a conformist bunch, all ambitious, focused on the careers that were going to emerge from our places on one of the BBC's elite training courses. We were the chosen few. Thousands had applied and eight of us had been selected. No one was going to make a scene about signing the Official Secrets Act, though even to my innocent mind it was a strange thing for journalists to do. I didn't take it seriously; I thought it was just one of those things that you would ignore if you had to. It must have been, because no one ever mentioned it again. In 1984, a representative of MI5 still had an office in Broadcasting House. Maybe as trainees who were seen as the future of the BBC, we had been vetted too; at the time the security service was checking thousands of BBC employees. I suspect it was done in as casual a way as the Official Secrets Act was pushed under our noses to sign. We were given a run-down of what we would be doing for the next two years, issued with an empty contacts book and, business transacted, a BBC hospitality trolley loaded with twiglets and bottles of wine was wheeled in, clinking. When it had been used up, we went to the pub.

I can't remember exactly when or how it happened, but through some sort of osmosis it started to become clear, to me at least, that one way to get on as reporter was to do dangerous stories. Correspondents would be brought in to see the trainees occasionally, and the bosses treated the ones who had come from somewhere dangerous with more respect. One of them was Gerald Butt, who did not seem much older than we were, and who was based in Beirut, which was a big story that summer. They played us tapes of his reports, which often had gunfire going on in the background. We joked before he arrived that he would be twitching at sudden noises, throwing himself under the desk if a car backfired outside in Portland Place. But he was calm and friendly and talked about living in Beirut when a war was going on around him. He had a suntan and a pale suit, and his life sounded exciting and glamorous.

On the day I joined the BBC a siege was going on in central London. The Libyan People's Bureau (Colonel Ghaddafi's revolutionary name for his embassy) was surrounded by armed police and soldiers. The week before a policewoman, Yvonne Fletcher, had been killed by shots fired from inside the building. Everyone was expecting the SAS to burst into it to end the siege, as they had done four years earlier at the Iranian Embassy, and our instructor, Alan Perry, twitched and darted towards the window every time he heard a police siren passing. I liked Alan, but I thought his compulsion to follow the story was funny. I still didn't get it. But I could sense that stories about life and death engaged journalists like no others.

After six weeks learning some of the basics, like news writing and law, we made a programme every morning, first radio and then, after a few months, television, in proper studios with the same studio managers who did the *Today* programme and the cameramen who did the main evening news. Most afternoons more grown-up journalists came to talk to us. Another one who made a big impression was Norman Rees. He was not from the

BBC, but from Independent Television News, ITN, which we learned later on to call 'the opposition'. Norman seemed slightly surprised to have been let into the building. He was gritty about coming first: 'I'd crawl over broken glass to beat the BBC,' he intoned with relish. He had been ITN's Washington correspondent, and was back in London in some executive job. He was dressed smartly, enthusiastic and dynamic in a way that many of our BBC managers were not. I was impressed. Not one BBC boss had talked about beating ITN. He invited me later on to the ITN offices in Wells Street, where he gave me a big whisky out of his cocktail cabinet.

The other thing that was never mentioned in the almost two years I spent as a BBC trainee was money. The tools we needed to do the job, like studios, or camera crews, were provided by the BBC and were available as long as you called the right number or filled in the right form. Money only came up in the session when the affable TV instructor, Peter Dorling, showed us how to do our expenses. He said a line called 'recip. hosp.' should always go in. Apparently it meant reciprocal hospitality and as long as it was not more than a couple of quid we would be allowed to claim. There were other allowances too, newspapers, even cinema tickets (supposedly so we could learn about the latest visual techniques), though the process of extracting the money was so complicated I never bothered. But we were all nervous and respectful about spending the BBC's money. After we finished work one afternoon I was making a few personal phone calls, conscious that some of them were long distance, back home to Cardiff. The office secretary came up to me making a 'T' sign with her fingers. I thought she was calling time on my personal calls, blushed and got off the phone. She was just offering to go and get a cup of tea.

After about nine months, we were trusted enough to be allowed out to work in newsrooms. I was sent to the regional television news programme in Belfast, *Inside Ulster*. Belfast in January 1985 was damp and smoky and turned in on itself. I rented a chilly room in a terraced house with some young people from BBC Belfast. Every morning I was woken by the sound of a shovel scraping over concrete as one of my housemates filled the coal bucket. I hope I offered to help. I was a little crass at times. The father of one of my housemates was an RUC reservist. I told her I couldn't understand why he would do such a dangerous job. She looked embarrassed and did not try to explain. Belfast was a prized assignment, because they would let us trainees do TV reporting. We all had a fantasy that we would somehow find ourselves doing the lead story on the evening news from the scene of some appalling atrocity.

The man who produced the programme most nights took the role of old-school news editor very seriously. He gave one of the female producers there such a hard time that she often had to leave the newsroom to cry, and for the first month or so gave me nothing to do except collect the names for the 'Astons', the captions named after the machine that generated them, that popped up on the screen for interviewees. David Shukman, who had been there as a trainee exactly a year earlier and done so well that they offered him a proper job as a reporter, had given me some advice. He said that in the first month he never sat down in the newsroom, so that he would always look alert and ready to go. Maybe he was busier than me, or had stronger legs. Standing up all day, doing nothing, even for a 24-year-old, began to get tiring. I had so little to do that I started looking forward every morning to my first sight of the canteen lunch menu in the lift. If it looked reasonable, the thought of what I was going to eat helped me get through the morning.

But slowly they gave me bits and pieces of work. The editor gave me a fierce ticking-off when I failed to find a student union official at Queen's University. Mobile phones still did not exist outside the City of London, so I left a few messages at the Student Union, and settled down to my lunch, which was fish and chips as it was Friday. He was livid, and loomed over me as I cut into my cod.

'Have you never heard of narrowing the distance between yourself and the story?' he spat. He should have been wearing a green eye-shade. 'Bloody well get off your arse and go down to the Union to find him! It's only just down the road.'

I found the missing activist, booked him for an interview and got back to my tray while the chips were still warm. I needed a few kicks up the backside. It was a basic lesson: if you can get to a story yourself you stand a better chance of doing it right, which is as important for the grandest foreign correspondent as for the most junior trainee. The real journalists at the BBC in Belfast, who dealt with big stories constantly, were actually very welcoming, since no one could have blamed them if they had lost patience quickly with a stream of British trainees whose ambitions were not, in my case at least, matched by either experience or even basic knowledge.

One morning I was sent to Crumlin Road Courthouse, to help out one of the reporters. It was covered with rolls of razor wire, and inside there were scores of men who were smart in their green uniforms and looked like soldiers. I was amazed to hear that they were police officers from the Royal Ulster Constabulary. I had no idea that the RUC wore green. No wonder Mr Eye-Shade gave me nothing to do. In the end, though, he sent me out to do my first TV report, on a new tourist guide to Downpatrick, a pretty little town not far from Belfast. I never did the lead story while I was there, though I did report, in successive weeks, on the competitions for both secretary and receptionist of the year, which were held in the same

15

hotel in Bangor and featured Dana, the singer, presenting giant-sized cheques to the lucky winners.

But by then I was feeling more like a journalist, and I was ambitious and persistent about getting near the kinds of stories that made Northern Ireland famous. When three IRA men were shot dead by undercover British soldiers in Strabane on 23 February 1985, I begged John Conway, the editor of News and Current Affairs, to let me go to help the BBC team at the funeral. I wanted to see what a big Republican funeral was like. Conway was reluctant, telling me that because I was a tall Brit with a moustache I might be mistaken for a soldier, which would get everyone in trouble. In the end he let me, and it was so silent when the coffins were taken out of a house that I tried not to breathe. I was not much help to the cameraman. When he sent me back to his car for a tape, I brought half a dozen, just in case. One would have done. Five days later, nine RUC officers were killed in Newry when the IRA brought a lorry loaded with home-made mortars close to their police station. I was there helping out again, when I realised that it was a very big story: it turned into the worst loss in a single attack suffered by the RUC. I didn't have much to do for the BBC, so I scribbled out a few lines, went to a phone box and transfer-charged a call to National Public Radio in Washington DC, where I had worked when I was a student. They took my story, and quite a few more. I still felt that I was impersonating a reporter, but I was discovering that if you are where something bad is happening, and you have the story, suddenly everyone wants you. In the news business, violence, especially political violence that needs some explaining, puts a desirable edge on the story.

But most of the reports I did in Northern Ireland were soft; apart from Dana's personal appearances there was a poker competition, and a new polar bear enclosure at Belfast Zoo, and the annual collection of shamrock for the Royal Irish Rangers on a mountain called Slemish. When I was struggling with the scripts for them I used to kid myself that it would be much easier to write a hard news report, on, say, a shooting. After all, you did not have to be inventive; you just had to write down what had happened. I was so wrong. Of course a script for a feature has to be accurate; but you can be creative. Hard news is much more pressured, details and nuance and tone matter enormously, especially in a place like Northern Ireland in the 1980s. One weekend, I persuaded them to let me be the on-duty reporter. Nothing happened until a few minutes before the shift was due to end on Sunday night, when the phones lit up. An RUC man had been shot outside his house. I had to write a report about it for the next day's *Breakfast Time*. Finally, a chance to be on the national news! On a serious story! Naturally, the last thing on my mind was the poor man who had been shot, who was badly hurt. The story ran but I did not do a good job. I had somehow got the impression that there were joy-riders – teenagers who stole cars for fun – zooming around in the area, and said so, based on nothing other than my hunch and the sound of a few revving engines. John Conway gave me an exasperated bollocking. It was another lesson: if in doubt, leave it out. When my time in Belfast ended Conway sent me back to London with a report saying that I needed more experience at the 'hard news coal-face'. He was a master of understatement.

But the first real violence I saw was in Britain, not Northern Ireland. It was later in 1985, at the riots at Broadwater Farm housing estate in Tottenham in north London. I was helping out again, so wet behind the ears that the editor who sent me, John Exelby, asked if I had a notebook and pen before I left the building. I met the crew at a pub somewhere in the wastes of north London. They were veterans, Keith Skinner and Robin Green, and they had been having a quiet day covering the tennis in Eastbourne until the call came to go to Broadwater Farm. I was twitching with keenness and anxiety, but they decided to stop to have something to eat before what they expected would be a long night.

They were right. It was a tough night for everyone, dark and wet and noisy, the only real light coming from burning buildings. It was the last night for a policeman, Keith Blakelock, who was hacked to death while he was trying to protect a fire crew. The police had the estate surrounded, and were lined up shoulder to shoulder, beating their riot shields with batons and making loud grunting noises that sounded like ape impersonations, which was shocking because as far as I could see the police were all white, and the rioters were all black. A big crowd, roaring and angry, was facing the police, pelting them with pieces of concrete, and attacking with what looked scaffolding poles. Police truncheons were coming up above the helmets and shields and whacking down again on the heads of the men who were attacking them. Petrol bombs would explode with a whoosh, which made the crowd roar more loudly and push forward, and then it would be the turn of the police to roar, do more ape grunts and push back. We were behind the police lines. Lumps of builder's rubble were coming over the tops of the riot shields. Keith Skinner stood on a small step-ladder to film, getting higher so he could see over the police, looking very steady, not even flinching when pieces of concrete whizzed past his head. Some thudded on the road near us; others were far too close to my head, and I did not have Keith's ability to ignore them. Robin the soundman was next to him. I was on the other side, wondering what I should be doing. Suddenly there was a bang. Robin went down, his hands to his face. He seemed to be tugging at his headphones. I wondered whether the noise had somehow deafened him. Then I saw there was blood running down his hands. He had been hit in the face by a blast from a shotgun. Keith went to help him and I tried to find a medic. He was bundled into an ambulance and I found a phone box and a couple of coins to call Exelby to tell him what had happened. I had not even found out which hospital they had taken him to. One of the shotgun pellets lodged in Robin Green's right eye, and the surgeons could not save it. He was fifty-eight, had been at the Hungarian uprising in 1956 and the war in Vietnam, but he lost his eye not too far from the old BBC studios in Alexandra Palace where he had started his career. After that night, he never worked again.

When the ambulance went away, the riot was still going on. I picked up Robin's gear, which was heavy because soundmen still had to carry recorders which included the tape and mixer, and were linked by an umbilical cable to the cameraman. Robin's blood was all over the cables and the headphones. I carried it while Keith shot more pictures.

It was a season of riots. Margaret Thatcher was reaching her zenith as Prime Minister and pressure was building in the inner cities. The next time was in Handsworth in Birmingham. By then I was a trainee with *Newsnight,* and I went up to Birmingham with them the night after the riot. All the lamps were out, and the streets were sinister, empty except for small groups of youths and the police. But the part that frightened me was dealing with Tim Gardam, who was editing the part of the programme that was coming from Birmingham. Tim had a terrible temper which he learned to control as he rose up the greasier, steeper parts of the broadcasting pole to a string of top jobs as a television executive and then to the headship of an Oxford college. For some reason, I lost the crew in the darkness. In 1985 mobile phones were still a novelty. I had one, only mobile if you remembered to connect the shoulder strap which helped spread the weight of the battery, which was the same shape and size as a couple of housebricks. The crew did not have a phone. So I phoned Tim to confess what I had done and to ask if the crew had been in touch.

'This is the sheerest fucking incompetence,' he began, and raved on for a couple of minutes until he slammed down the phone. Tim was always at boiling point as the transmission time of his programmes approached. But the rest of the time he was amiable, gave me chances, and when I plucked up the courage to tell him that maybe he was not getting the best out of people by yelling at them, he said he only did it to me because he knew I could take the pressure and it would make me a better journalist.

Back on the streets in Handsworth, I felt queasy as I wondered what to do. A voice inside started to tell me that I had no need to put myself through such agony. There were plenty of trains from Birmingham New Street to London. I could just walk away. Just as I was fantasising about my resignation speech the crew swept up in their huge BMW. Their driver had panicked because the dark, empty streets scared him and he had roared off in the wrong direction. We still had time to do our filming. Back at the BBC's Pebble Mill studios, when I brought in the material, Tim was much calmer. The reporter I was working for, Steve Bradshaw, said the pictures I had got for him, of a local band rehearsing and talking about the riots, were the best bit of television in his piece. I decided resignation was not the only option after all.

My first job after I finished my training was as a financial news reporter. I had no real interest in the City of London; unlike some of the striped-shirted 1980s people I had to interview, I didn't think that greed was good. But they gave me the job even though when I was trying it out as a trainee I overslept one morning and did not get to the studio in time to broadcast an early programme. That time I really was convinced that my career was over before it had begun. Desperate and unshaven, I had gone into Broadcasting House by tube (it was Monday morning and I had no cash for a taxi), marking items in the *Financial Times* that I planned to read out on air instead of what was supposed to be an eight-minute summary of market prices. The only part of the programme I liked doing was the first line, which was always a stately 'This is London', which made me feel as if I was broadcasting to occupied Europe during the Second World War. Luckily for my future prospects, they had cancelled the programme by the time I burst into the office, covered in sweat and carrying my dog-eared copy of the *FT*. The World Service read out a few prices and played solemn music instead. Some listeners thought the Queen had died.

I took the job as a financial reporter because I wanted to be a broadcaster and the offers I had in television were for producers' jobs. I had studied some economics, so the subject matter was not mysterious. I told the personnel officer after I accepted the job that my plan was to do it for a couple of years to help me get into straight news reporting, preferably abroad. He looked worried.

'My dear fellow, you could be doing the wrong thing. Most people who have had your job tend to move into the City, to do financial PR.' I told him cheerfully that I would break the mould, but when I left his office I felt ill.

I worked at Broadcasting House where some of the older hands instructed me in the traditional practices of radio news, many of which revolved around going to the pub. Each programme had its own pub in the area around BH. The newsroom people were generally in the Crown & Sceptre (usually known as the hat and stick) or the Yorkshire Grey. The Radio 1 programme *Newsbeat* went to the Stag. More arty types were in the George, where Dylan Thomas used to get drunk while he worked at the BBC. I enjoyed lunchtime drinking until one afternoon after a few pints followed by a long lunch at a Turkish restaurant and then a few more pints I barely managed to write and then broadcast my report. After that I decided to be more careful. I desperately wanted to be one of the people who did the big stories, one of the grown-ups in the reporters' room, where they had a dartboard and made check calls to the police when there was nothing else to do, and when there were stories they went off in a hurry to Brixton or Bradford or even Beirut.

Going abroad for television news, which was what I really wanted to do, still looked many steps away. I just wanted to get on the right track. But it turned out that there were some good stories for financial and business reporters at the height of the greedy 1980s. I managed to do well with a scandal that revolved around a controversial takeover of Guinness. I covered the story for a couple of months. One freezing morning I hung around for hours in front of the house of one of the principals in the scandal, who gave me an interview, partly because I was the only reporter there but mostly because I got into his taxi with him and refused to get out until he spoke. Then I had the chance to interview the chairman of Guinness and gave him such a good grilling that the editor of the *Today* programme congratulated me. It was all progress.

After about eighteen months they offered me my dream job as a radio news reporter, but I turned it down because another one had come up in Geneva, to cover the United Nations European office and to act as a low-level fireman in the Alps, for floods and disasters. Geneva was hardly exotic, but it was a chance to be a foreign correspondent. It started badly. I sold a story to the *Today* programme about Swiss preparations for nuclear war. But I managed to miss the train that was taking the Geneva press corps into the mountains to a road tunnel that the Swiss authorities were turning into a field hospital and shelter. Facing disaster once again, I thought about re-creating what I might have seen with my microphone in a pedestrian underpass at Geneva station. Luckily I remembered something about fabricating news stories, got a later train and managed to come up with a report that might have been dull but was at least honest. Later that year, there were

Alpine disasters, a flood in Le Grand Bornand and then a tragedy on the annual skiing trip of the Prince of Wales. I had wanted an excuse to go skiing in Klosters and offered to monitor the Prince's activities while he was there. The urbane foreign editor in radio news, Chris Wyld, told me loftily that I could of course go, but only if a mountain fell on the Prince's head. A day or two later, I left the office for a coffee and came back to find about a dozen messages from Wyld telling me to get to Klosters because the Prince's party had been hit by an avalanche.

Then UNICEF took me away on my first proper foreign adventure, to Ethiopia. It was a couple of years after the catastrophic famine of 1984, and as well as UNICEF, Bob Geldof was going back to check how the Live Aid money was being spent. In Mekele in Tigre things were not going so well; aid flights were not arriving as promised and a priest told me that 'if they don't arrive soon, they might as well load them with shovels to dig graves'. As it happened, the aid did start arriving, so they didn't need the shovels, but it was a great quote. I spent an evening drinking, Soviet-style, with the Russian flight crew of one of the transport planes. They had a case of Asmara dry gin, which was a local speciality, so rough that after they had downed a tumbler of it in one, they would drink another tumbler of Coca-Cola to kill the taste. I was rescued from their room by the hotel receptionist and a chambermaid who thought that my new friends were trying to make me pass out so that they could inflict on me a fate worse than death.

The next morning I had to travel, with a tremendous hangover, on the aircraft that was being flown by the Russians, who must have still been drunk, to get to a remote patch of desert where about 25,000 people were being given food. I was so dehydrated from the Asmara dry gin that I had to be talked out of lapping up the dark brackish water that the Ethiopians were carrying in metal pots.

Later on, I went to Asmara in Eritrea and admired the fascistic Fiat garages left by the Italian colonialists. In a restaurant an old man speaking perfect Italian served me *fegato alla veneziana* and a bottle of Ethiopian Soave. At the end of the trip, I went out to a dirt landing strip before dawn to wait for the light plane that was going to take us back to Addis Ababa. Women were picking up water for their families, pushing along copper barrels that had been so well made for the Italian air force in the 1930s that they were still useful fifty years on. The sun rose over the mountains and my boots kicked up red dust as I walked around listening to the BBC World Service on my shortwave radio, waiting to hear the piece I had filed, and I realised that I wanted badly to have this kind of life, and that it might even be possible.

Geneva was dull after Ethiopia. I decided that I wanted to spend no more than a year in Switzerland. I was a young man in a big hurry and the stately pace of the UN headquarters, the Palais des Nations, drove me mad. When the doors of a lift opened, the UN functionaries, who never had to rush, would perform a stately quadrille.

'Madame, after you.'

'*Non, Monsieur, après vous.*'

'Madame, I insist.'

I fumed behind them, mouthing *just get in the bloody lift*. It was a lonely life. I didn't have many friends and most evenings I worked late, on good days filing Geneva's best stories, which were the nuclear arms reduction talks between the United States and the Soviet Union, and the UN's response to the new pandemic of Aids. On bad days I squeezed as much news as I could out of the stacks of press releases that the UN produced every day. On the way home I usually stopped to eat a plate of pasta on my own at an Italian restaurant run by a Portuguese family. Deliverance came from Channel 4 News. It had been taken over by Richard Tait, who had edited *Newsnight* when I was a trainee there. He offered me a job as a reporter. I asked the BBC if they could do something to make me stay; I asked nervously for a job as a current affairs reporter on *Newsnight*. I didn't dare to name the job I really wanted, one that the BBC called 'Reporter, Television News', because it still seemed too grown-up. But *Newsnight* did not want me, and Chris Cramer, who ran Television News intake, did. He gave me the TV news job. I was twenty-eight, and couldn't believe my luck. When I rang Richard Tait to turn down his kind offer, he told me what a mistake I was making and warned me about my first day back at BBC Television Centre.

'Just remember, Jeremy, to listen hard as you cross the threshold of the West London Palace of Varieties . . . Because as you go in, you will hear the picks and shovels of the people in the basement trying to tunnel their way out.'

I think he was trying to make me feel bad. In fact 1988 was a good time to be joining BBC TV News, though I didn't realise it at the time and neither did anyone else. After a couple of months as a general reporter, I was offered a job as a correspondent, which was supposed to be a big step up. The trouble was that it was the wrong job, doing business and economics. Cramer rang me with the good news.

'Chris, do I have to take it? You know I want to do foreign.'

'Bowen, it's a fucking correspondency! You'd be a cunt to turn it down.'

But a few months later the BBC started a new office, the foreign affairs unit, for a small group of correspondents to travel from London to the places where the BBC was thin on the ground. I applied for a job covering the developing world. I loved the line in the advert that said that the successful candidate would have to travel frequently. I worked hard for the board; the BBC convention is that you have to show at the interview that you are as knowledgeable as if you had been doing the job for two years. My shirt under my jacket was wringing with sweat at the end of the interview. I walked out of the room desperately wanting the job, worrying that I hadn't done well enough to get it. I hadn't. They gave it to George Alagiah, a good-looking and talented journalist from *South* magazine.

Cramer rang me later that day. It seemed the board had gone a lot better than I thought. He said I hadn't been a cunt when he needed help in the business unit, so he was going to give me a job in foreign affairs anyway. I was overjoyed. It was less than six months since I had left Geneva. My colleagues when the unit started, apart from George, were my old friend David Shukman and Brian Hanrahan, who was back in Britain after a posting in Moscow. I was in awe of Hanrahan. I was a student in London doing my finals in 1982 when he was counting Royal Navy warplanes out and counting them back in again during the war for the Falklands. When I was a trainee, one of the editors in radio played us some of his dispatches, holding them up as perfect examples of broadcast journalism.

'Listen to them and remember,' he said. 'Only clear and direct words, and only one fact in each sentence.'

John Simpson, elegant and charming, another foreign correspondent who had hit heights of which I could only dream, was the editor, though he didn't want to be in charge.

'Listen, chaps, I'm not a housemaster. I'm not going to tell you what to do. We'll just all go out to lunch together when we're all at home. It's going to work splendidly.'

And it did. It was the end of 1988, the end of the old world in which my generation had grown up, of the Cold War, and the crazy superpower logic of intercontinental ballistic missiles, first strikes and MAD, mutually assured destruction, that I had studied in

Washington. There were already signs of change, of course: Poland had the Solidarity trade union, Mikhail Gorbachev was trying to reform the Soviet Union and its empire, which he realised, far more clearly than its enemies in the West, was collapsing from within. But they looked more like variations on an old theme rather than the beginning of something utterly new, and it was still too much to try to imagine a world without the division of Europe, the Iron Curtain, Checkpoint Charlie and the Berlin Wall. I wrote scripts in London about that world, about the latest arrest of the Czech dissident Václav Havel, and more strikes in Poland. In the early summer of 1989, one of the great turning-points of the century, I was sent to West Germany to do some features.

I went to a camp full of Volga Germans, descendants of ethnic German settlers in Tsarist Russia who were being allowed to leave the USSR, people with German names and blond hair who spoke Russian to each other. I travelled from Hanover on the British military train, which ran every day, even if it did not have any passengers, to keep open the railway line to West Berlin. It was an obscure backwater of the Cold War, part of the agreement between Britain, France, the United States and the Soviet Union, the victors of the Second World War, which still regulated the status of the former capital of the German Reich. The train was a little bubble of Britain that no longer existed on British Rail. The status quo was everything in the four-power agreement, because changing something small might end in an attempt to change something big, like the fact that Westerners could travel through communist East Germany to get to their half of Berlin, so they hadn't even put up the prices on the train since 1948. You could get a 1940s kind of drink like a brandy and soda for the equivalent of about 2s 6d, or a brown ale for less, and a proper breakfast or chops and two veg. When the train stopped at the inner German border, a detachment of British soldiers, boots, belts and brims burnished and shining, stamped down the platform and crashed to a halt outside the window of my compartment. A squad of Soviet troops goose-stepped towards them. They all saluted and went into an office with a briefcase that supposedly contained the train's documents; a steward told me that it also hid a bottle of scotch that they would swap for a bottle of vodka.

Before it reached West Berlin, the train went through East German territory, a strange land of cobblestones, smoky factories and small, fragile-looking cars, where blocks of flats that had survived the downfall of the Nazis in 1945 were still pitted with bullet holes. Then in an instant it crossed into suburban West Berlin, an outpost of capitalism, with swimming pools, BMWs and Mercedes. I had a beer with the BBC's long-established Berlin correspondent, who was leaving his post after many years out of boredom as much as anything else. 'This bloody place is covered with concrete, literally,' he complained. 'Physically it's paved with concrete, and politically too. Nothing's going to change here. I'm fed up. I'm getting out.'

A couple of months later, the citizens of Berlin were dancing on top of the Wall and knocking lumps out of the concrete with hammers. The East German border guards who had been shooting people on it for nearly thirty years leaned on their rifles and let them do what they wanted. In Czechoslovakia, Václav Havel went from a prison cell to the president's palace. The Soviet empire in Eastern Europe disintegrated and by 1991 the Soviet Union itself collapsed. The old Cold War division of East and West, the balance of terror that inflicted an odd, frightened stability on the world for more than forty years, vanished in front of our eyes, though it did not go quietly. The Cold War had been full of violence, but the competition between the two superpowers, and the fear of what might happen if they got out of control, had put a limiter on conflicts. They could not be allowed to get out of hand because of the appalling consequences of the superpowers sliding into a nuclear crisis. Suddenly that fear was not there any more. Wars around the world that had been held down by the weight of the Cold War started popping up. Within a year, Iraq invaded Kuwait and touched off a confrontation with the United States whose consequences are still with us and are escalating. Within two years, Yugoslavia fell apart and subsided into war.

Times of change are great for journalists. I came into international reporting at a time when a new cycle of global politics was beginning, and when the news business was about to be forced, by technology and by the pace of the new connected world, to transform itself to keep up. The reporting that I have done around the world since then has had one big theme: the violent division of power that followed the Cold War, and the painful birth of a new world order. It took more than ten years of confusion and false hopes before a pattern began to form after the attacks on the United States on 11 September 2001; it is disorder not order, unstable, increasingly dangerous, and looks as if it will be the global story of the next twenty years, at least.

Six months after I joined Television News, on 21 December 1988, the ghost of Christmases yet to come ruined a lot of lives. It was the night of the newsroom party. I had been working all day, so I turned up early in the canteen where it was being held. The organisers had made a big effort. A live band was playing, but as time went by, the women who had planned it all looked more and more desperate. No one was turning up. It was too depressing, so I slipped out. On my way down the corridor, a producer came running towards the party, to stop it and to grab the people who were there to get them to work.

'Haven't you heard?' he shouted, hardly stopping. 'A jumbo jet has crashed into a town in Scotland.'

My shift was over, but I went up to the newsroom. The boss, the mighty Cramer, was standing at the news intake desk, on three phones at once.

'Bowen, what the hell are you doing here? Get up to fucking Lockerbie now.'

I borrowed one of the crew cars, a powerful Vauxhall Carlton, and set off. One of the senior reporters, Michael Cole, made a big impression on me when I was a trainee when he told us what he did after the phone went in the middle of the night to tell him to go to Brighton because the IRA had blown up Mrs Thatcher's hotel at the 1984 Conservative party conference. Instead of rushing off straight away, he had a shower while his wife cooked him some breakfast. He knew it was going to be a long night and a long day after that, so he reckoned that a quarter of an hour to set himself up would be time well spent. So following the Cole dictum, I went to my flat in south London, even though it was in the opposite direction, to get some proper outdoor clothes and something to eat. The next couple of weeks in Scotland were cold and wet but at least I had the right gear. Somewhere on the M1 the car needed fuel, so I pulled into a service station. Jennie Bond was there too. Later she became famous covering the Royal Family, but then she was an ambitious news reporter like me, rushing to get to Lockerbie. We eyed each other without speaking and ran to the cash desk to pay, then went back to our cars like Le Mans racers, wheels spinning away from the pumps to see who could get back on the road first.

I had never been to a war zone, but Lockerbie looked like one. Part of the town had disappeared, vaporised when a wing of the Pan-Am airliner that was fully loaded with fuel for the trip across the Atlantic crashed on to it. The main street was covered with hundreds of twisted pieces of metal, pieces of the destroyed 747, so sharp that one of them cut through the sole of the boots

I had gone home to get. Small fires were burning in a lot of places; firemen had run hundreds of yards of hoses down the roads; it was chaos. It took days to collect all the bodies of the passengers. They were scattered around the town, on the golf course and on the rolling hills around. Some of them, still strapped into their seats, were stuck in rooftops and had to be winched down by the Fire Brigade. A few miles out of Lockerbie, the nose of the Pan-Am jumbo had smashed into a hill, and come to rest on its side.

I had nothing to do that first morning for *Breakfast Time*. But I did a report for the *One O'Clock News*, which we cut in the back of a Renault Espace that had been fitted with all the machines necessary to make it into a mobile edit room. I sat with Tim Platt, a very talented editor about the same age as me, and as new rushes tapes came in from camera crews around the town they were shoved in through the door. A couple of minutes before the news was going on air Tim put in the last shot, which was of an old lady, looking bewildered and terrified, standing by her front door holding on to her cat. The BBC News management liked the report. On huge news days like that, they worry not just about reporters hitting their deadlines, getting the right pictures and writing vividly and accurately; they are also concerned with using the right tone. It turned out that the report that Tim and I had cut satisfied all those requirements. They let me stay with the story. It was my first real breakthrough. For the first time, but not the last – not nearly – someone else's catastrophe was my piece of good luck.

2

The War Drug

El Salvador in 1989 was my first proper war. I was only there for a couple of weeks, but it was enough for me to get hooked on the war drug. It started seeping into my bloodstream before I had even heard a shot fired. It was late afternoon when the BBC team landed at the airport in San Salvador, which is a little way out of the city. A shoot-on-sight curfew started at six, and it was already getting on for half-past five. The taxi drivers were nervous about driving into town but we persuaded someone to take us into San Salvador in his pickup. My colleagues sat in the cab and I sat in the open on the back, on the silver boxes of TV equipment that we had brought. There was probably enough room up front but I wanted to breathe everything in. The sun was setting, making the rocks and red earth glow as the driver hurtled down empty roads. I could not see any signs of war, except for a few checkpoints manned by suntanned men with wide cheekbones and dark eyes and scratched, used-looking guns. It did not matter. The wind was warm in my hair and there was dust in my eyes and I wanted everything that was waiting at the other end of the ride. I was nervous because I had been watching the street fighting on television in America and a lot was happening. It was violent. But I wanted to get into it. I wanted to prove that I could do it.

I count El Salvador as my first war because it was the first time I was close enough to the action to get killed. I had been to another war, in Afghanistan, earlier in 1989, but I did not think of it as a proper debut at the time because the explosions were too far away, just a distant, lazy crump coming out of the mountains. It seems like a daft distinction but it was important to me. I had respect for experience and I did not want to claim it before I could justify it. My first attempt at getting to Afghanistan was not distinguished. When the call came to go to Kabul I was recovering at my parents' house in Cardiff after a fight outside the Old Arcade pub in the city centre following a rugby international. Because I am no kind of fighter, I had two black eyes and a swollen face. But I was very keen to go to Afghanistan – ten years after they invaded, the Russians were admitting defeat and getting out – so I told the foreign editor, John Mahoney, disingenuously, that the swelling was going down and that all he had to do was to arrange for a make-up artist to meet me in Television Centre to show me how to hide the green, yellow and brown bruises around my eyes. An elegant woman called Marilyn was waiting in foreign news when I arrived, with a plastic bag full of powders, liquids and sponges. She looked very doubtful about whether it would work, and tried to say so, but I manoeuvred her away from Mahoney's desk in case he heard and decided I couldn't go.

I flew out to Dubai, where I had to get another plane for Kabul. It was disappointing to find out that the way to Afghanistan was not in a jeep through the Khyber Pass but in an airliner from Dubai. But Ariana Afghan Airways was no ordinary airline. After so many years of war the fact that it was still flying at all was a miracle of aerospace. In the next few years, as I became a relatively frequent flyer on Ariana, there were many times when its planes could not take off because of shelling in Kabul, and almost as many times when you wished that they had not, as take-off would be followed by some emergency or other. In 1989 I was told that the only place I could get Ariana tickets was at small shop deep in the bazaar. Dubai was much smaller then. Not far behind the avenue that ran along the creek, where there was a strip of high buildings and posh hotels, there were scruffy, narrow streets, full of people, small shops and interesting new smells. It was my first trip to the Middle East, so it felt exotic. I found the shop and bought a ticket with some of the $10,000 in cash that the BBC had given me in London for expenses. It was in small bills which meant quite a big bag, which I tried to open non-chalantly in the shop.

The first time I turned up at the airport the flight was cancelled because, yet again, Kabul airport was being shelled. The next day, and the day after that, we sat on the tarmac in a mouldy old Boeing for hours while they waited to see if things were any better in Kabul. Each time the flight was cancelled and the passengers had to get off, again, I saw that the aircraft was dripping important-looking fluids from its orifices that pooled on the runway as it sat in the desert sun. By the time it was considered safe enough to take off the next day, Ariana's flight crew, cheery moustachioed men and pleasantly buxom air hostesses, told nervous passengers not to worry and we rattled off down the runway. All that was lacking was an Afghan visa in my passport. The BBC people in Kabul had sworn that I would be able to get one at the airport.

It was not that simple. 'Ah, welcome,' said a man in uniform at Kabul airport, 'where is your visa? It is forbidden to enter our country without one.' He looked at my face. 'Are you a boxer? Maybe you can fight again while you are in our country.'

It got worse when they went through my luggage and found a copy of a Sunday newspaper magazine with a cover picture of the country's greatest warlord, Ahmed Shah Masoud, on horse-back as he led the fight against the Russians and their puppet government in Kabul. If I had had a chance of talking them into issuing me a visa, it vanished at that moment. Barry Meadows, the BBC producer who had come out of Kabul to meet me, took delivery of the $10,000 and went back into town to start doing my job. As he was being filmed strolling in the garden of the presidential palace interviewing Moscow's friend, President Najibullah, I was being told politely and very firmly that they would not let me in and that they had no immediate plans to let me out either. I was held at the airport for three days, in a small locked room, until the guards took pity on me and let me join them next to their one-bar electric fire, and to pace up and down a small patch of grass outside. I saw the last Soviet plane leave, with no ceremony and the last few gaudily made-up wives grumbling their way out across the tarmac to the steps. I suppose it was a world exclusive as I was the only journalist there, watching one of the crucial moments that hurried the USSR down the road to collapse, but I had no chance of filing a story: the shadowy parts of the military might have had satellite phones in the 1980s, but journalists didn't; mobiles were still status symbols for yuppies who worked in the financial markets. Even if I had possessed one, it would not have worked within thousands of miles of Kabul airport. Perhaps it was something to do with the mountains, but I could not even get the news, in any language, out of my shortwave radio. I had no idea if anyone knew that the last Soviet plane had left Kabul. I was in the back of beyond.

Once the last Russian had gone, nothing was landing or taking off. The area around the runways was silent, littered with broken aircraft and the skeletons of helicopter gunships so smashed up that the Soviets had abandoned them. I cheered myself up by sitting on the grass outside the guard room in thin, wintry sunshine, reading *The Bonfire of the Vanities*, the novel about a Wall Street trader who feels he is the master of the universe until his life collapses when he takes the wrong exit off a road. It made Kabul airport feel less of a disaster. The night after the last Russians went I sat with my new friends, the guards, eating their potato curry garnished with coriander and drinking my Johnny Walker Black Label whisky, which they liked more than my company. Exploding shells made distant thumps. Before I left British newspapers and television bulletins had been full of breathless reports about how the mujahideen rebels would sweep into a defenceless Kabul the minute the Russians departed. One of the guards spoke a little English.

'Are those mujahideen shells?' I asked.

'Oh yes.'

'I suppose this airport is a big target now?'

'Of course.'

'So it must be well defended?'

'Yes.'

'How many soldiers are here?'

He pointed to his comrade who grinned and drank a bit more of my whisky.

'Me and him.'

Not for the first time he eyed up my brand-new Timberland boots. 'What size are they?' he asked, greedily. I poured some whisky for him and then a bigger one for me. I was convinced that the mujahideen were about to come bursting in. I was safer than I thought. It was another three years before they took Kabul.

I got out the next day, when I found an Ariana pilot who was prepared to help me. We went to the airport's administrative offices, on a corridor lined with aircraft seats, which was their way of recycling their grounded DC-10 airliner. More of the seats, which could still recline, were in the offices. I settled down in one that had been in Business Class and dozed while the pilot negotiated my freedom. He even let me call Barry Meadows at the BBC office in Kabul. They had not noticed that I was missing.

'We were wondering where you were, old boy. We assumed when you didn't get the visa that you'd left on the Delhi flight and were sulking in the Oberoi hotel about not getting in.'

That night the pilot was taking a cargo flight to Dubai loaded with carpets and oranges. The pilot got permission from the men in uniform for me to come too. They seemed to have become bored with keeping me there, and after some form-filling they sold me a ticket. The carpets and oranges never turned up, so we flew out in a plane that was completely empty, with just one seat bolted to the floor for me. After that Ariana was always one of my favourite airlines. Not many of their rivals would spring their passengers from jail. They took off from Kabul by climbing steeply in a series of sharp, banking turns, to outwit the men sitting in the mountains with anti-aircraft missiles. They landed the same way. Life for an Ariana pilot did not have much routine about it.

I liked Afghanistan. I went back about ten days later, with a less swollen face and a visa in my passport, and I was a fairly regular visitor until the mid-1990s. For a country that had suffered a vicious war it had some gentle moments. The foreign ministry in Kabul was in an old building with verandahs, Afghan carpets and functionaries who murmured quietly in French. One of the engravings on the wall inside was called *Scenery Near Winchester*. It must have been brought in by some homesick British official. I sat once on the grass outside the ministry, waiting for a meeting of tribal chiefs – proud, bearded men dressed in robes, or baggy trousers and combat jackets, all carrying Kalashnikovs. The translator was not very Islamic.

'Look at the dandelions, let's make some wine!' He looked at the fighting men who were swaggering around the lawn. 'We were a timid people. You used to be able to walk unmolested in the hills and valleys. We should not have beaten the British. Then they might have stayed here and built something.'

Kabul finally fell in April 1992, to the mujahideen guerrillas who had defeated the Russians, and there was still some hope for a better future. A one-eyed truck driver, who attracted the attention of men who were ignoring him at a checkpoint by leaning out of the window and firing his pistol in the air, sat back in his cab and complained to me that life during the war with the Russians had been very hard. 'There was no time to sit, no time to eat our mulberries. We were always out in the sun and the snow. God willing, it will be different now.'

It was different, but it wasn't better. On the morning of the final collapse of the regime led by Mohammed Najibullah, the secret policeman that the Soviets had left in charge, Kabul was quiet. Heavily armed mujahideen, followers of Ahmad Shah Masoud's group, fanned out around the city, while Najibullah was prevented from leaving and took refuge in the UN compound. Najibullah, who had been responsible for the imprisonment, torture and death of thousands of Afghans while he was head of the KHAD, the secret police, stayed there until he was dragged out by the Taliban when they captured Kabul in 1996. He and his henchmen were shot and their bodies displayed on a traffic island outside what had been his presidential palace.

Quite a few of the bands of mujahideen who were driving round the city when they arrived in 1992 had a younger man with them, with long hair, painted nails and eyes black with kohl.

When I asked one of them what his job was, he giggled. I presumed he was the unit catamite. Most of them had spent years in the field, fighting the Russians, fighting each other sometimes. A small boy came out to cheer and to welcome them, but he asked too many questions and got too close so one of them picked him up and threw him in a ditch. He burst into tears and ran home. 'There will be many other cruelties, much worse,' the BBC's translator said darkly. Some of the mujahideen found their way into the only decent hotel in Kabul, the former Intercontinental that was still decorated with Pan-Am posters from the late 1960s, where white-coated stewards served cold beer and villainous Afghan brandy in the Nuristan bar. The mujahideen who wandered into the foyer had hardly ever seen a two-storey building, let alone one with half a dozen. The day that Kabul fell I was in the hotel with a group of journalists (there weren't any other kinds of guest in the hotel) waiting for the lift to arrive. A fighter, carrying a Kalashnikov and wide-eyed at the extraordinary sights around him, lined up politely behind us, and when the lift came and the door opened, he followed us in. When he realised the room he had entered was tiny, with no other exit, he turned to leave, then looked close to panic when the door closed in front of him and we started to move. At the first floor, he staggered out, even more alarmed when he saw that he was somewhere else.

There wasn't much light relief, though. From the north came General Abdul Rashid Dostum's Uzbeks, with turquoise turbans and a big reputation as fighters to do the mopping up and the carrying away. Looting was a perk of their work. Coming from the south were the Hezbi Islami, followers of a warlord called Gulbuddin Hekmatyar. As they approached the city, I went out to find them with Rory Peck, a BBC cameraman. We drove out in a taxi, past the citadel of Bala Hissar that rises high above the plain and has been a fortress since the fifth century. In 1879 Sir Louis

Cavagnari, a representative of Britain, was cut down, along with his escort, in one of its palaces. Britain's response to the killing of Sir Louis was to send an army, which hanged rebellious Afghan chieftains in the courtyard of Bala Hissar and then did their best to flatten it, to create, as General Roberts put it, 'a lasting memorial of our ability to avenge our countrymen'. More than a century later, Bala Hissar was being shelled again. The taxi parked and we walked closer to get some pictures. After each salvo Rory ran into the hole made by the newest shell.

'By far the safest way, old chap,' said Rory, who had the same sort of accent and background as the British officers who came to take Bala Hissar for Queen Victoria. 'They're far too inaccurate to hit the same place twice.'

When Rory had filmed enough explosions to satisfy both of us, we drove on until we came to a checkpoint which was manned by fighters whose ammunition pouches were decorated with pictures of Gulbuddin Hekmatyar. Our bad luck was that they were looking for some revenge of their own. I asked Rory to film them. 'Listen, Jeremy, I don't think that's a good idea. These chaps can get angry very quickly.' He had years of experience in Afghanistan, but I was impatient. 'Just bloody film them, Rory, for Christ's sake.' As soon as he lifted his camera the man it was pointing at lifted his gun back at us and started to shout. The taxi driver pulled at Rory's arm and told us to get in the car straight away.

'What the hell was all that about?' I said as we bumped down the road away from them, irritated that something was coming between me and the story.

'Sorry, sir, it's just that he was saying, "Kill the Westerners, kill them now." I thought you'd better leave.'

We went back to Kabul, which had survived the war against the Soviet Union relatively intact. The competing groups of

mujahideen that had beaten the Soviets and removed the government soon fell out, and started an artillery war that flattened the
centre of the city and killed a lot of people. The wounded would
travel to the hospital crammed into cars and taxis that ran with
blood, dozens at a time. I find it hard to forget the desperate eyes
of a teenage boy shoved into the boot of a taxi with both his legs
blown away, lying in a pond of his own blood.

When the time came to leave in 1992, with the war between
the guerrillas getting worse but falling off the end of the news
bulletins, Ariana was still flying – just. Half-way up the steep,
twisting take-off, my ears started to pop fiercely. A wind blew
through the cabin and the door of the flight deck banged open. I
noticed that the flight crew were wearing their oxygen masks.
The next moment the flaps above the passengers' heads opened
with a horrible plastic snap and oxygen masks dropped down.
Mine came away in my hand. I looked back and saw the rest of
the passengers struggling with their masks; a few of them were
screaming. I got out my camera to take a picture and thought
better of it. What if the camera survived the crash? I could see the
headlines in the *Daily Mail*: 'Last terrifying moments of doomed
Afghan flight'. I put the camera away. The intrepid Ariana pilot
performed an emergency landing. After a few hours they tried
again – and the same thing happened. We did another emergency
landing as the aircraft depressurised, but Afghans are tough and by
then we had some faith in the pilot, so far fewer people panicked.
We had to go back to spend the night in Kabul, where the Hezbi
Islami was rocketing Masoud's men, pulverising the city. By the
next morning the irrepressible Ariana crew had fixed the plane
and we got out.

The only thing that El Salvador had in common with Afghanistan
in the 1980s was that it was one of the hot fronts in the Cold War.

The fighting was very dirty: insurgents from the Farabundo Martí National Liberation Front (FMLN) battled an unjust government; civilians were massacred; an archbishop who had criticised the government's brutal tactics was murdered in his cathedral. The Americans bankrolled the Salvadorian government, trained its forces and turned a blind eye to their barbaric behaviour because of their global competition with the Soviet Union. In November 1989 I was there because the FMLN had launched one of their biggest offensives. They had taken the fight into the capital, to the suburbs and the playgrounds of the ruling class as well as the slums, and the regime was shaking. The ruling elite in Salvador and their American friends still talked about dominoes falling to communism but only two weeks before I landed at San Salvador airport the Berlin Wall had come down and the Velvet Revolution was under way in Czechoslovakia. By the time I arrived San Salvador was the Cold War's last bloody sideshow.

I was twenty-nine. I had been with the BBC for five years and a foreign correspondent for three. I was a little old to be experiencing a real shooting war for the first time, but that might have helped; 29-year-olds are normally more sensible than 21-year-olds. Going off to report on a war had never been one of my targets, though I suppose somewhere in my mind was the idea that if I wanted to do the big stories I would have to try it. Now I was in a war zone, I wanted to make the most of it. I was determined to get close to the fighting at the very first opportunity, because I thought that it was the best way to report the story, and the best way to make a mark in television. I was never a hothead. Some people like danger just because it is dangerous. I was never that crazy. I just accepted it, like bad weather, right from the start. I was very rarely scared, not because I am brave, but because, for a long time, I was able to put the thought of being killed right out of my mind. I was not gung-ho about war. What I wanted to be, more than anything else, was a good journalist. I wanted to tell the truth about what was happening. Until I arrived in El Salvador, it had never occurred to me that doing that in a war could also be fun and exciting and in the end would start consuming my life.

I was there only because Martin Bell, the BBC correspondent with whom I was working in Washington at the time, couldn't make it that particular week. He was the guy who normally did El Salvador. When he asked me if I wanted to go instead, I was very excited because it was a chance to do a demanding job in a demanding place. Central America had been one of the big stories of the 1980s, and when I was starting out in journalism I had wanted to have a go at it. And I saw a chance to start making a name for myself.

The next day, my first morning reporting war, I was fighting panic; not because I was worried about being killed, but because I was worried that the Salvadorians had stopped killing each other. I had overheard a cameraman from another network telling someone that he was a week late. He said that the story was over. I still did not understand that reporters and crews with a few days' seniority on a story often say that to new arrivals. Depressed, thinking that I had missed the party, I rode in the back of a pickup truck to Mejicanos, the place in San Salvador where the war was hottest that day. The cameraman was up front with the driver. I cheered up a bit in the back as I started to hear the snap, crackle and pop of gunfire.

Mejicanos was a desperately poor slum. As soon as the pickup stopped, about a dozen civilians surrounded us. They pulled at my sleeve and pointed down the road, shouting in Spanish. The cameraman, Guillermo Duran, translated. He was Salvadorian, stocky and strong, and sounded like a man who was having a routine day at the office.

'They're saying that there's the body of a dead guerrilla down the road, and they want to know if we want to film it.'

He shrugged that it was up to me. I felt like a boy on his first day at school. I had never seen a dead body before, though I did not tell him that.

'OK, then, let's take a look.'

I tried to sound nonchalant, but I was excited and apprehensive. We followed the crowd down the road. I could hear bursts of gunfire. The body was in some kind of sunken drain. Guillermo put his camera on his shoulder and went to the edge of the hole, and started filming.

I hung back, nervously, bracing myself before I took a look. Would I faint? Or lose control of myself? I forced myself to look. The corpse had been burned. The skin was shrivelled and black-brown. It wasn't very recognisable as something that had been human until that morning. Thankfully I didn't make any kind of embarrassing exhibition.

We moved away from the hole, along a dusty street towards some low buildings made of breeze blocks with corrugated tin roofs. It was getting towards lunchtime and I was hungry. A strong barbecue smell wafted around. It made my mouth water. The cooking smells were coming from a fire just around the corner that was blazing in the middle of the street. In the heart of the flames what looked like a side of pork ribs sizzled and spluttered. The meat was human. Just above the ribs some charred hair still stuck to fragments of skin on a human skull, which was the colour of greasy fried bread. I felt less hungry. Guillermo Duran explained that the people burned the bodies of rebel guerrillas where they fell. They threw wood on top of them and petrol on the wood. He said it was because if they were left they would rot in the sun and spread disease. And I suspected that if it was the security forces who were doing the burning, they wanted to deny the guerrillas they had killed a decent burial and a grave that might turn into a shrine. Guillermo kept on filming.

Later on there was some shooting. I lay on my stomach in the gutter, hoping that the six inches or so of cover from the kerbstone might help. For the first time I heard the *psst psst psst* noise, like mad insects whispering, that bullets make when they go over your head. It was hard to believe the bullets were real, even though across the city civilians, government soldiers and guerrilla fighters were dying. Then, when it was over and I got through it and wasn't dead, it was fantastically exciting. That was the first big burst of the war drug, pulling me towards addiction. It was also frightening, but to start with, anyway, you forget the fear and remember the excitement. I liked it. It was an action movie and I was in it.

We had more pictures of bodies. By the end of the day I had also done what I hoped was a gritty piece to camera, a 'standupper'. I was moderately pleased with my day's work. Our material went well with other pictures shot by our allies that the picture editor and producer had assembled while I was out. The best television news reports are usually the result of one team's hard work. But most of what is on the news is a collaboration between broadcasting allies. Sometimes their crews have been in different places. Just as often, they have been in the same place but can offer a different angle on the same story. We went back to the hotel to feed the story on the satellite to London. Fifteen years later I saw the report again for the first time. It was an ordinary compilation of the day's pictures, with a not terribly informative piece to camera. But after we fed it that night I was exhausted and elated. Just getting through the day was an achievement. I had produced a passable piece of work, but on that day, the quality of the journalism was secondary. I was just pleased to have got something out and on to the satellite. And I was in a war, and I had the responsibility of trying to work out what was happening and to let our viewers know about it. I couldn't wait to go out again the next morning.

In 1989 BBC TV News was not the twenty-four-hour operation it is now, so after the feed we were done for the day. I went to the hotel's terrace to have dinner and to get drunk. Was this what being a war correspondent felt like? If it was, this was the life for me. We were staying at the Camino Real hotel. I'd always wanted to stay in one of the famous war hotels I heard about from the big boys in the reporters' room. They talked about the Caravelle in Saigon and the Commodore in Beirut and the Camino Real, and I'd made it. It felt like every room was packed with news people. TV editors had set up their gear in the rooms. The screeching gabble of tapes being played fast, backwards and forwards, filled the corridors. Cables dangled out of windows to generators and live positions. You couldn't go out because of the shoot-on-sight curfew, so at night we ate and drank on the terrace. Multi-coloured tracer looped around the volcano that dominates the city. The war went on as dinner was served. I loved it.

In the next few days other journalists with more experience told me how to try to look after myself and the people with me. Don't look like a soldier, don't run fast, make sure you always look like a journalist, a non-combatant. Most journalists covering urban wars in the 1980s did not have flak jackets or helmets, because the theory was that it was better to look like a civilian. On the streets in El Salvador the custom was to wave white flags and yell '*periodista*', Spanish for journalist, in the hope that the gunmen would not shoot. I thought I'd pinch a towel or a pillowcase to make into a flag. But the hotel was wise to that. Everything in my bathroom was yellow – presumably because so much hotel linen had already been stolen and ruined by journalists who needed white flags. The only special equipment that I had with me in El Salvador in 1989 was a pair of training shoes; I thought I might need to run away. I saw one reporter with a very lightweight piece of body armour that might just about have stopped a bullet from a Saturday night special. It was nothing compared to the heavy-duty pieces of carbon fibre that news people wrap themselves in these days to stop high-velocity bullets. People said behind his back, in a tone that suggested he was slightly damaged, that someone had been killed very near him the previous year, so he was nervous. I just nodded. I had very little real understanding of what they were discussing; they could have been talking about the difficulties of declining verbs in Sanskrit.

One day guerrillas took over a hotel in the rich part of San Salvador, trapping some American soldiers inside. We hung around outside, as government soldiers occasionally blazed away with their heavy machine-guns, enjoying seeing the guerrillas trash the official version of the war, that the Salvadorian government was winning with the help of American military advice. Now the Americans were barricaded into their hotel rooms and the rebels were in the middle of the city. A burst of gunfire sent a group of us leaping into a ditch for cover. We discovered as we flew through the air that some soldiers had been using it as a latrine. It was full of shit. We jumped out again, hooting with laughter, drunk on the noise of the battle.

The BBC was trying not to spend money in the Americas at the end of 1989, because it was spending so much in Central and Eastern Europe, which was why in El Salvador we were borrowing cameramen from Visnews, a friendly news agency which produced pictures for TV networks around the world. In turn, not being able to contribute very much, I followed Guillermo, his colleague Maite Galeano, a cool Salvadorian woman, and a painfully handsome Frenchman called Jean-Jacques around the city. Jean-Jacques' Argentine girlfriend Marina was one of the sex-iest women in the Americas and also a producer for Visnews. One day, after a lot of gunfire, some local cameramen plunged into a field where the grass was more than head-high to find who was responsible for it. That day I was with Jean-Jacques. We looked at each other, thinking the same thing. Shall we follow them? Bullets had already been whizzing round quite a lot that day and even though I was full of my freshman excitement, I didn't fancy it and neither did he.

When we went back to his office with what we both thought was good material, his boss tore into him.

'Jean-Jacques, this is crap. We need stronger than this. You're doing this kind of work, you just have to get stuck in.'

Actually the pictures were very good, and told an interesting story, but what he meant was that there was not enough 'bang-bang', Hollywood-style shots of gunmen blazing away.

I liked getting out with the crews. It felt right, and it would have been dishonest not to share the risks that they were taking. I was bemused to find that some TV correspondents did not spend much time in the field. One morning I saw an American, experienced-looking, quite a bit older than me, whose reporting from El Salvador for one of the top US television networks I had admired from Washington. He was sitting in the back of a car, about to go out to Mejicanos where more fighting was happen-ing. I introduced myself, hoping to get some tips. He said there was not much he could tell me. His producers made him stay in the hotel because he had to go live on air a lot. This was his day off; his cameraman was taking him into the field so he could get an idea of what was happening. Rooftop journalism, pontificating from a safe distance without seeing things for real – a danger and sometimes a curse for everyone by the late 1990s – started for the Americans a decade earlier.

The War Drug

There was another lesson that started in El Salvador and sank in slowly over the next ten years. I wanted to tell the story of what was happening, in Salvador and everywhere else. But television does some things very well and other things very badly. It is excellent at simple messages. Thanks to the bang-bang that Guillermo, Maite, Jean-Jacques and the others were picking up in San Salvador, it was easy to tell a very simple story in two minutes on a news bulletin: a war was raging between two sides. Civilians were caught in the middle and were suffering. A government that had close ties to its powerful northern neighbour, the United States, claimed to be in control. But guerrillas (largely invisible) were advancing. It was very hard to go beyond that, to explore some of the subtleties of the story. The reason is that it is not easy to illustrate complicated ideas on TV. It is impossible to fight pictures. A reporter can hint at the background to a civil war over images of a gun battle, but if gunmen are still blazing away while he drones on about politics, the audience will get distracted and will not listen. Anyway, I knew that the people back in Television Centre did not want a forensic analysis of the way power worked in El Salvador – and on my first visit to the country, I was not very qualified to provide it. After all, the civil war was no novelty. It had been going on right through the 1980s.

We went to do the story of the FMLN offensive, late, only because of the quality of the pictures that were coming out of El Salvador. My editors wanted the drama of the battle on the streets of San Salvador. We had been covering the story from Washington, compiling pieces for the BBC with facts from wire service reports and pictures from the satellite feeds of NBC News, among others, which we could access from the ease and safety of our offices in M Street. That wasn't rooftop journalism, it was worse – armchair journalism with time off for lunch and drinks after work. The reason for sending me was to have a reporter on the spot; part of that, I understood, though I was never asked for it directly, was the need to establish myself on the ground by doing dramatic pieces to camera somewhere dangerous. I had seen producers and programme editors grouped round monitors in Television Centre, watching feeds coming in and I knew what they liked. I did not disapprove; I thought it was understandable, and felt the same way.

Despite its restrictions, television done properly by reporters who have been at the sharp end of a story is tremendously powerful and can help people understand what is happening in parts of the world that seem a long way from home. When pictures, sounds and words are put together in the right order, they are unbeatable. One notch down from that, when you have some of the ingredients you need, but not necessarily enough of the right ones, there are still ways of getting round the restrictions of the medium. But with no pictures at all it is virtually impossible to do anything. Sometimes the logistics of shooting any pictures, never mind the right ones, get in the way of finding out what is really happening, even for experienced reporters and crews. And the time spent in the edit room is crucial. A good picture editor, and a reporter who understands the story and knows how to magnify the power of the images by linking them up with the right words, can achieve a lot.

In El Salvador, I was starting to realise how difficult it is to report a war. It took much more time to get a clearer idea of what journalists in war zones have to do, and how they should do it. But I was already starting to understand why human beings like wars, despite all the pain they cause, because I had felt a flash of it myself. For the first time I was discovering that war creates a special – and terrible – atmosphere that can weigh humans down and destroy them but also lift them up. Wars are for high stakes; they give the people caught up in them the worst experiences they will ever have, sometimes their last ones, and sometimes their greatest moments. Being in danger, and then escaping it, is a great feeling. In a war you discover your limits. Doing a job in a war zone, handling it well and coming out alive can give a man or a woman the confidence to face anything, for a while. Do too much of it and it will destroy you – if not physically, then mentally.

When I was growing up in Britain in the 1960s and '70s the television and the radio were full of people reminiscing about how wonderful the Second World War had been. I couldn't understand why they missed something so terrible so badly. Over the next few years that changed, as I began to understand the relationship that humans have with war, their greatest vice. Wars are horrendous and awful but when they are happening they are not always terrible, as long as the worst things are happening to other people, who you don't know and better still don't love. Life stops drifting along and suddenly has a sharp purpose. It gets reduced to a very simple and fundamental equation about death and survival, and the complications and the nonsense fall away. Peace is better, but it is complicated and it can be dull.

The thought of going to a country at war and then working hard to get to the most dangerous parts of it had made me nervous before I left Washington for San Salvador. But once I had heard a few bullets shot in anger, I stopped thinking that anything bad was going to happen to me. I did not want anything bad to happen to anyone else either, but if it did, I wanted to be close to what was going on, and to be the one who went on television to tell the viewers what was happening. I was young, I was full of ambition and energy, and I was already developing one of the most vital skills of war journalists – denial. All around was the evidence that we are fragile, not immortal, but I could ignore it when it came to my own life. I was going to be fine. I wasn't stupid, I would be careful and I would live. If someone had asked whether the story was worth my life, I would have said that the question was wrong. I was not going to die that day. In my head, I realised that my life could be at stake but I couldn't feel it in my guts, which made it easy to deal with.

The day I travelled to San Salvador David Blundy, a famous British foreign correspondent, was killed, shot by a sniper in Mejicanos. It made me a little more apprehensive that one of my colleagues, a man of great experience from the same country as me, was dead. But to be honest, it didn't bother me too much. I suppose I thought that if this was the sort of story I wanted to do, this is the kind of risk I would have to take. I felt sorry for him and for his family, but only in the most distant way. I was not thinking too hard, either about him or even the suffering that the local people were experiencing. I wanted a life like his, without the death. Blundy had not been late on the story. He was at the fag-end of an assignment that must have seemed routine to him on the day that he was killed. I never knew him, but later on I read the obituaries his friends had written, about his distinguished reporting from the Middle East, about his charm and charisma, about the women in his life. The *Sunday Times* gave Blundy a write-up the weekend after he was killed that is still moving to read. The story of his death went across six columns and you can feel the shock and loss of his friends who wrote it. It said that after he was shot he did not have a chance and that he died later in hospital. They reprinted one of his reports from earlier in the war, a brilliant, forensic reconstruction of a massacre. And the obituary said: 'No grave will inter his reputation as one of Britain's best narrators of war and other social and political ineptitudes. No editor who knew him will bury his or her grief, no journalist will dispose of his memory.'

I am thinking of him as I write this, but I wonder how many people apart from his nearest and dearest have thought about him in the intervening years. Reporting the news is about the moment, and when it has gone, and the people who did it are gone, we should not kid ourselves too much about what is left. I have done obituaries on television and in the papers for colleagues. You cannot get much more sincere than in an obituary of a friend. But in the end, they are still the story of someone who is dead and who should be alive. And any journalists who want to go to war ought to be told that that is how they could end up. If they are like I was in 1989, they won't listen, which is just as well, because wars need reporters.

Blundy's daughter Anna was a student at Oxford University when he was killed. Later, when she wanted to find out about what had happened to him, she went to a library to read the cuttings about how he died. She could imagine her father's friends crying into their typewriters as they wrote them. For a television documentary I met Anna and she took me to her father's grave in Highgate Cemetery. It was a handsome place to end up, and he had a fine gravestone, with his name and the dates of his life and death carved elegantly into it. (At some point in the 1990s, probably in the Balkans, I had decided that if I ever needed a gravestone it would be made of Welsh slate.) Anna was calm. She had thought a lot about her father's death, and written about it, so her answers were fluent. The only time her voice cracked – and we were standing at his grave – was when I asked her what she would say to him if she could. She said she would ask, 'Dad, why did you do it?' By the time I met Anna, I had imagined my children asking the same question at my grave, over the Welsh slate, and I was looking for a better way to earn my living as journalist.

But the week that David Blundy died in 1989, I was still in my late twenties, I had seen dead bodies and heard shots fired in anger for the first time, and I was having fun. I was starting to feel like a proper reporter. I was indestructible. What I didn't realise was that I was drinking a potentially lethal cocktail from a very dangerous cup. It is still there in wars, waiting for the young to try it and for the regulars who should know better but want more. It is a mixture of fun, fear, excitement, adrenaline – and a sense of mission. It helps reporters ignore the big drawback of a great job. You can get killed.

3

All Flesh is Grass

John Simpson leaned against the wall of one of the circular, endless corridors in BBC Television Centre and was sympathetic and not even slightly reassuring.

'My dear chap, you simply must have a good war. If you don't, you might be better off trying to find a job somewhere else.'

Reporters are always insecure. It is like being in love with someone who doesn't always love you. When I was still in the first flush of my life as a foreign correspondent, infatuated with every part of it, I could have wonderful moments, so completely satisfying that nothing came close. And then there were terrible times when my passion was not returned by the BBC, and this was the worst so far. I had just discovered that I was not in the starting line-up for the biggest story in years, the Gulf War of 1991, and I felt rejected, knocked back, smashed. It never occurred to me to go to the boss concerned and ask what the problem was and how it might be fixed. That was not how things worked, and anyway it would have been difficult, since I had unearthed the BBC's masterplan for the war in a wastepaper bin. Rooting around in the bin was not dignified, but everyone else seemed to be getting their invitations and I was not, and unrequited love does strange things to you. BBC News was expanding and an extra layer of management had been grafted on; the man in question was freezing me out. The crumpled bit of paper proved it. Everyone else had a good assignment and I was on the replacements' bench, plunged into gloom about the crap war they were planning for me. In the next few days, the only thing that made me feel better was going for long runs, throwing imaginary punches at the imaginary head of the man who was ruining my war. I was deranged. I had no sense of proportion. I could not get it out of my mind. I was desperate to be somewhere dangerous and interesting when the war started. I wanted to see some history happening in front of my face. Nothing else mattered.

I was already hopelessly wrapped up in my new life, and I worried that someone could still take it away. In a couple of years I had spent big chunks of time in China, the United States, the Middle East and Latin America. I had seen wars in El Salvador and Afghanistan and a revolution (or what looked like one) in Romania. My thirtieth birthday party on 6 February 1990 was under the Hapsburg chandeliers of the Athénée Palace hotel in Bucharest. Its façade was peppered with bullet holes and draped with Romanian flags with holes in the middle where the emblem of Nicolae Ceauşescu's communist state had been hacked out. Opposite the doors of the hotel were the burned-out remains of the Romanian national library. In the foyer broken glass and rubble crunched under my boots, a sound and a feeling that I had already got to like, because it made me think I was in the right place. The entrance to the Athénée Palace was guarded by student revolutionaries who sported berets and believed they were changing their country. Bits of paper with V for victory daubed on them in paint were pasted up all over what was left of the hotel windows. Inside, under the chandeliers, there was dark red wine and a big dinner arranged by the BBC's fixer, an elegantly dressed, moustachioed Romanian called Tibi who adapted so well to life in the new Europe that he surfaced in London a few years later as the translator for a Romanian football star. Tibi had acquired a big joint of meat which he had delivered to the hotel to be roasted, and once it had been eaten he replaced it with a large-breasted gypsy singer who covered my face in violent red lipstick as her song reached its climax. Then there was dancing with our dark-eyed translator girls in nightclubs where rich gypsies had punch-ups to win the honour of paying each other's bills. Getting to thirty was making some of my contemporaries nervous. But I was reporting on foreign news for BBC TV, doing what I had dreamed of doing, and it had happened so fast.

Now the bastards, who had helped me get addicted, were cutting me off from the life, the love, the drug that was so all-consuming. John Mahoney, the foreign editor, was the only friendly face in the management; he tried to help but could not do much. In a muttered conversation in a corridor – a lot of BBC business is done in corridors – he explained, low-voiced, that he had been outranked, that I was fine before they put someone in above him, and would be again, and that I would be held in reserve, and that something would come up. He was being rational when I was anything but. For the time being all that he could produce was a pre-war swing through the Gulf on board the British foreign secretary Douglas Hurd's VC-10, and the number-two slot at the UN in New York once the killing started. It was not what I had imagined. I was going to be stuck in New York, watching it on TV. I felt sick. It was the first time I had felt the power that the boss class had over people like me. They could take it all away, they could stop me going, decide someone else should have a chance, and there was nothing I could do about it.

The trouble, as far as I could see, went back to the summer before, after Iraq invaded Kuwait on 2 August 1990. Kuwait was closed off, so the closest place to get to it was Saudi Arabia. Once the Saudis had decided to let us in, I was sent there in the first wave of news people, and the person in the management who I thought was persecuting me felt I could have done a better job. The truth was I didn't do too badly, but I was not experienced and Saudi Arabia was a hard place to work. Early on in that trip, I learned a couple more important journalistic lessons. Half-way through the first day there, with the temperature about forty-five degrees in the shade, when we still trying to fix up cars and maps and accreditation, I came out in a cold sweat. It was suddenly glar-ingly obvious that the only story to do was to get up to the Kuwaiti border to see what was going on. My rival from ITN was certain, at that moment, to be hoovering up an exclusive from the border on account of my naïve stupidity in not going there first. For a couple of hours I was near panic, trying to work out if we could get there and back from our base in Dhahran before the evening deadline. The answer was that we could not, so I awaited the news of ITN's big story. I shouldn't have worried. They had not thought of it either. The first lesson I learned on that trip was not to worry what the opposition is up to. It is a waste of energy to fret about things you cannot do anything about.

The next lesson was to do the story you find, not the story you expect. The day after, we set off at first light to drive through the desert to the border, which sounded difficult and romantic until I saw that there was a well-paved highway to Kuwait, unsur-prisingly considering it was the main artery through the most important oil-producing area in the world. We sped along in an air-conditioned Mercedes. It took a couple of weeks after the invasion for journalists to get into Saudi Arabia and by then the first wave of American troops had arrived. I assumed they would be dug in along the border. After all, George Bush Sr. had drawn a line in the sand, on television. The script was written in my head. Along Bush's line an iron wall was waiting to stop the Iraqis moving into the Saudi oil fields. When someone asked Bush what he was going to do, didn't he say watch and learn? At the very least, that ought to mean that the US Marines were ready to fight. The last town in Saudi Arabia was al-Khafji, sleepy and spread out on the Gulf coast. And there was nothing there, not even Saudi soldiers, let alone Marines. But I thought the fact that I could not see any defences meant that I had not tried hard enough to find them. It was a long drive up there and back and I wanted to get a story for that night. There was not much time to work. We got a few pictures, on the end of the lens, of some sort of armoured vehicle. It was too far away to tell what it was, but with a bit of careful packaging maybe it looked like it was part of an iron wall.

What was really happening hit me a couple of days later, but by then it was too late. We were probably the first newsmen to get up to the Kuwait border and a great exclusive story was there yelling at me and I hadn't noticed. The border was defenceless, wide open. Saddam's men could have started their tanks and driven into eastern Saudi Arabia, the greatest oil field in the world, without being molested, at ground level at least. They would have raced along, because the desert was flat and firm, covered with small pebbles that had such perfect shapes and beautiful colours that I took a bag of them home. When the war started the following January the Iraqis crossed the border and seized al-Khafji. It took a fierce fight before the US Marines, who were there by then, pushed them back, once they had also fought off the journalists who invaded their battlefield. When the Iraqis

59

started shelling them, the Marines took cover in their fighting holes, amazed that news crews who had turned up were 'blatantly stood in the open to "get that perfect picture of history"', as one later reported. When I got back to London the manager who decided to spike my guns when the war was starting five months later wasn't too impressed, not because I had missed the story that the border was without defenders and the road to the oil was open, but because I had not been able to find the iron wall, which existed in his head too.

Everyone was in limbo in Saudi Arabia in the months between the invasion of Kuwait in August 1990 and the start of the war on 17 January 1991. The hotels in eastern Saudi Arabia were full of Kuwaiti refugees. Their children made a nuisance of themselves by playing in the lifts and pressing all the buttons. One evening we were told to go back to al-Khafji on the border to meet a group of people who called themselves the Kuwaiti resistance. Some plump young men appeared, their faces wrapped in chequered red and white Arab headscarves, self-consciously nursing brand-new assault rifles.

'Soon we will fight,' one of them proclaimed. 'Our young men have been spending the hot months of the summer in London, in the south of France, and now they are returning, to liberate their homeland!'

Thousands of US troops were flooding into Saudi Arabia though, and after a few more weeks ships were coming into the docks at al-Jubail and unloading everything big you need in a war. Huge trucks, Vietnam-green, not yet resprayed the colour of desert sand, and long convoys of transporters carrying tanks and armoured personnel carriers rolled off and headed into the desert. One afternoon, about sixty miles from the Kuwait border, I noticed some strange humps and drove down a track that led off the highway to investigate. It was a US Marine infantry unit, astonished that I had seen through their camouflage, which they thought was foolproof. The Marines were friendly and going stir-crazy. They had rushed over in the first wave thinking they were going to fight and had been living in tents for a couple of months realising it was not going to be that simple. The officers hardly ever saw newspapers and the Marines had no idea what was happening outside their little patch of desert. In the absence of war, about the biggest thing in their lives was what they called 'hydration', drinking vast amounts of water. Dozens of pallet-loads of it were stacked up in their camp, covered in camouflage netting. Before and after patrolling, or training, or just because they had not drunk anything in a while, they would down bottle after bottle of water. The Palestinian businessman who got the American mineral water contract became a billionaire. The Corps had ways of testing if the men were drinking enough.

'It's a buddy system,' said the Colonel. 'We told the guys to sniff their buddies' piss. If it stinks, they need more water. Same if it's yellow. Not enough water.'

The piss tubes, pipes pushed into the sand, were never busy enough for his liking. At night the blackout was strict. No torches were allowed. In the dark desert, under blankets of stars but no Moon, I ripped open the vinyl cover of my MRE, meal ready to eat, the food made by scientists rather than chefs that the US military eats in the field. It was so dark that the only way to tell what was in the packages inside was to try them. I nibbled some tissues and mints before getting to a piece of something that was supposed to be meat. The next day there was a big celebration when hot chow – meatloaf and mashed potatoes – arrived suspended in canisters from the bottom of helicopters, cooked miles away and flown into the desert. The Americans' huge logistical power really hit me the following year, when more than 100,000 Bangladeshis were killed by a cyclone. The Bangladesh Air Force only had half a dozen serviceable helicopters, one of which they used to fly us about, reckoning that getting their story out was worth more than the tiny amounts of food and relief that it otherwise would have been carrying. The Bangladeshi pilot was unsurprised and unamused when he heard that the Americans had enough helicopters to fly in lunch.

But even though the Marine unit I had gatecrashed was well nourished and well hydrated, they did not know where they were. They had been told that they were close to the Kuwaiti border and that the Iraqis could invade at any time. I felt cruel when their faces fell as I told them that they were about sixty miles away from the border, much closer to the five-star hotels of Dhahran, the oil capital of eastern Saudi Arabia, than they were to the Iraqis. They were young men cut off from the world and time was heavy. Some of them asked for newspapers, so for a couple of days I collected a bin-liner full and went to drop them off when I was passing. It was getting towards dusk when I drove down the track towards their camp. But they nearly shot their paperboy.

'Man, we were locked and loaded, we were ready with the claymores. You should have fucking told us you were coming. We thought you were a fucking Iraqi. Man, you got to be more careful.' I didn't bother to help them out again.

After more than five months of a phoney war, the Americans and their allies started bombing Iraq on 17 January 1991. I was in Julia's flat, watching TV with her late in the evening when the programmes were interrupted with the news that the bombing had started. It was the moment that I had dreaded. War in Iraq, and I was stuck in London. While the Americans were smashing Baghdad, CNN, the broadcaster that invented twenty-four-hour satellite news, was smashing its rivals. We were not really rivals, though – we weren't even in the game. The BBC had a team in

Baghdad, led by John Simpson, but the Iraqis forced it to work under heavy restrictions. John and his unrelated namesake Bob Simpson managed to get out some vivid reports, but on that first night, the BBC carried hours of live CNN output. Their three correspondents sat in the hotel and commentated on what they could see out of the window. It was compelling. Their exclusive made one of them light-headed. When someone knocked on the door, he quipped that it was the pizza arriving. And that was what the war seemed like for a while: the latest TV entertainment, which you could watch with a pizza and a beer.

The next morning Julia and I went to Heathrow. She got on a flight to Washington, where she was going to be one of the producers for the duration of the war. I flew to New York to take up my spot on the subs' bench. I was depressed because I was not at the war and bored because nothing was happening at the UN. I sat in our office in the Rockefeller Center watching snowflakes blowing around outside the windows. I saw the bare minimum of news. It looked unreal, a TV drama with pyrotechnics but no blood. Stormin' Norman Schwarzkopf, the American commander, gleefully showed video of tiny cars moving off bridges just seconds before they were blown away by precision-guided munitions. We were learning new things about war; modern weapons did not miss, and that you could get it all live on TV. But it was too painful to watch for me, the rejected lover, the addict without his drug. So I went shopping. In Bergdorf Goodman, a fancy department store on Fifth Avenue, a flirtatious saleswoman with red lips and nails got to work on my wilting self-esteem. She helped me into a brown check Ralph Lauren suit.

'Hey, this looks great, you know, really good,' she cooed as her talons arranged the collar and scraped down my back as she smoothed out imaginary wrinkles in the jacket. It worked; I bought it, and never wore it again. It might have been right on an off-duty bond trader at a charity fundraiser in the Hamptons, but it did not do much for me.

Back at the Rockefeller Center the phone rang. It was foreign editor Mahoney, the master of the terse phone message. The previous summer, the weekend before the Chinese crushed the pro-democracy demonstrations in Tiananmen Square, he decided we needed reinforcements. When he phoned all he said was, 'Honkers, then Pekers. OK? Well done.' I guessed he meant that I was flying to Hong Kong, and then on to the Chinese capital, and that I ought to feel pleased about it. I was delighted, but I had to call his deputy in case there had been a terrible mistake. This time there was more to explain.

John Simpson had been expelled from Baghdad with the rest of his team and most of the foreign press after the first few days of the war. When he got out to Jordan he had collapsed and was too ill to go back. He had collided with a piece of heavy wooden furniture during a blackout in Baghdad and bashed his ribs, and he was run-down after months in Iraq. They needed someone to replace him. I had done a stint in Baghdad before Christmas. Did I want to go back? Normal people, not suffering from the war-reporting virus, might have been a bit nervous. After all, the Americans and their allies were bombing Iraq every day and every night. Hundreds of warplanes, thousands of tanks and hundreds of thousands of soldiers were in the Saudi desert, waiting for the order to charge. But I was relieved. If it all went to plan, I would be heading to Baghdad on my thirty-first birthday. What a present! Mahoney, who was a very decent man, was pleased to be telling me I was back in the game. My depression went away. I thought that the bosses had forgotten about me, that my career was on the skids before it had properly got started. The truth was that they had not started to love me; they were stuck. They had deployed all their favourites already, so when they had a vacancy for the biggest reporting job in the war, I was the only one who could fill it. I agreed straight away to do it and got on a plane that night with my Bergdorf Goodman suit-bag – picking up something a little more appropriate in London before I went out to Jordan, the jumping-off point for Baghdad.

Before I left for Amman I went to Television Centre, a little patch of west London that was consumed by war fever. Because the Iraqis were expected to use chemical weapons everyone who was going to the war had been given a protective suit and gas mask. During the months of the phoney war we had all been sent on a course to learn how to use the kit in a Nissen hut somewhere on Salisbury Plain. The trousers were cunningly designed so that a flap would open to allow the user to take a dump. A friendly NCO instructed us in the correct way to decontaminate the backside with something called Fuller's Earth, which had some magical effect on whatever Saddam Hussein was going to be throwing at us. We lined up in the hut, solemnly miming the procedure. Back in London, a researcher was sent out to a pet shop on the Uxbridge Road with the names and blood groups of everyone who was going to the Gulf to get them engraved on dog tags to be hung around the neck. We had been told not to take the anti-gas kit to Baghdad because it has been developed by the British army and could fall into the hands of the enemy. I thought my skin was more important than Britain's military secrets so picked up my suit to take to Baghdad. I left it in a bag for a moment by the lift while I went back to the office to get the rest of my stuff. When I returned, about a moment later, it was gone. I went to a security office to report it missing, and found it sitting on the supervisor's desk while he stared at it wordlessly, twitching, angry, enjoying every second of his work-up to giving me a bollocking for leaving it unattended. Didn't I know there was a war on? Pathetically, small-mindedly, I got much more pleasure in cutting across to tell him what was in the bag, that I would need it at the real war, where I was going and he was not. My ego, ragged and bruised a couple of days before, was surging back to full strength. My narcotic, war and television news, was back in my veins, and I was good and whole again. At Heathrow paranoid, short-tempered officials demanded to see my notebooks and press cuttings. When I asked them how that would help Britain's national security they said that if they didn't get them I wouldn't be on the plane. The war drug was getting to them too.

Amman was cold and quiet. The streets were emptier than usual. The war was squeezing Jordan hard. King Hussein, as ever, was balancing his instinct to stay close to the West with his fear that he could be unseated by the Palestinians who made up at least 60 per cent of Jordan's population, and were solidly behind Saddam Hussein. In shops in Amman enamelled replicas of the missiles Iraq had been firing at Israel were the souvenir of choice. The result for the King was an uneasy middle course: not backing Saddam and not condemning him, and not joining the US coalition but trying to help it in private. In the foyer of the Marriott Hotel the Christmas decorations were still up. A witch's cottage towered over the reception desk. It was made of slabs of gingerbread, baked rock hard and nailed in place. Upstairs in my room, I started to realise what I was about to do and what could happen. Back in London, David Shukman, one of my best friends in the BBC who was by then the defence correspondent, had given me a mild lecture. He tried to make me think more about the risks.

'Look, Jeremy, at the MoD they're telling us that if the Iraqis do something stupid, like drop a missile laced with gas on Tel Aviv, the Israelis could nuke Baghdad.'

David pointed out that I would be sitting in the middle of it.

I appreciated what he was trying to do, but it did not put me off for a second. I was going to be part of the biggest news story in the world, and that was that. But in my room in the hotel in Amman, with the still, grey city on the other side of the glass rolling away towards the desert which led to Baghdad, I started thinking harder about what was going to happen. I was too far in to turn back, and I didn't want to, but suddenly I felt lonely and scared about what lay ahead. I wrote letters to my parents and to Julia in case I was killed. Big fat tears splashed on to the paper as I tried to tell them how much I loved them and how much they meant to me and how they weren't to be sad. I sealed them up in envelopes marked to be opened in the event of my death, and left them in a bag with my sports kit which I had decided to leave in Amman as there would be no time for jogging in Baghdad. The tears felt even more like self-pity an hour later, when I was refilling my bravado tank in the bar. But looking back, they were intrusions from a real world of danger and loss which was touching me, if only briefly, for the first time. They were a flash of realisation that there were people who cared if I lived or died, who were worrying about me at that moment. At least I had started to think in a serious way about danger, which was probably good, but that did not make me any less keen to hug it and keep it close. When I got back from Baghdad in March and I was not dead, the first thing I did was to rip the letters up without opening them.

The Iraqis had issued a raft of visas in Jordan and had told all the journalists who wanted to get in to meet on their side of the border, where they would form us into a convoy to drive to Baghdad. I rang London to tell them the good news. I respected and liked my boss Chris Cramer most of the time – he had given me all my first breaks, so I owed him a lot – but that day I thought he was a shit. Brian Hulls, one of the cameramen who hadn't managed to get a visa for Baghdad, who was twelve years or so older than me, married with children, asked what I was doing about life insurance. I hadn't thought of it. I assumed the BBC would take care of it. In the 1980s the BBC had persuaded quite a few reporters, myself included, to leave its pensionable staff to take an annual contract, by offering pay rises and pointing out a loophole which cut tax bills by a third or even a half, as long as you had an aggressive accountant. I rang Cramer to ask him about insurance. He was as straight as ever. 'You haven't got any,' he said. 'As a freelance, it is up to you.' That's nonsense, I protested, people are getting quoted premiums higher than their entire salaries, and I am only a notional freelance, since I work full-time for the BBC.

'Look, Jeremy,' he said, not unkindly, 'the BBC's record is second to none in these matters. If anything bad happens, we'll look after you.' I didn't know whether to believe him or not, but I put it out of my mind. I had made my decision. I was going, and nothing was going to stop me.

The night before we were due to leave, some American reporters asked everyone who had been given a visa to meet them in a conference room at the Intercontinental Hotel. They had been rattled by a warning from the Department of Defense in Washington, which said that the road from the Jordanian border to Baghdad was being attacked from the air and that it was too dangerous to go down it. The Pentagon had told them they could give no guarantee that our convoy would not be hit. In the previous few days the Americans had been killing the drivers of Jordanian petrol tankers, whose long tubular trucks were supposed to resemble Scud missile transporters. Our nervous colleagues proposed the journalistic equivalent of mutually assured destruction. None of us should go. I suppose they were trying to find a way to make their own second thoughts more palatable to their management. You can imagine the phone call: 'Well, the BBC isn't going either . . .'

I had got over my own little wobble of the previous night. I was nervous, but I was excited too. I thought that the Americans who were trying to stop our trip had lost their bottle and, even worse, were trying to sabotage my war. I stood up and said that the BBC would be going, that everyone knew this was going to be dangerous before we got into it, and that it was too late for second thoughts. Rory Peck, who had been given the BBC cameraman's visa for Baghdad, was full of contempt for our American colleagues. In his languid, posh voice, politely and firmly, he told them so. Rory was an adventurer who got into journalism during the Afghan war against the Soviet Union. He started taking a camera with him while he walked deep into the interior with mule trains full of CIA cash for the Afghan mujahideen. His appetite for action was endless, until he was killed during a shootout at the television station during the attempted coup in Moscow in 1993.

I was also well aware that I had to get in because the BBC had nobody in Baghdad and Brent Sadler, the top foreign correspondent at ITN, our opposition, was already there, filing some very strong stories. One had even shown a cruise missile, the wonder weapon of that war, flying towards Baghdad in broad daylight. We had nothing and nobody in Baghdad. The ITN team had been kicked out at the same time as John Simpson and the others a couple of days into the war. John and the rest of the team went back to London where they were all fêted by a grateful management. But ITN stayed in Amman, pushing for visas, and got them. When I arrived in Amman I found that in all the excitement nobody had remembered to apply for the next lot of BBC visas. Not for the first time, the BBC had taken its eye off the ball, losing out to a rival that did only news, so it had no distractions and was lighter on its feet. The result was that we were at least a week behind our biggest rivals.

Rory Peck and I left for Baghdad the next morning, with Allan Little, who was doing radio. He was a Scotsman who could not be stopped, intelligent, funny, almost exactly the same age as me and with the same taste in alcohol, who was becoming one of the best journalists of our generation. When the phone call from the Iraqi Embassy had come in, offering visas, another reporter was dozing on the sofa of BBC Radio's office in Amman. The BBC can be Darwinian, letting correspondents fight it out between them; nobody in the ranks of the management in London had said exactly who would be staying in Amman and who would be going to Baghdad for Radio News. Allan answered the phone, crept out so that his sleeping colleague would not stir, and went down to the Embassy to claim the visa for himself.

The BBC convoy was made up of two Toyota pickup trucks. At first they had olive green canvas covers over their backs which I thought would show up nicely against the desert sand for the American pilots, so they were now painted white with 'TV' written in big black letters. The pilots might not see the markings, but I didn't want to give them the excuse of saying that our convoy had nothing on it to say that we were journalists. The trucks had been rented from two young Jordanian entrepreneurs. We were so anxious to get moving that the BBC producer who did the deal had paid their asking price of US $25,000. At the last minute, the two junior capitalists revealed that they would not be driving us themselves to Baghdad. Instead they paid two Palestinians about $100 each to take us down what was then the most dangerous road in the world. A nervous-looking Christian Palestinian called Issa had the keys of the pickup that carried our fuel supply, hundreds and hundreds of litres of petrol that we needed for the vehicles and for the generator which had to keep our operation going in Baghdad. One spark would have turned him into a bomb. Rory felt sorry for Issa, and went to sit next to him. Brian Hulls filmed us as we left. 'It's for the obit,' he said, cheerfully.

On 8 February 1991 we trundled up towards the border with Iraq. A few lines of tents were standing flapping and cold in the black fields of volcanic rock a few miles inside Jordan, where the landscape was already turning into desert. The summer before, after the invasion of Kuwait, big camps had been set up on the Jordanian side for tens of thousands of migrant labourers, mainly Asians, who were getting out of Iraq. At the border post, King Hussein's troops were businesslike, with uniforms that looked as if they had come out of a catalogue of 1950s British military tailoring. When they handed back our passports and waved us on, it felt like we were cutting the last ties with home. We were off to war. The unknown was the right direction and I felt excited and liberated. After a mile or so the Iraqi border post came into view. A portrait of Saddam Hussein stared down from the gate.

It took hours for the Iraqis to go through all our gear and to organise themselves into a convoy. The rain spotted on and off as we drove fast down the highway that leads to Baghdad, away from the volcanic rock of Jordan and through a flat plain of sand and shale. Any anxieties I had left about the trip lifted away. There had been plenty, almost all about things that would stop me getting to Baghdad. What if the Iraqis decided my visa was wrong in some way? Even worse, what if John Simpson rose from his sick-bed to bigfoot me? (Bigfooting is the practice in journalism of a more senior person taking over the story. John Simpson has never actually applied his perfectly polished brogues to my head and pushed down. It just felt like that sometimes. 'Think of me as the dentist,' he said to one correspondent who resented him coming on to his

71

patch. 'It's jolly painful to see me, but it only happens a couple of times a year.')

The war, or maybe just the rarity of traffic, was confusing the dogs. Dead ones were everywhere, squashed flat on the highway or decomposing in the gutter, their bellies bloated and their tongues lolling out. Grey clouds churned across the sky and the drizzle wet the dark sand and grit of the desert. Every now and then we had to bump down off the road to avoid places that had been bombed. The remains of the oil tankers that had been heading for Jordan lay broken-backed on the road, gutted and burnt. Sometimes vapour trails showed where warplanes were passing, and there were wrecked communications towers and power lines and bridges to mark where they had already been. I felt calm. There was no point worrying if they were going to bomb our convoy. We couldn't stop them.

The sun started to set when we were still a couple of hundred miles from Baghdad. The convoy stopped and the Iraqis gave us instructions. We were not to use our lights. Air raids were expected, and there was a blackout. When the convoy moved again our drivers were exhausted as well as scared. They were nodding off over the wheel as we raced along, without lights, far too close together. Rory took over in Issa's petrol wagon, and I did the driving in the other pickup. We were blind and fatalistic, ploughing on into the blackness. Faint moonlight was reflecting off the white lines in the road, and I tried to follow them and the dark shape of the vehicle ahead. Sometimes there were flashes on the horizon. The BBC's war in Baghdad nearly ended prematurely when a pile of rubble grew out of the motorway, close to where a bomb had exploded. I braked hard, swerved and raced on, through the town of Fallujah. A few people were running along the pavements as men on bicycles whistled and shouted at them to take cover, like the air-raid wardens in *Dad's Army*.

The streets of Baghdad were empty and dark. We drove along deserted flyovers and expressways. There was no power or light because the bombing had smashed the electricity grid. Men carrying Kalashnikovs were at the gates of the Rashid hotel, and pulled back the iron gates. The hotel was the grandest in Baghdad, a concrete monolith, built 'in the era of Saddam Hussein' according to a plaque inside the door that was cordoned off with a satin rope. Now that his era has ended it is in the heart of the American 'green zone' in Baghdad, walled in by miles of razor wire and fortifications. The last time I saw it an American tank was parked outside. On that winter's night in 1991 it was gloomy, freezing cold and unwelcoming. My footsteps echoed on the marble as I approached an angry-looking woman behind the desk. A black and white portrait of Saddam Hussein, young and spruce in the late 1960s or early '70s, gazed down on the foyer, his eyes focused somewhere off-camera, perhaps at some vision of Arab unity under his firm and benevolent leadership.

The receptionist looked at me, and then at my passport, as if she couldn't decide which was more poisonous. At first she refused to re-open the BBC office, which was in a suite half-way up the hotel. Then she wanted money, and with her face stubborn with satisfaction she produced sheaves of receipts to prove how much we owed and shone her torch through the gloom at the bottom line of the invoice, which was a very big number. The last BBC team had left in a hurry – in too much of a rush, it seemed, to pay their bill. I can't remember how much cash they demanded just to let us into the hotel, in payment for a bill that may have been real or may have been fake. It didn't matter because there was nowhere else to go, and we had to be there, no matter how much it cost. I gave her maybe twenty thousand dollars, maybe more, I can't remember exactly. After I handed it over she agreed to let the three of us check in for a single night. She gave me a hotel ID card, and wrote 'one night only' on it in big letters.

Down at the end of the dingy marble vault of the foyer, I could see torches and camping lights shining out of the Sheherazade bar, a piece of 1970s kitsch where I had drunk Jordanian beer before Christmas and which had now been annexed by the CNN news machine as their forward base near the garden, where their satellite dish was pitched. They were well set up, with cables snaking out on to the terrace outside and someone talking loudly on the phone to Atlanta. They probably thought it was basic. From where I was standing, it looked cosy. They had a world-beating operation and we had to start again from scratch. Explosions rumbled in from the city, and from the roofs close by there were odd cracks and ripples from anti-aircraft guns as they launched green and red tracer at the invisible bombers.

I went to find Saddoun al-Janabi, the Iraqi official who looked after most of the dealings with the foreign press. The surly woman at the front desk said he was in the Rashid's bomb shelter, under the hotel. Down in the basement I pushed open the steel door. A stink slapped me in the face, the kind that humans produce when they have been living in a confined space without running water for the best part of three weeks. I decided that I would not be visiting there again. The shelter was lit by candles and a few lanterns and families were camping there. I stepped over some sleeping bodies and found Saddoun sitting on the floor wearing an overcoat, with a red and white chequered *keffiyah* wrapped round his head. He struggled up to his feet.

'Jeremy, welcome, you are back, it has been hell here.'

Saddoun was an amiable man, proud that he had studied at a Scottish university, where had developed a liking for whisky and shortbread biscuits. He gave me a stubbly kiss on the cheek.

Saddoun's eyes were red and exhausted. Later in the war he was demoted because he was not nasty enough to the foreigners.

If the hotel had a generator they were not using it. Just like the rest of the city, there was no power, no lifts and no lights. We slogged up a dark staircase by torchlight to the fourth floor with our supplies and the gear. Bags of rubbish were decomposing in the corners of the office. A half-eaten meal was fossilised on a plate. I had no idea how long our predecessors had been given to get ready when they had the order to get out. Perhaps the Iraqis had gone through the room after they left. More likely, in the pressure of the moment they didn't think about taking the garbage out. The place was a slum. In the next few days (they allowed us to check in properly after I paid them even more money) we made it even worse. There were only three of us and we wanted to get stuck into the story, not do the cleaning. But the chaos in the office reflected our feeble, disorganised operation and made it even worse. Doing TV news is impossible without the right logistics, and we had almost nothing. The first few days were a huge struggle. Once I had to go down to the ITN office for something. It felt clean, efficient and peaceful. Someone was selecting a Marks & Spencer's long-life microwave meal for his dinner, which was haute cuisine for Baghdad in February 1991. They had light, from an adequate generator. Music was playing softly in the background. Their reporter, Brent Sadler, was friendly enough but his eyes were hard. Never mind who was winning the real war. In the Rashid hotel no one wanted to come second either.

Sadler was ITN's best man, ten years older and much more experienced than me. I was a better writer, but I was less experienced and against him had to pedal very hard in every other department. His crew treated Sadler with a lot of anxious deference. He was an 'operator', the highest form of praise for a news reporter at that time, when the ability to get into places you should not be, against the odds, was more important than how you performed live. Brent's crew looked nervous around him. So was I. (He was replaced by the urbane and charming Edward Stourton towards the end of the war. A few hours after he left I saw the ITN crew, without the camera, relaxing in the sun, which was starting to get hot in the middle of the day. 'Day off,' the camera-man said triumphantly. They looked relieved. So was I.)

I had gone back to our dark, filthy cave feeling depressed. But cleaning the office was the least of it. CNN had a very well-organised operation which they had been allowed to keep going, and then reinforce, when other broadcasters were thrown out. They were Iraq's route to the outside world, and from our posi-tion as the regime's most hated foreign broadcaster they seemed to be treated like royalty. Iraqi officials would stop the BBC using a small light for a piece to camera, on the grounds that it violated the blackout and would attract bombs, while twenty-five feet away CNN's Peter Arnett stood in a blazing pool of light, on air non-stop via a satellite dish that was pumping out a signal that must have shown up on every piece of American surveillance equipment from Riyadh to Langley. The Iraqis loved CNN, and hated us. Arnett covered America's war in Vietnam from the beginning to the end, winning a Pulitzer Prize along the way. He was the reporter who got the quote from an American major in the ruins of Ben Tre in 1968 that 'it became necessary to destroy the town to save it'. By 1991, being in Baghdad had made him the most famous journalist in the world by a big margin. After John Simpson and the others were expelled he was for a few weeks the only TV reporter in Baghdad. CNN often called him the city's only Western journalist. That infuriated Alfonso Rojo, of the Spanish paper *El Mundo*, who was one of my friends in the Rashid. He had been told to get out like John and the rest, but persuaded the Iraqis to let him stay.

'What are these Americans saying?' he used to demand. 'Are they saying I am not a journalist? Is that because I am not on CNN? Or because I am Spanish? Is that not Western?'

Alfonso was furious with CNN because Arnett had been told not to let anyone use their satellite equipment to file. They were number one on the story, and were so hard-nosed about staying on top that even Spanish newspaper reporters were treated like rivals. CNN exploited their moment brilliantly. Their campaign to stay in Baghdad had been masterminded by an exceptional producer, Robert Weiner. He schmoozed with the Iraqi officials from the Ministry of Information, stockpiled food and water, and made sure they had the right equipment. Weiner, and CNN, saw what was possible long before anyone else. They realised what the new satellite technology could do, and made sure that they had everything they needed to win the media war and to invent a new way of doing TV news while they were about it.

In the first few evenings, after we had fed our stories from a satellite uplink that had arrived in the same convoy that we did, Rory and I would sit slumped in our filthy and dark office, watching the air raids, relieved that we had at least got a piece out. We camped in the middle of our slum, eating stews out of hotcans, a strange and useful delicacy I had brought out with me from London. When they were pierced the food inside them would heat up, thanks to a magical chemical process. Huge flashes, like sheets of lightning, would break over the flat skyline of Baghdad. A Ba'ath party building a few miles away was a favourite target. Even though it was pulverised they would keep coming back to it. We wondered whether that was because it could be seen clearly from the hotel, and filmed. The crash of the explosions which followed a few seconds after every flash often shook the glass, which we had taped up, and sometimes shook the hotel, but we never went to the shelters, because they were so stuffy, stinking and crowded. Green and red tracer bullets went up slow and lazy into the sky. Often sirens would sound the all-clear, then start wailing again a few minutes later because another raid was coming. There was no warning for cruise missiles. I was knocked off my feet by the blast when two of them destroyed the conference centre opposite the hotel.

In the office we drank beer and ate more stew and listened to a few music cassettes Rory had with him. My favourite was Brahms' *German Requiem*, especially its dark and glorious second movement, 'All flesh is as grass.' After Rory was killed two and half years later I played it again and again, and it helped me remember how much of a struggle it had been in Baghdad, and how much we had enjoyed it. We may not have looked young and carefree in Baghdad in 1991, but to me it felt like a kind of freedom, away from the world, responsible only for what we did, in a place that felt so isolated that it was almost on another planet.

Getting the story in Baghdad was easy and difficult at the same time. The easy bits were the air raids. Every night there was tracer, and then the flash of an explosion, instantly if it was near, and after a few seconds if it was further away. The hard part was everything else. None of us had any way, however indirect, into Saddam's circle. The Associated Press correspondent, an Iraqi called Salah Nasrawi, would help out with tips and explanations. One of my colleagues before the war started to attribute Salah's sayings to 'a highly placed Iraqi source', which was too strong for me. It would have been more accurate to call him 'the highest placed Iraqi source we have'. Without thinking about it too hard, probably because there was no other choice, I relied instead on being an eyewitness, trying to give viewers an idea of what it was like to be

78

in Baghdad, and better still, when I could manage it, because it was not easy, what it was like to be an Iraqi in Baghdad.

The main streets of Baghdad were empty and still. Tens of thousands of people had left for the country to get away from the bombing. Most mornings we asked for permission to film in a small vegetable market. We did it because we knew they would let us go there, and because there were a couple of good kebab shops. I thought that if we always went to the same place people would get to know us a bit and start to relax, and we needed to eat. Rory and I would do some filming, then eat lamb kebabs and drink glasses of hot, sweet tea. Because there was no electricity there was no refrigeration. Animals were driven into the city close to where they were needed, then slaughtered on the spot. One day about a dozen sheep and goats and a big cow were standing peacefully next to the entrance of our vegetable market. We went off to do our pre-lunch filming and came back to find them all lying dead in pools of blood. The man with the knife had just dispatched the cow, in the approved Halal fashion with a clean cut across the throat. It produced another lake of blood that had oozed along the paving stones and was starting to congeal in the sun. We picked our way through it and sat down to eat our kebabs, which we knew now were definitely fresh. It was chilly and the sky was dark from the smoke coming from an oil installation that was burning on the edge of the city. We had not been allowed anywhere near it. The ash floated down and settled gently on my kebab.

One day, as usual, we did vox pops, which are those random snippets of interview that crop up in news reports, filmed in cafés or on street corners. A man who could speak passable English, which was unusual in poor parts of Baghdad like the one we were in, took the lead. He came out with an almost perfect soundbite, about how the resistance to the foreign invaders would continue to the glory of the leader they all loved, Saddam Hussein. When we were packing up, he came up to me. 'That stuff I was telling you . . . it was all lies, rubbish.' He spoke English because he had dreamed of being a hotel manager. But when he was a student in the early 1980s, he was conscripted into the army to fight Iran. Ten years on, he had not been released, and now he was on the run.

Everything broadcast from Baghdad had to be censored. Normally there were not many problems because I knew we were not allowed to film military installations, or bridges, or government buildings. Everyone who spoke to us on camera, like the deserter in the market, said they loved Saddam Hussein and that America would bow down before him. But I could not report what he said away from the camera, because the censor would cut it and the act of defiance would have got me expelled. But it was another fragment of what was happening, a little nugget that helped me understand a bit of what was going on. When sometimes I tried to get something through the censor, like a picture that might be giving a location away, I would try to distract him at the key moment, by knocking over a chair, or opening a shaken-up can of beer next to him, so that it would explode over his trousers. In fact there was little that I left out that I would have liked to report. The best way to censor journalists is not when they write scripts but when they are gathering information, which the Iraqis were experts at doing.

We called the men who did the censoring 'minders'. They called themselves 'guides'. They spoke English very well; many of them had been to university in Britain, quite often in Scotland like Saddoun, and often shared his mania for whisky and shortbread. They were usually employed by the Ministry of Information to work on the *Baghdad Observer*, the official English-language journal that came out every day on inky, grimy paper. It was never more than eight pages long, mainly official communiqués about the president. Some of the minders looked like they could have had a stab at being proper journalists in another life. They even looked like journalists, untidy and ready for lunch or a drink. But I always realised that however sympathetic they seemed, they would be expected to report back everything we said to the authorities. So would the drivers, an amiable alcoholic called Ramadan, who never drove sober; a stout, sorry-for-himself man called Hassan who wore a suit made of ticking; and a little bantam cock called Hattam, who would dart his head forward to land a kiss on his employer's shoulder if he was treated with kindness. Allan Little was horrified when Hattam's head darted forward after he gave him some tea bags and landed a kiss full on his lips. A few years later, Hattam was murdered, probably for his car. Our regular minder was a decent man called Faris, who had the pained look of someone for whom life had become much harder than ever he dreamed. Towards the end of the war, we passed the headquarters of Tariq Aziz, the foreign minister, which had been bombed. When I asked testily exactly why we couldn't film it, he looked at me wearily.

'I am tired, so are you, you know the rules. Do we have to have this argument today?'

My attempts to prod the system, until the system, in the form of Faris, pushed back, had become a ritual. And he was right. It was exhausting. One day Faris was joined by another minder. He did not look like the men from the *Baghdad Observer*. He was too tall, too tough-looking. One of the other minders, a Kurd who would criticise the regime openly when no one else from the ministry was around, warned me that our new friend was from the security police, was therefore armed, and that the BBC was the only broadcaster to get a real secret policeman to itself. I asked him if it was a back-handed compliment.

'Not really. It means you have enemies here.'

Once we were allowed out of Baghdad to go to Basra, in the south. On the way the road went through a town at a crossroads, where thousands of Iraqi soldiers were milling around. They looked like unwilling conscripts, with scruffy, faded uniforms, and they were mostly unarmed. Presumably they were only issued with weapons when they were close to the battlefield. As we drove at night, the horizon lit up with huge flashes of light. They were narrow when they started at the ground and broadened as they rose into the sky. There was a line of them, one after the other. Quite a few seconds later, a rumbling noise like distant thunder came in our direction. I ignored the minder's order and told Rory to film it. When we got back to Baghdad, they took our tapes and never gave them back. I was given a lecture by Naji al-Hadithi, the head of the press centre, who went on to be Saddam Hussein's last foreign minister, about the untrustworthiness of the BBC. I protested, asking at least for tapes that had pictures of civilians in Basra who had been badly burned. He refused, and not for the last time during that war, threatened the ultimate sanction, the hold he had over all the foreign press, to cancel my visa and kick me back across the desert to Jordan. I grovelled and he gave me another chance to mend my ways.

We grovelled when it was necessary to officials like Naji al-Hadithi so that we could stay in Baghdad for days like 13 February, when the American air force killed at least 314 people, including 130 children, in a bomb shelter. For months after I had waded through the water in the basement of the shelter I could not get the smell of human fat out of my boots. The water came up to my thighs. It had been pumped in to put out the fire that was started by the American bombs. A scum of rendered-down human fat floated on the surface. Afterwards I kept getting sick-making whiffs of it. I scrubbed my boots, but the fat-smell would not go away. I was picking it up when nobody else could. After a while I realised that was because it was in my brain, not my nostrils.

On the morning that it was destroyed, we arrived at the shelter, which was in Amirya, a suburb of Baghdad, at about eight o'clock. It was a low, concrete building. Smoke was pouring out of a hole in the roof. Bodies on stretchers were being carried out, and then the empty stretchers were passed back inside to be refilled. Sometimes instead of a whole body there were just sections – someone's torso, a pair of legs, a shoulder. They were passed down a human chain wrapped in polyester blankets, made in China, with yellow and brown checks. Those blankets always remind me of corpses, because so many ended up wrapped in them. Since that day in Baghdad I have seen them in the West Bank, in Lebanon, in Bosnia, Kosovo and Grozny, covering bodies and then discarded in piles as if they had died too, with the red blood on the polyester turning black and stinking. You get the blankets on beds in cheap hotels too, in the sort of places where people kill each other easily, which made going to sleep feel like a rehearsal for being a corpse. But that day at the shelter there was not too much blood. High explosive makes blood flow when it tears bodies apart, but the American bombers had started a fire that cooked it all away. Most of the bodies that were still recognisable as human beings were those of women, old men and children, who had been alive the night before, and by the time I saw them were gnarled and black, like charred logs.

The minders said we could go wherever we liked, interview anyone we wanted and that there would no censorship. At other places where they had claimed there were civilian casualties they would take on a very official tone, like a propaganda broadcast, making speeches about the perfidy of their enemies. But at Amirya they were very different, shocked, with eyes full of tears.

It looked like a straightforward story. An air-raid shelter had received a direct hit from a bomb powerful enough to cut through yards of reinforced concrete. (After the war it emerged that the Americans had attacked it with two 2,000-pound laser-guided 'smart bombs'.) But I knew it would be controversial, because the Americans had just killed hundreds of civilians and they would not want to take the blame for it. Amirya was a middle-class area, full of officials and other educated, relatively privileged Iraqis. Outside the shelter were crowds of frantic middle-aged men. Some of them were wearing old-fashioned striped pyjamas and dressing gowns, and they told similar stories about the evening routines that had developed during nearly a month of bombing. As it was getting dark the men would bring their wives and children and elderly relations to the shelter where they would spend the night. It reassured them because it was big and strong, built by a Scandinavian company. Then the men would go back to their homes, to watch over their property. But that morning they were woken at about dawn by the crack of two monstrous explosions. One bomb blew a hole in the concrete roof of the shelter and another smashed in after it and exploded inside. The ceiling was low and the intact concrete walls channelled the blast around the building. That day there were very few wounded in the hospital. Most of them were dead.

I assumed that the Americans had made some sort of mistake. Killing so many women, children and old men made them look so bad that I could not believe they had been stupid enough to do it deliberately. At Yarmuk hospital, a couple of miles away, fragments of people, burnt pieces of meat, had been laid out in the car park. The headless torsos looked even more like blackened tree stumps that had been burned and ripped out of the earth. I noticed that Rory Peck was shooting some tight shots. I told him not to do it, because we would never be able to use them.

'I know, but I just want those bastards back in London who don't like the truth to see it.'

He kept on filming. I made sure he had the kind of 'tasteful' shots that we use to sanitise our news coverage – close-ups of fingers, or feet, or cutaways of people grimacing down at the contents of the hideous butcher's shop that was spread out on the tarmac in front of them.

I think it sounds patronising when news presenters or reporters say that there are pictures 'too distressing to broadcast'. Far better, when the story warrants it, to warn people that something horrible is coming, and to show a nasty burst of the truth. It was lucky that I had paid so much attention to the corpses. On air that afternoon I was interrogated endlessly about what I had seen. The Pentagon and the Ministry of Defence were claiming that the Amirya bunker was a military command centre. The aggressive tone of some of the BBC anchormen surprised me. I was being treated like an Iraqi spokesman. In London, they must have been feeling the pressure. The idea that the war was a grown-up version of an arcade game, which had been so carefully nurtured by American and British spokesmen with their talk of precision bombing, had taken a big knock and the spin-doctors were counter-attacking by making false claims about the shelter. The bombing was precise all right – so precise that it killed most of the people in the building. The trouble was that they were not the people that the Pentagon and the Ministry of Defence said they were. For the first time, Western reporters had more than just gun-camera video games to work with: for the first time we had seen dead Iraqi bodies, piles of them, to add to the thousands who had died unseen in air raids in the desert.

It was such bad news for America and its friends that it was time to shoot the messenger. Again and again I made the point that I was just reporting what I had seen and heard with my own eyes and ears. No, I hadn't seen any soldiers. The bodies were of women, children and old men. And there were hundreds of them. The Americans and the British would have done better to admit their mistake, and point to the true fact that, considering the massive weight of bombs that had been dropped, civilian casualties in Baghdad were surprisingly low. The more they stuck to an explanation which contradicted the evidence from the scene, the more incredible they sounded. (About a year later I met a general who had been in an important job at the Ministry of Defence in London during the war. He confirmed that the attack had been a mistake. Their information about the building had been wrong.)

The dead were buried at a mass funeral. Dozens of coffins were carried down the road at the head of a procession of thousands of chanting people. Many of the mourners had Kalashnikov assault rifles which they were firing into the air. When they saw our group of foreign camera crews they exploded with anger. Rory Peck, his camera on his shoulder, plunged right into the middle of them. I followed him nervously, wishing that he hadn't, expecting a shot in our direction at any moment. I could smell the smoke from the guns as the Kalashnikovs were emptied into the sky. For a couple of seconds it felt very nasty. The crowd was pushing in around us, shouting, firing. The gunfire was very loud and spent cartridges were flying around, bouncing off people in the crowd. Then about a dozen men materialised between Rory, me and the mourners, pulling weapons out of the half-zipped fronts of their leather jackets. The crowd did not need to be told. They moved away, very fast, to wave their Kalashnikovs somewhere else. I was never so relieved to see Saddam's security police.

I knew that we were being watched but I had no idea we were under that much surveillance. Perhaps they were reinforced because the authorities knew there would be a lot of angry people at the funeral. It was the only time in the whole war that I was scared in Baghdad, the only time that Iraqis showed any hostility – in fact the only time they were not welcoming. Being a foreign correspondent in Baghdad in 1991 was very different from the way it was fifteen years later. Usually, the only physical danger came from the sky, from the bombing. But most of that was so accurate that unless you were sitting in a place they decided to hit, like the Amirya shelter, it was always manageable. Iraq and the Middle East have changed since then. The deep cultural tradition of offering hospitality to strangers still holds among most people, but the rise of militant, political Islam and the activities of Western governments are changing attitudes fast. In 1991 in Iraq, the diehards in Saddam's regime were unfriendly; most other people were not. I was pretty sure that if the Iraqis had managed to plant a bomb in London at that time and killed 314 people, including many children, an Iraqi TV reporter would have had a good chance of being strung up from a lamp-post if he had tried to report it.

On air that day I was still getting the third degree from our presenters in London. How did I know the shelter was not a command post? What evidence was there of secret passages under it? The Pentagon in Washington and the Ministry of Defence in London and every spin-doctor the military had everywhere else were all insisting that they had knocked out a military target. I was politely and firmly insisting that civilians had been there, and that I had seen the bodies. When the live broadcasts were over, some of the management came across the line to talk to me. I became suspicious when one of them, who I knew had not helped my cause before the war, told me that he had '200 per cent' confidence in me. Maybe he was trying to convince himself. Perhaps he was being truthful and I was getting paranoid. But reporting the attack on the shelter was the biggest journalistic test I had faced, and I was passing it. I stuck to what I had seen myself and it seemed to be a winning formula. The BBC editors in London, even if the propaganda onslaught had given them doubts, decided to trust the judgement of their man in the field, which was the custom, and correct.

The next day we went to the mortuary. It was a square, old building with a courtyard in front of it. A lorry had been backed into the courtyard. It was full of bodies, still loaded because they had run out of space. The ground around the lorry was covered in more bodies. Men were walking slowly among them, leaning down, turning them over, trying to identify the women and children they had left settling in for the night in a modern shelter that was supposed to be strong enough to resist a nuclear explosion. The banal details struck me, like the knots they used to tie their laces or the colour of their socks. I couldn't stop thinking that when they tied that knot, or put on a pair of clean socks, they were not expecting to end the night dead.

It was hard to see inside the building, which had very few windows and no lights; like everywhere else in Baghdad, there was no electricity. We had to pick our way over and around the bodies. Quite a lot of them were burnt and unrecognisable. Some of them looked like shrivelled piles of old clothes. The yellow and brown Chinese blankets still wrapped some of them. Out of the sun and at night, Baghdad in February is chilly. Perhaps because so many of them had been cooked by the fire the Americans started, they had not begun to smell. Bodies, and parts of bodies, had been dumped everywhere. There were bodies on the doorstep, in the entrance hall and in the corridor leading to the pathology lecture theatre, which must once have been used by medical students. Inside the theatre, natural light streamed in through windows in the roof, washing over more bodies that were piled up on marble slabs in the centre of the room. Corpses spilled down across the floor, and back up the raked tiers of students' benches.

A man was looking for his children. He had just found his wife. He identified her from her rings, which he was now clutching in hands that were sticky and sooty from the congealed blood of the charred corpses he had moved to find her. Spending time with so many dead people was numbing. When I interviewed the man with the bloodied, heat-tarnished rings, the cameraman, Brian Hulls, who was part of a small team of reinforcements that had reached us from Amman, tried to set up his tripod. There was so little floor space left that he had to take off the spreader at the bottom of it and put its legs either side of a corpse. I suppose he was working automatically, but it would not have been a professional sin to film with the camera on his shoulder. I set my feet one in front of the other, as if I was walking a plank, between two bodies. As I talked I could feel the weight of one of the corpses pressing into my ankle, getting heavier every minute. Back in our office at the Rashid hotel, Allan Little and I talked about the best way to describe the scenes at the mortuary. He wanted to say that the bodies had been dumped 'like rubbish'. I thought that was too dehumanising, too harsh for victims of our side. But he was probably right. War always spits people out when it has finished with them.

We weren't really guests at the Rashid. We were just people who paid a couple of hundred dollars a day for the privilege of sleeping in a hotel that had no power and half an hour's water a day – which was thirty minutes more than most of the rest of Baghdad was getting. I built our filming day around the three o'clock water ceremony. Everyone would be in their rooms, waiting for the pipes to start gurgling. The first and most important job was to flush the lavatory. Then I would have a shower. The water was always ice-cold, but after an agonising few weeks I started to quite like it. The last job was always to refill the bath. There was no guarantee the water would come on tomorrow. Life without electricity is fine, as long as you have a torch and batteries and, if you are in TV, a generator to power your equipment. Life without water becomes disgusting very quickly. The hotel provided no food. It also tried to stop people cooking in their rooms. We had a terrifying Syrian-made primus stove that Rory had bought in Jordan. He pumped it furiously; it hissed and spluttered until flames roared out of it and licked the curtains and the ceiling. I had made the mistake of letting him do the shopping in Amman. Rory had a genuine liking for spam. We had hundreds of tins of spam. Rory liked fried spam best. He would crank up his Syrian stove and fill the room with smoke. Every few days the hotel would try to take it away, on the reasonable grounds that it was a fire hazard.

I decided to stay in Baghdad until the bitter end, whenever or whatever it was. Nothing was going to shift me. John Simpson was getting better in London and I knew he would have loved to come back. But I had no plans to leave. No one from Television Centre said anything, but I sensed I had passed some sort of test when the Amirya shelter was hit. I had also discovered one of the fundamental truths about reporting wars, the one I remembered again when Abed Takkoush was killed in Lebanon nine years later. For us to have a good day, someone else has to have their worst day or their last day. In this case, the deaths of 314 people and the misery of their friends and relations allowed me to make the most important breakthrough of my career. On the day that the Americans and their allies carried out the worst single atrocity against civilians of the war, I had produced some decent and honest coverage, and I had not embarrassed the BBC. I could almost hear the sigh of relief from the management in London.

On 24 February I turned on my shortwave radio as usual to listen to the seven o'clock news on the BBC World Service as soon as I woke up. I nearly fell out of bed. The ground war had started. The Americans and the British and the rest of them had attacked on a massive front from Saudi Arabia, going into Kuwait and into

Iraq itself. Not much information was coming out, except that it was going well. Later on I found Naji al-Hadithi in his little office at the back of the reception desk at the Rashid. He parroted the official line. Iraqi forces were fighting bravely against the latest act of aggression and would drive the invaders back. OK, I said, so take us to the front line. 'We will see what can be arranged.' No chance, I thought, the Iraqis haven't got a prayer. In the next few days the other Iraqi minders kept saying the same thing. Naji kept his head down. The atmosphere was different. Some of the more unpleasant minders were cracking uncomfortable smiles. The nicer ones were more friendly than usual. They felt that something was changing, that our side would be arriving in Baghdad soon. I had always tried to behave like a neutral, but I started to feel a little triumphant. I was looking forward to seeing the Iraqi regime getting what it deserved, but I also wanted to see the worst of the minders going down with it. A few old Middle East hands in the hotel started talking about the coup of 1958, and the slaughter of the royal family, reminding anyone who cared to listen that political change in Iraq usually meant a lot of bloodshed.

Once the ground war started, the BBC wanted less news from Baghdad. It had teams of reporters with the ground troops, who had been sitting in the desert for months waiting for their moment. I spent a lot of time listening to the World Service, trying to piece together what was happening. The details were sketchy, but Kuwait had been recaptured and the tanks seemed to be moving towards Baghdad. We couldn't wait to see them. I was exhausted, hungry most of the time because there was not enough food, and ready to get out. The night before the ceasefire the allied air forces seemed to be using up all their leftover ammunition. There had been bombing every day and night I was there, but this was especially heavy. The hotel was shaking. In our office we could hear jet engines screaming low across Baghdad. Up to that moment they had always been invisible, high in the sky. They were rubbing the Iraqis' noses in their superiority. The Rashid was like a grandstand, looking down over the bombers' playground. The Ba'ath party building that we could all see from our office windows, which had been bombed at least once a week, was hit again and again. It was almost as if they were putting on a show for the cameras that they knew were watching them. Rory Peck got more and more excited. He leaned out of the windows and shook his fist at the sky.

'Come on Biggles, come on Ginger, hit the bastards!'

I did a piece to camera at the window of the office, trying to time it so I started after the whoosh of an engine and ended with an explosion. It was so noisy that the microphones started complaining, the sound distorting as they refused to take any more decibels. I could feel the force of the explosions, which were at least a couple of miles away, lifting my shirt off my shoulders. But it felt no more dangerous than a firework display. We were not even slightly frightened. We knew that they knew where we were, and felt certain that they would not hit us. I also thought that the attacks were mostly for show. They were hitting empty buildings that they had hit before. After Amirya they did not want more bad publicity about mass civilian casualties. All the same, it must have been terrifying to be closer to the explosions.

On the morning of 28 February I was woken early by gunfire, lots of it. Christ, the Americans must have arrived. I lay there for a few moments listening, wondering what to do next. Then I realised that the Americans could not have entered Baghdad, because it was only small-arms fire. There was no heavy stuff. I got dressed in a hurry. Rory was already in the office. We dashed down the stairs and towards the gates of the hotel compound. Outside in the street dozens of men were firing their Kalashnikovs into the air, as if they had won the war. Rory Peck ran around filming. I hate it when armed men empty the magazines of their weapons into the sky. If the bullets don't get you as they spray them around people's heads, they can kill you on the way down. Then the police came and marched us back into the hotel. Naji al-Hadithi was shaking with rage.

'Why did you leave the Rashid? Your lives were in danger. You know you are not allowed out without one of our guides . . .'

Once again the threat of expulsion was waved around. But they were all relieved. They were shooting because, amazingly, a ceasefire had been declared. The Iraqi officials could not believe it. They had thought the game was up. Mentally, they had been preparing for defeat, and now the regime had survived. The minders who had been trying to ingratiate themselves switched back to the way they had been, only worse. The gates of the hotel were locked. Every request I put in for filming was refused. We were prisoners.

A week or so later we were expelled. The order to go came very quickly. This time the offices had to be cleared out. No one was coming back for a while. We had only a few hours to find some transport for the BBC team, which had expanded since Rory, Allan and I arrived a month earlier. There was only time to throw thousands of tapes that had been shot since the previous August into the back of a truck and to cover them with a tarpaulin for the drive across the desert to Jordan. By midnight an extraordinary convoy had formed up, of taxis, trucks, old American sedans. They were going to get an escort to the border. But they pulled out of the hotel compound without the BBC party. A member of our team had gone missing. I roamed the dark corridors of the hotel, with just my torch to light the way, banging on doors, trying to find our missing comrade, who emerged bleary-eyed an hour later. Our colleague had been conducting a romantic tryst with another journalist, and they wanted to prolong their personal siege of Baghdad for as long as they could.

The Iraqis had given stern instructions not to lose touch with the convoy because special security measures were in place. Now we were at least two hours behind them. What I did not know much about at the time was that Saddam Hussein was taking his revenge on Kurds and Shia Arabs who had tried to rise against him. In the Kurdish north and in the Shia south a slaughter had begun. They did not want us to see it, and they succeeded. Our drivers talked us through three rings of roadblocks around Baghdad and as the sun came up accelerated down the highway towards Jordan. The journey across the desert was long and the lights of Amman that evening looked like Paris.

4

The Wired World

I was too busy during the war in the Gulf in 1991 trying to do my job to think deep thoughts about the future of my trade. It was CNN's war, and the rest of us were just trying to keep up. CNN were the big boys in Baghdad, with the best office and a satellite dish they could use whenever they wanted. The rest of us were poor relations, having to ask permission from the Iraqi minders to make a simple call on the satellite telephone to talk about a broadcast later in the day, while Peter Arnett and his CNN colleagues were busy pontificating live on TV. I was jealous of CNN's resources, of their well-organised, highly professional operation, and of the way that the Iraqis gave them preferential treatment. Even then, it was obvious that CNN had found a new way to report the news, by recognising that broad-cast technology made it possible to be on air twenty-four hours a day, covering events as they happened and pumping them out to the world. But at first I thought it was just another way of doing the news. I did not realise that we would end up copying them, and that a global twenty-four-hour cycle was being created that would change everything about the news business.

I found out how TV news was going global a few months after the war in Iraq, when Yugoslavia started to break up. It was a hot day in the early summer and I was standing on the banks of the River Danube with a Serb pointing a cocked machine-gun at my chest. He was not doing it because he thought I was one of the Croatians he was fighting, but because he hated the way that the BBC was reporting his war. The man with the gun was part of the Serb minority in Croatia, who were also fighting against the new nationalist Croatian republic, because they thought that if they stayed in it, they would be second-class citizens, or dispossessed of their property, or dead, or all three. The Croatians, who were also fighting the federal Yugoslav army, were besieging a string of villages of stubborn and desperate ethnic Serbs on their side of the Danube. The only way in and out was from the Serbian side of the river, on a raft made of planks lashed to oil drums. I felt like an emissary to a remote land as the raft was pulled on a steel cable through the soupy green water, and in a way I was, because for the BBC at least the Serb side of Croatia's war for independence was undiscovered territory. That was why the man with the gun was so angry.

On the Croatian side of the front line Martin Bell had been doing heroic work for the BBC but we had been slow to report from the Serb side, which was why I was on the raft, trying to reach them. It jammed itself into the marshy bank on the Serb side of the Danube and the BBC team jumped off. Someone must have warned the local Serbs that we were coming, because the welcoming party was already waiting. I stepped off the raft, smiled, offered a handshake and said who I was and who I worked for. The answer was the oily rattle of a weapon being cocked. Even though I guessed he was doing it for show, to make a point, not because he wanted to pull the trigger, you can't ignore a machine-gun heavy with bullets pointed at your breastbone; you feel a strong connection with the person holding it, as if some sort of invisible beam is coming out of the barrel and fixing you in one place. They were big men, dressed in bits and pieces of combat fatigues and carrying an assortment of hunting rifles and ancient submachine-guns, which looked like the ones that Richard Burton used in *Where Eagles Dare*. When we had got over our bad start a few days later, they told me that they were indeed German weapons, taken by their grandfathers from the Wehrmacht in the Second World War and buried in their orchards until they were needed again. But it was still too early to try to start a conversation by admiring their guns.

A man with a beard and a nasty look made a speech. BBC reports had been rebroadcast on Serbian TV and they had not liked what they had seen. They were not happy that all the reports had covered the Croatian side and not theirs, which was why they were requesting that we got back on the raft and left; presumably the guns were there to help the message stick. None of the men spoke English, but they had seen the BBC pictures, and heard Serbian TV's commentary that the BBC was with the Croatians, and that was enough.

Something had changed. TV foreign correspondents had always been much less visible abroad than they were at home, because no one in the places where we worked saw the stories that we produced. BBC World Service Radio had always, by definition, been global. But BBC TV reporters abroad had been about as invisible as you can be with a camera crew. Once in Afghanistan in 1989 I asked, through a translator, whether some soldiers who were emptying their Kalashnikovs up at the stars to mark the New Year would mind being filmed by the BBC. One of the soldiers stopped firing and said something. 'He wants to know if you're Lyse Doucet,' the translator said.

Lyse, a talented Canadian journalist, was in Kabul for the World Service and her reports had been translated and read out on the BBC Pashto service. They must have liked what she had been saying because they were very co-operative. I told them I was not Lyse, not even the same gender, but they did not mind, and went on pouring streams of green tracer into the sky over Kabul. If they had not liked her reporting, it might have been very different. The point is that they had an opinion about the BBC, for good or ill, formed through listening to one of its language services that was aimed at them. Now the men on the banks of the Danube had an opinion about English-language TV reports that they had seen but could not understand.

In the village next to the river, which was called Borovo Selo, I managed to placate them enough to let us stay. Even better, they uncocked their weapons. In their village hall, they were serving food for Serb families who had been kicked out of their homes in other villages by the Croatians. Over a big dinner of roast pork, I tried to explain that what we had been doing from Croatia was good and honest, and that they should not assume anything just because they had seen pictures of a BBC reporter standing next to their enemies, speaking English. In the isolated and besieged Serb villages along the Danube in the summer of 1991, a certain amount of paranoia was understandable. They had been brought up on stories of Croat brutality during the Second World War. Now everything that their grandfathers had said – and that Serbian TV, which was pumping out fierce nationalism, had underlined – was happening again, or so it seemed to them. It took a lot of drinking home-made plum brandy and talking to extract even an ounce of trust from them. In the end one of my reports made it on to Serbian TV, pulled down in Belgrade off a satellite, and they liked what they saw, not because of what I said, which they couldn't understand, but because I included a section of a Serbian propaganda broadcast that showed pictures of Nazis and Second World War atrocities. It was there to show our audience what viewers in Serbia were getting, but my new friends in Borovo Selo assumed I put it in because I was with them. I didn't try to change their minds.

In their village, I was discovering that the spread of global television news was going to be messy, because different and competing groups of people would understand the power of pictures and would resent it or want to control it; you don't have to understand the words to have an opinion about what you think you can see, and men with guns have ways of making their opinions count. In the next few years television went global so fast that most of us in the TV news business did not realise the enormity of what was happening. It changed the way that we worked and the impact that the news had, and it happened so quickly that we are still trying to keep up.

What made the revolution possible was technology. And as the 1990s wore on, it became lighter, more portable and cheaper. When it was heavy and expensive and had to be moved by lorry rather than on an airport trolley, it was much easier to control the news. In 1982, Britain went to the South Atlantic to take the Falkland Islands back from Argentina; the only way to get to the war was on one of the Royal navy ships and auxiliaries that sailed there from Portsmouth. The navy took only a small pool of journalists, all of whom were British, and it had complete control of the equipment that transmitted their stories back to London. All print despatches and voice reports from the fleet and then from the Falklands once they landed had to be sent on military communication channels. There were no others. TV pictures had to be carried back physically to Britain. In 1854 it took twenty days for *The Times* to receive William Howard Russell's report on the charge of the Light Brigade in the Crimea. In 1982 it took twenty-one days for pictures of the destruction of HMS *Sheffield* in the Falklands to get to air. Even pictures of the Argentine surrender took eleven days.

Transmitting videotape and brief live reports by satellite was already routine in the 1980s, but the technology was cumbersome and not always reliable. They talked about ways of trying to feed pictures from the South Atlantic, but it would have taken a ten-metre-wide satellite dish, and it was not certain that it could have been done at all from the heaving deck of a warship. Anyway, the discussion was theoretical, because the Royal Navy task force sailed without the right dish, which some of the journalists concluded suited the British government just fine. The Pentagon in Washington was so impressed with the job that Britain's Ministry of Defence did with the news from the Falklands that when President Reagan ordered the invasion of the island of Grenada in the Caribbean the following year, it tried something similar.

Controlling the news agenda in a war is much harder now. Anyone with a hand-held satellite phone, which are about the size that ordinary mobiles were in the mid-1990s, can file words in reasonable quality, and call home afterwards to say goodnight to the kids. Still photographs can be sent from a laptop computer, as long as you have a reasonable phone signal. Sending moving pictures down satellite phone lines is slightly more complicated, but not much, and the technology is getting lighter, more flexible and more reliable all the time. Satellite dishes can be fitted to vehicles so a reporter can go live on the news as he drives through a war zone. In Baghdad in 1991 we did not even have a night-vision lens, vital for getting pictures of air raids after dark. They were expensive and complicated pieces of professional equipment, and once the BBC had equipped the teams in the Saudi desert they did not have any money left to get one for us. Now anyone can buy a point–and–shoot digital camera with full night–vision facilities for about the price of a good bicycle.

But because it has become virtually impossible to stop pictures getting out does not mean that people with power have stopped trying to control the mass media. Honest journalists can be manipulated in lots of ways, if they don't notice what is happening and don't take precautions. We deal in information, which has to come from somewhere. Every reporter cultivates people who might be helpful. It is now more important than ever for the powerful to control the news agenda, so it is up to journalists to be on their guard, to fight back.

Access is everything. It was ironic that in the mid–1990s, as the world was going digital and the twenty–four–hour news cycle was tightening its grip on journalism, that Iraq, a story with the potential to be one of the biggest in the world, was more isolated than ever. It took me a couple of years to get back after the 1991 war. I was blacklisted by the regime as someone considered untrustworthy and anti–Iraqi.

By the time I returned, the authorities had repaired all the visible war damage. In Baghdad the buildings that had been favourite targets of the coalition air forces were up again, reborn as replicas of their former selves. Even the same portraits of Saddam Hussein had been put back on their old sites, although none of them rivalled the magnificent portrait that hung in the visa section of the Iraqi Embassy in Amman, which showed him as a hunter, knee-deep in the snows of Kurdistan, with a shotgun, a tweed suit and a Tyrolean hat.

The visa section was a necessary way-station for anyone wanting to take the highway to Baghdad. It was hard even to get through the door; most of the business was done through a barred window in the wall. It was progress to get inside, to see Saddam as a hunter, and there were plenty of hours to study the brushwork. Until Saddam was overthrown in 2003 the BBC had problems getting Iraqi visas, because the regime did not trust us. They did not like the way we reported them; other broadcasters were much better at buttering them up. My nemesis was an official called Uday al-Taheri, who rose from being a particularly spiteful minder of people like me to being director of the Ministry of Information and head of the Iraqi Press Agency.

Uday was a nasty piece of work who had been expelled from France for using his job as a journalist as cover for something dirty in the world of intelligence. Our relationship started badly and got worse. In 1993, on my first time there since the war, Uday welcomed me back to Baghdad outside the Ministry of Information, drawing smoke from his cigarette through his horrible blackened teeth, luxuriating in the power he had over the Western press, as he was the man who decided whether we could stay or go.

'My dear,' he said, with no trace of affection, 'some of my biggest friendships started with quarrels and the biggest quarrel I ever had was with you, so I am expecting that we will have my biggest friendship.'

But a couple of days later Uday decided tough love was better: he expelled me and my team after I used the phrase 'Saddam's network of repression and coercion' during a report on a cruise missile attack by the Americans. Uday summoned me to his office where his display of faked rage could not hide his satisfaction that he had the BBC bang to rights so easily and quickly. We were told to cross the border with Jordan by midnight. In my last few hours in Baghdad, in a last attempt to save my visa, I went to see Naji al-Hadithi, the most powerful Iraqi we had dealt with during the war, whom Uday had temporarily supplanted.

I had wondered about Naji's habit of always playing music in his office and realised why he did it when he turned it up loud, and then went into the bathroom and turned on all the taps. With the music high and the water gushing he mouthed, like a crazed lip-reader, that he couldn't help, that I could come back some day if he was in charge, but for now I had to go, sorry, sorry, but it's a difficult time for me. Naji's career revived. He grew a dark, Saddam-like moustache and eventually, under the name Naji Sabri, became the regime's last foreign minister before it fell. He was not pursued by the Americans – according to one retired intelligence official he was Washington's man on the inside. Naji denied it vehemently when I contacted him. But he is allowed to live quietly in Qatar, America's staunch ally, teaching part-time at the university.

Getting Iraqi visas during Saddam's last ten years was a messy and potentially corrupting business. Some of it was harmless. Later in the 1990s, when Naji, who liked the British, let us in again, I used to play tennis with him at the Rashid hotel. He would claim that balls were in when they were yards out, enjoying the fact that the reporter on the other side of the net had to agree. I was a useless tennis player, but better than him, and he always won, because I had the impression that losing at tennis might make getting a visa easier.

On another visit I was approached by an attractive woman with long black hair. She said she worked for Iraqi youth television, which was one of the playthings of Saddam's psychopathic younger son, Uday. I assumed from the way she spoke of him that she was one of his playthings too, and tried to befriend her to get closer to the most sinister man in Baghdad, who was feared even more than his father because at least Saddam's cruelties had a certain logic. She told stories about a hunting club where she hung out with Uday's circle. 'Of course, His Excellency and I go back many years, to when we were teenagers, and so close . . .' she would purr, suggestively, looking down demurely at her manicured red talons.

She hinted that she might be able to arrange an interview, and could certainly guarantee visas in the future. But we would first have to do her a favour. If we could lend her some small items of television equipment, who knows what would be possible. The

BBC management in London agreed to leave behind some edit gear. Even though it was getting to the end of its useful life, the thought of what we were doing made me feel sick. More than anything else it was a con trick, which I fell for. Other networks were rumoured to be doing much worse things, paying off officials who granted visas, bringing in expensive presents, or suitcases of cash, across the desert from Jordan. But if it helped us report from Iraq, then it was probably worth it.

In the end, of course, we got nothing out of the deal: no visas, no interviews, no access to the court of Prince Uday, which in a way was a relief. Someone I knew in Baghdad used to frequent a brothel that was used by members of the elite. One of the girls there, he said, was very beautiful, except that she had terrible damage to one of her eyes. The story in the brothel was that she had been picked off the street by one of Uday's thugs and turned into a sex slave. When she got pregnant, another of his men pistol-whipped her so severely that he almost took her eye out.

The worst part of the fight to get visas was the risk that it could insidiously affect the way that stories were covered. The dilemma was simple. If we could not get the visas, we could not report the story from inside the greater part of Iraq that was controlled by Saddam Hussein. That meant that we would not be able to get at the story of how the severe United Nations sanctions that were imposed after 1991 were killing innocent Iraqis. But if we did get visas, the authorities wanted us to do the story their way, which meant when we were in Baghdad we could not touch Saddam's bloodstained, totalitarian police state. The challenge was trying to find an honest way of building up a comprehensive picture from both inside and outside Iraq, while at the same time persuading the officials in the Ministry of Information in Baghdad to issue another set of visas. The ministry dominated the lives of the foreign press corps. We all had to work out of its gloomy halls,

where the BBC had two small rooms partitioned off from a corridor. Every month, a book-keeper would make the rounds of the
foreign news teams, extracting thousands of dollars in cash for the
privilege of being there and using our own equipment, like satphones and satellite uplinks.

The UN sanctions included a ban on flights, so after Iraq
eventually started to give the BBC visas again we would rent a
couple of enormous GMC Suburbans with drivers from the taxi
office at the Intercontinental Hotel in Amman. It was a fast drive
to Baghdad, and during the 1990s it felt like taking a spaceship to
another planet. The desert all around was flat, stony and uninhabited, stretching away on every side, and it was as if we were
racing down a long tunnel to a city under a dome where the usual
rules no longer applied. The people who lived there were trapped,
and the subject of savage experimentation, by a dictator who
regarded them as expendable, the raw material of his glory, and by
an outside world that claimed it was containing Saddam by
squeezing Iraq's people to death.

The road in from Jordan ran past Abu Ghraib prison, which
everyone knew was a place where people were tortured and
killed. The drivers would drive even faster as we went past it, and
were nervous if anyone even looked in its direction. Only part of
the reason for not actively pursuing the network of repression and
coercion was the fear of losing a visa and not being allowed back.
Any of us would have been glad to pay that price if we could have
done the big exclusive about Saddam's police state right under his
nose and moustache. The question was how to get to the people,
if they existed, who were brave – or suicidal – enough to talk
to us.

The only journeys we were allowed to make without a
minder were from the hotel to the press centre and back, or to go
out to shops and restaurants, and then we had to assume we were

being watched too. We had to give the Ministry of Information a list of places we would like to visit; we were not allowed to do any filming or interviewing without one of the ministry's minders. Requests to film at Saddam Children's Hospital were never denied, because that meant we would be reporting what the sanctions were doing to civilians. Sanctions were a blunt instrument. They gave the regime and its cronies a chance to get even richer, by controlling the black market, but they were also killing people. The Iraqis did not want to talk about corruption, but they liked us to report the deaths of civilians, because they made the West look bad. The doctors at Saddam Children's Hospital, always English-speaking, generally educated in the West, would show off wards of dying children. We did the story, because it was true, but I would also try to explain why the sanctions were considered necessary.

Anyone breaking the rules would get expelled and blacklisted. It was a fair assumption that every Iraqi we dealt with would inform on us if they had a visit from the security police. Who could blame them? Towards the end of the 1990s, more people would talk privately about what was happening. But interviewing them on camera was impossible. Even if they wanted to do it, which they didn't, filming the interview would have been like assisting at a suicide. The only way to cover the brutalities of the regime was from outside Iraq, through the accounts of defectors and émigrés, or from the northern provinces that were controlled by Kurds under the protection of the West.

I went to Halabja, where at least 5,000 Iraqi Kurds were killed by Saddam's chemical weapons in 1988. That massacre was part of Operation Anfal, a genocidal campaign that killed between 50,000 and 100,000 Kurds. And I reported from a small town called Qush Tape, where all the men, 8,000 of them, were marched away and killed during Operation Anfal. When I was there the oldest male in the town was only sixteen. Until Saddam's men were forced out after the 1991 war the women had to live in the village with their children in isolation; anyone trying to visit was shot. Sometimes the women themselves were shot at random when they were working in the fields; they said that graves of the dead women were dug up by Saddam's security police to see if symbols of Kurdish nationhood had been buried with them.

No one watching the BBC could have missed the fact that Saddam Hussein was a bloodsoaked dictator. But we could not pursue the story in Baghdad, and that was a weakness. Even so, I always thought it was worth being there, despite the difficulties and constraints. Half the story was better than no story at all. Still, the holes in the coverage of Iraq were not difficult to spot. They prompted two kinds of criticism. One was that foreign journalists were soft on the regime. The other was that we were soft on the West, because we were supposedly not doing enough about the impact of the sanctions. Neither accusation was true.

One very well-known London-based journalist once claimed that the BBC had never bothered to interview the UN humanitarian co-ordinator in Baghdad, Hans von Sponeck, who was a strong critic of sanctions. In fact, I spent a lot of time with Von Sponeck and filmed him in Saddam Children's Hospital, before and after UNICEF said that sanctions could have caused the deaths of half a million Iraqi under-fives between 1991 and 1998.

People cared about how close foreign reporters were getting to the truth in Iraq because they recognised that a great struggle was going on for control of the country between the West and Saddam. In 1991, there had been a hot war, and it continued at a lower level throughout the rest of the decade, mainly through American and British air patrols to enforce the no-fly zone that the UN Security Council had established. Occasionally it flared up into big air strikes on Baghdad. But for the most of the time, the real fight was on the airwaves and in the newspapers.

In 1998, just before Christmas, there was a crisis centred on the UN weapons inspectors. After they withdrew, and as President Bill Clinton faced impeachment over telling lies about his affair with Monica Lewinsky, the Americans bombed Baghdad. Before I left Jerusalem, where I was then based, for Iraq I wrapped all my Christmas presents because I assumed I would not be there to do it on 25 December. But after a few days of spectacular raids, huge thunderclapping explosions and technicolour light-shows, it was all over and our circus was able to leave town and get home for Christmas. As we all celebrated in the bar of the Intercontinental Hotel in Amman on the way out, I heard a strange story. One of my TV colleagues, admittedly drunk with beer and exhaustion, talked of a tip from the Pentagon to an American TV network. They were told they had to make sure that they were ready to broadcast at a certain hour in the middle of the night, which is early evening on the east coast of the United States. All the TV networks had live positions on the roof of the Ministry of Information. They had a good view over half of Baghdad, which is completely flat, but couldn't see the other half because of a higher section of the roof behind them. My informant said that just after the appointed hour, a big raid started, which ended punctually in time for him to round off his broadcast just before the bottom of the hour. None of the explosions happened on the side of Baghdad that was obscured by the high roof. Everything worth filming was in front of their live position. The bombing sounded ferocious but there were not many casualties because the Americans bombed places they had hit before. The mind of the man who told me all this was reeling at the idea that the Americans were launching made-for-TV air raids. He didn't want to believe it, but the circumstantial evidence was interesting, at the very least.

★

In modern wars, everyone needs the right pictures. Control the pictures and you control the argument. In a suite at the Intercontinental Hotel in Geneva during the first winter of the Bosnian war, Radovan Karadžić, the leader of the Bosnian Serbs, and Ratko Mladić, the commander of their army, showed me their snapshots. They had hundreds of them, in paper wallets of the kind that people used to have when their holiday pictures came back from the processors. When we had shuffled through the contents of one of the wallets, Karadžić sent Mladić to get the next from the top of the minibar, where they were stacked up in a neat pile. Most of the pictures showed corpses, generally mutilated, and often partly decomposed and smeared with earth because they had been exhumed from mass graves. Karadžić gave a running commentary on each picture.

'Look, an innocent man dead because of those Muslim terrorists. Terrorists! And see, another . . . and one more . . .'

Why, he asked, in one of the favourite Serb litanies, did the British not remember the old Second World War alliance with their brothers in Serbia, and fight Islam together as they had fought the Nazis? Look, he said, waving another photo, which like the others had a glossy finish, these are dead civilians and they were killed by Muslims! I asked why all the corpses were male and why most of them were wearing olive green trousers and black army boots? Didn't that suggest they might be soldiers? Perhaps they had been killed in battle . . .

An enormous bodyguard stood at the door of the hotel room. He stared down at me and there were a couple of seconds of silence. Then Karadžić smiled and delivered his answer, and it was as if he was glad that I had made the point because it proved everything he was saying.

'They are farmers! Serb farmers always wear green trousers and strong boots.'

He gave Mladić another command and he disappeared into a bedroom and came back with a video, full of more pictures of dead bodies. I could take it and watch it at my leisure, said Karadžić.

'Use it on your news. You have my permission.' Karadžić waved a hand, like a king granting a favour. He wanted to at the very least plant the idea in my head that here was definitive proof that the Muslims were carrying out a campaign of genocide against the Serbs. It was nonsense. The truth was the other way round, and since I had been in Bosnia and seen it for myself, his attempt at manipulation failed. Mladić and Karadžić went on the run when the war ended in Bosnia and they were charged with genocide and crimes against humanity. Their prosecutors have more than just a few wallets full of snapshots to use against them if their cases ever come to court.

Karadžić and Mladić were making a crude attempt to get the story they wanted on the news. Others worked out more sophisticated techniques. In the 1990s, when the world was being wired together, when the internet was taking hold and digital technology was beginning to revolutionise the TV news business, it was more and more important for people who wanted to get and keep power to put the image they approved on people's screens, to seize the news agenda. Now, in the twenty-first century, where instant communications are taken for granted, it is all-important, in wars as much as any other branch of politics. Winning the media battle, creating the idea that you are winning and your enemies are not, is a vital part of modern warfare.

General Wesley Clark, who was Supreme Allied Commander, Europe when NATO forces went into Kosovo in 1999, recognised the power of instant news and, especially, pictures. In his book *Waging Modern War* he wrote that they 'could overwhelm the ability of governments to explain, investigate, co-ordinate and confirm . . . It was clear that the new [media] technologies could put unrelenting heavy pressure on policy-makers at all levels from the very beginning of any operation.' When General Clark was commanding NATO in Kosovo he had the television on constantly, and after the war took away the lesson that Western governments were going to have to accept that they would be getting scrutinised by journalists who 'were a battlefield fixture, driven by entrepreneurial spirit, a thirst for the real stories, and a quest for personal respect and recognition'.

The best way to get ahead in the media battle is to control access to the war. TV journalists can have the cleverest, most lightweight technology at their disposal, but if they have no story, and no pictures, they have nothing. Politicians, generals and war-lords need to have the right pictures transmitted, to justify what they are doing and to prove that they are winning, even when they are not. Sometimes this shared need leads to alliances between our side and theirs, which can get uncomfortable or even unholy. During the invasion of Iraq in 2003 hundreds of reporters traded independence for access by agreeing to be 'embedded' with units in the invading forces. Every favour has a price. Armies can affect what is filmed without directly imposing censorship by controlling where news teams are allowed to go. Or there can be more insidious pressures. If, as a journalist, you spend time with soldiers who share their food, and protect you from danger, it is easier to give them the benefit of the doubt, to see things from their point of view, to lose some of the distance that you need to be a good reporter. We do our best work as outsiders. If reporters think of themselves as insiders they risk getting too close, and sharing the assumptions and prejudices of the people they are meant to be fol-lowing.

Those kinds of dangers are not new. In 1944, just before D-Day, BBC correspondents who were about to be landed in occupied

Europe received a letter from their boss, A. P. Ryan, the Controller of News. He warned them to make sure they turned in

> enough good stuff to make the grade. We shall edit hard at this end and kill everything that is not worth using . . . There are no back pages in a broadcast. Everything we put out is in the nature of front-page stuff . . . This does not rule out simple and homely stories dealing, for instance, with the everyday life of the men in the field . . . but such stories must be good. The faintest suggestion of insincerity about them, of telling the families at home something that we think they would like to hear though it may not be quite true – and they're out. Never seek to 'jazz up' a plain story. You are not dramatists . . . You are broadcast reporters sent out to observe and tell us what you have seen . . . If a correspondent is in the front row on an historic occasion – as some of you will be with luck – then he should let his story run . . . [But] it is a very good broadcast indeed that stands more than five minutes.

Ryan's words are as relevant now as they were in 1944. The fundamentals of journalism are the same. What has changed enormously, even in the years I have been in the news business, is the technology, and the fact that everyone from governments to insurgents knows that the best way to communicate with their supporters, and to win over new ones, is to get their version of what is happening on to the airwaves. Winning the information war is no longer incidental; it is a top military priority.

During the invasion of Iraq in 2003 some people thought being embedded was a cop-out, a betrayal of important principles of journalistic integrity and independence. I did not think it was, as long as the reporters who did it remembered why they were there, and the basics of journalism. That includes being careful about language, remembering not to write sentences like '. . . and then the enemy opened fire on our position'. Journalists should do journalism, not the official history of the unit to which they were attached. I have spent a lot of time with armies, from well-organised Western soldiers to ragged guerrillas, as a 'unilateral' as they were called in 2003, joining them for a couple of hours or even a couple of days, to see what they were doing or to get a ride towards the action. I have never been an 'embed'. But I do not have a problem with the idea of doing it. Some of the people who were embedded during the 2003 war, like the BBC's Gavin Hewitt and David Willis, or James Mates of ITV News, among many others, did excellent reporting from places they would not have had a chance of getting to had they not been attached the military. Problems only start if viewers are led to believe that the very focused and narrow look at the war coming from an embedded reporter is the whole truth, when it is only a fraction of it.

One journalist on the *Washington Post* who was with an American unit said it was 'like being the second dog on a dogsled team. You see and hear a lot of the dog directly in front of you, and you see what is passing by on the left and right, but you cannot get out of the [harnesses] to explore intriguing sights you pass, without losing your spot on the moving team.' Inexperienced reporters in that situation can produce very superficial work, and their audiences were short-changed if that was all they were getting. Now that working as a reporter in Iraq is so dangerous, the only way to get to many parts of the country is to join an army unit. One British journalist I know, who works for an American broadcaster, told me that when he was in Iraq recently he was attached to a unit of US soldiers in an armoured Humvee and told to do whatever he wanted. He got to a town that would have been inaccessible on his own, managed to interview the mayor, and to get out on the streets, none of which would have been possible without his escorts. The other soldiers had more important things to think about, like survival, and were not bothered about what a journalist was doing.

Embedding is not a new idea. War correspondents have been attached to army units formally or informally since *The Times* sent Russell to the Crimean war in 1854. In the first few years of the Second World War, the BBC had trouble finding the right reporters – or news observers, as they were known at first. On 3 April 1942, Ryan, the Controller of News, wrote a gloomy memo, stamped very urgent, private and confidential, to Sir Cecil Graves, the Director General. Ryan was blunt: 'We have been criticised by the Board of Governors, by the Ministry of Information and by No. 10 for not having a high enough standard of news observing. We must, you will agree, admit that this criticism is justified.'

There had been complaints after the BBC put out a commentary on an aerial dog-fight during the Battle of Britain. The BBC was accused of treating combat in which men were being killed 'as if it were a cricket match or a horse race'. Only Edward Ward, who covered the war in Finland in 1939, had 'added to the prestige of broadcasting', and by 1942 he was in a German prisoner-of-war-camp. So the BBC set up a 'War Reporting Unit' to prepare journalists and technicians for the invasion of continental Europe. Just like the journalists and technicians who were sent to Boot Camp at Quantico before they were embedded with the US Marines in 2003, Ryan's reporters were sent to Salisbury Plain to learn about working with the army, and practised by doing dummy dispatches on some of the exercises that were held in the run-up to D-Day. In 1944, the BBC produced a typewritten guide for staff who were about to splash ashore from landing craft or be parachuted into battle. It told them that 'war reporting is a strenuous job and a war reporter is entitled to make himself as comfortable as he can – but he must strike a balance between taking everything he might want and carrying more than he can conveniently manage'.

For bedding, the BBC recommended: 'Hounsfield bed [a folding camp bed], quilted sleeping bag, Jaeger bag or two blankets, ground sheet, sheets, pillow and pillow cases.' Everything except the sheets, pillow and pillow case would be provided by the Corporation. A long list of military must-haves followed: 'Battledress, service dress or second battledress, greatcoat or detachable lining for Macintosh, four shirts and six collars . . .' It went on for almost a page. Again, the BBC would pay for everything, except pyjamas and underwear. The list ended with a stern reminder, in capitals: 'SUITCASES MUST NOT BE TAKEN'.

In the Gulf war in 1991 journalists were attached to the allied forces in Saudi Arabia as they got ready for the invasion of Kuwait. It did not work particularly well once the fighting started. Their reports were pooled and it took time to get them back to a place where they could be shared out and transmitted, and the ground war was over so quickly that they waited weeks for just a couple of days of action – while reporters who got into cars and drove to Kuwait from Saudi Arabia beat them to the story. Vaughan Smith, a freelance cameraman from Front Line News, had a uniform run up by a tailor in Bahrain. He was a former officer in the British army, so he knew how to talk his way through checkpoints and up to where the fighting was happening. He got some of the best pictures of the war. The BBC reporters with the British army in the desert wore military uniforms, and were honorary officers, like the correspondents in the Second World War. I regarded the likes of Brian Barron, Martin Bell and Kate Adie as proper grown-up reporters – I was still usually the youngest person in any team I worked in. I respected what they were doing, and I knew that the uniforms were probably very practical. But I wondered about the impression that their outfits left with the viewers. On the other side of the lines, in Baghdad, perversely, I tried to wear a tie and jacket for live shots, to look different. I resented the fact that every report I did was broadcast with a warning that what I said was subject to Iraqi censorship, while the pooled reports that my colleagues were sending from the desert, which were also subject to military censorship, did not carry the same warning.

The BBC correspondents who were going to battle with the soldiers on D–Day could not have had any doubts about whether the war was right or wrong. Their country was fighting for its survival. But these days plenty of journalists do not agree with the wars that are being fought in the names of their countries. That does not mean that their views will slant their coverage. If they are professionals, they ought to be able to put their own beliefs to one side. But it does mean that governments do not feel safe enough to assume that just because someone is from the same country they can be trusted to say the right things. Controlling the message is a modern science, at the heart of politics and government, and journalists need always to remember that if they get help and co–operation it is for a reason. And if journalists produce work that challenges the chosen message, they can expect a difficult reception from governments and their friends.

In the Gulf war of 1991 one of the key underlying messages that military briefings were putting out was that modern weapons somehow made the war cleaner. The Americans released videos taken from aircraft as they dropped precision–guided bombs, knocking out bridges as if it were an arcade game. But war is never clean, and my reports of the destruction by the Americans of the Amirya shelter in Baghdad on 13 February 1991 were badly off message. As I have described, a strong line came from Whitehall and from the Pentagon in Washington that the shelter was a command bunker, with the implication that reporters who saw civilians there were being manipulated by the Iraqis. I had some hostile interrogations from BBC presenters. I am not saying that they were fed questions by the Ministry of Defence, but what I was reporting was shockingly different from what they had seen until then. The images of the war on people's screens had become familiar and uncontroversial – grainy gun-camera video of air strikes, green night-vision pictures of anti-aircraft guns firing into the night over Baghdad, cheerful allied soldiers in the desert preparing to fight – but now for the first time, on TV, was the blood and guts of real war. In Britain, it was too much for the tabloids. The morning after my report the *Daily Express* and the *Daily Star* decided that the main news of the war was not the fact that more than 300 civilians had been killed; much more interesting was my coverage of the attack.

I had no idea of what they were saying until a couple of days after the Amirya shelter bombing. Because the Americans had destroyed Baghdad's electricity network, there were no lifts at the Rashid hotel so guests did a lot of walking up and down an unlit emergency stairwell. Journalists puffed up carrying torches, in wobbly bubbles of light like out-of-shape fireflies. Brent Sadler, my ITN opponent, loomed out of the gloom.

'Understand there's a big row about your coverage,' he said maliciously. 'And that it's gone right up to the Board of Management.'

'First I've heard about it, Brent,' I said lightly. It was.

'Well, it's a big row,' Sadler said, to make sure I had heard. I thought he was trying to play mind games.

I asked John Mahoney, the foreign editor, what was going on during a call on the satellite phone. The satphones were the only link we had to the outside world, other than going live on TV, and the Iraqis restricted the length of time that we could use them. The phones were set up on a long terrace overlooking the Rashid's extensive gardens so that the Iraqis could keep an eye on them. By the standards of the digital world that was to come we were very isolated – no e-mail, no mobiles, no internet – but the satphone was a huge advance. Just hearing a voice at the other end rather than fighting for time on a telex was a big change.

'Don't worry about all that now, old fella,' John said, blithely. I sat on some steps in the weak sun of a February afternoon in Baghdad listening to his voice, which was slightly squeezed and distorted by its trip up to the satellite and down again, like a Dalek in training. 'You can read all that nonsense when you come home.'

But John, kind as ever, had spared me from knowing that my reporting of the attack on the Amirya shelter was being severely criticised in London. My crime was to undermine morale at home in time of war by telling the truth. Only that was not exactly how it was put. Some of the tabloids said I was inexperienced, naïve, and malicious. The *Sun* said I was 'stabbing Our Boys in the back . . . swept along on a stinking polluted tide'. *Today* newspaper, now defunct, had a personal message. Jeremy Bowen, it said, your 'impartial' reporting had made you a 'disgrace to your whole country'. But the worst of all was Express Newspapers.

'Complaining viewers jam BBC switchboard' ran the headline in the *Daily Express*. The *Star*, its stablemate, was just as bad. 'Lord Haw-Haw reborn at the Beeb' it said, with a big picture of me next to a smaller picture of William Joyce, the American-born Irishman who was given a joke title when he broadcast propaganda for Nazi Germany from Berlin during the Second World War. Joyce was the last man to be hanged in Britain for treason, on the gallows at Wandsworth prison in 1946. The mood was picked up in the House of Commons. On 19 February, the Tory backbencher Sir Nicholas Fairbairn stood up to ask, 'Is not it strange that in the alleged attack on the bunker only women and children were in that air-raid shelter? When on earth have only women and children entered a shelter during an air raid? Can the BBC please not provide propaganda for the enemy by suggesting that it was an attack on a civilian target?' (As a matter of fact I never said that there were just women and children in the shelter; I said that the only men, as far as I could tell from the state of their bodies, were old.)

When I got home after the war my brother Nicholas, who is a barrister, told me I had to sue Express Newspapers. He did occasional shifts as a libel lawyer for them, though he was not on the night they had a go at me. But their chief lawyer had told him that he had been horrified by the headlines, was amazed that they got into the paper, and that Express Newspapers did not have a leg to stand on. Nicholas recommended a top solicitor. Express Newspapers, he said, was expecting to hear from me. I wanted some sort of redress. I thought if I did not challenge what had been written about me it would follow me around for years. It was a gross libel. They had compared me to a man who was executed for broadcasting propaganda from the enemy capital. But the libel courts can be hugely expensive, and I was put off when my boss, Chris Cramer, told me that the BBC would not back me. In fact I was more than put off. I was disgusted that after what I had done during the war in Baghdad the BBC would not underwrite my legal costs, when I knew that they had done it for other employees who had not just spent five or six weeks risking their lives. Cramer said that an article had been written defending me at the time, and that was enough. I was not earning much money so I decided not to take the risk of going it alone. But Nicholas told me to do it, and my posh new solicitor said that there might be a way. He would write a letter to Express Newspapers, threatening legal action and demanding an apology and damages. If he could not extract anything from them, we would let it drop and I would pay only a few hundred pounds for the letter. But if they could negotiate a deal, I would pay his fees out of the damages I received.

A couple of executives and a lawyer from Express Newspapers came to my solicitor's very smart offices in the City of London. My team did not say that they were not being backed by the BBC. If the men from Express Newspapers drew a different conclusion from the fact that they were in the grand offices of a top City firm, that was their business. The bluff was not called, and a few days later they offered to settle the case for about half my annual salary. My solicitor told me that if I took it to court I might get five times more – or the same – and that if I didn't get costs in my favour as well I would be in trouble. So I took the money.

If it is hard to tell who's winning, the media war is more important than ever. Unequal wars, especially ones between states and guerrilla armies, are all about perceptions. Look at Vietnam. In military terms, the Tet offensive in 1968 was crushed by the Americans. But politically, it was a victory for North Vietnam and the guerrilla groups in the south; the impact in the United States of pictures of fighting in the heart of Saigon, even in the grounds of the American Embassy, fatally undermined anyone who said the war was going well. And if pictures were powerful then, when they were not broadcast live, when film had to be shipped out to be processed and cut before it could be transmitted, their impact has increased exponentially in the wired world.

More than thirty years later, the people who planned the attacks on the United States on 11 September 2001 chose deeply symbolic targets. Even if they had happened before the age of twenty-four-hour global communications, that guaranteed the attacks would have a huge impact. But the fact that it all took place live on television across the world multiplied its effect many times over; the collapse of the twin towers of the World Trade Center, first one and then the other, as well as the other attacks, created an atrocity that unfolded slowly enough for people to hear about it and to switch on their TVs in time to see it all live, amplifying the event in ways that al-Qaeda could only have dreamed about. TV made it into the greatest and most gruesome live global moment there has ever been. So many people seeing it at the same time magnified enormously the pain, humiliation and rage in the United States, the support it received from its allies, and the satisfaction felt by its enemies.

Since 2001 the big war going on in the world is America's 'war on terror'. The US is so far ahead of every other country as a military power that no other state or group can ever dream about defeating it, in strictly military terms, on the battlefield. So the only way to fight it is asymmetrically, like the Vietnamese did in the 1960s and early '70s. In a war like the one that started in Iraq after the Americans and its allies invaded, the big side knows that it has so much firepower that it cannot lose any kind of straight fight, but also knows that military power on its own will not bring it victory. In the last few years insurgent groups in Iraq found a simple way of seizing the news agenda. They have filmed bombs exploding that they had planted at the sides of roads to kill foreign troops, and kidnapped foreigners and cut off their heads in front of video cameras, then put the pictures on the internet. They used modern technology that provides direct access to the world as a weapon of war, to achieve the classic military and political objective of breaking the will of the enemy to fight on.

No weapon in asymmetrical warfare is more important than the media. The enemies of America and its Western allies in the war on terror use the media to prove that the US military leviathan, for all its power, cannot touch them. Their aim is to rally their own supporters and undermine public opinion and belief in Washington's camp. Every TV or audio tape from Osama bin Laden and al-Qaeda dents American prestige. Bin Laden's deputy, Ayman al-Zawahiri, put out a broadcast during the war between Hezbollah and Israel in 2006 that was recorded in what looked like a modern television studio. His words were all about trying to exploit Hezbollah's success against Israel for al-Qaeda's benefit; but the underlying message coming from his surroundings was that these are not men on the run, being forced to live in caves, but an organised group, worthy of support; still capable of hurting the biggest military power the world has ever seen despite being its main target for five years. Maybe Bin Laden and al-Zawahiri are on the run; maybe they spend a lot of time in caves in the tribal regions of Pakistan. It doesn't matter, when their media message gives the opposite impression.

During the same war Hezbollah's leader, Hassan Nasrallah, appeared regularly on his group's own television station, al-Manar, which Israel's air force, despite repeated attempts, could not bomb off the air. Nasrallah's appearances, mocking Israel and promising that more 'surprises' would be coming their way, were much more than an embarrassing irritant for Israel. They cemented Nasrallah's place as the new hero of the Arab world, and were broadcast and rebroadcast on Arabic-language twenty-four-hour news stations, giving the lie to Israel's claims that it was destroying Hezbollah's capacity to fight and strengthening the conviction in Nasrallah's audience that he was winning the war.

Nasrallah and Hezbollah were organised enough to have their own TV station to carry their broadcasts. In case people who had lost their homes in the bombing of Beirut no longer had televisions, they also pushed their message from loudspeaker vans, sent out to cruise the streets. When al-Manar was not broadcasting its leader's messages, it carried news bulletins and propaganda videos. Bin Laden and his associates know their messages are newsworthy enough to get picked up around the world once they are transmitted on one of the Arabic satellite channels. Leaders of powerful Western countries have a direct line to the people too. But below the level of leaders staring solemnly into cameras, most of the messages put out by all sides, from members of the UN Security Council to insurgent groups, have to go through journalists.

That makes us, when the world is watching our broadcasts, very powerful, because what we say and how we say it is influential. Our reports can sway public opinion or sometimes create it.

I am very conscious of the need to use that power responsibly, which means, essentially, getting the story right. Some people do not trust us to be responsible. They find the influence that news broadcasts have alarming, and assume that journalists are either biased or incompetent. The BBC is often their target, because of its size and importance and because it can look like a mysterious, secretive institution. Sometimes people outside the BBC think that journalists inside it are pushed in one direction or another by dark, powerful forces, beholden either to the British government or to some powerful lobby. It is not my experience. Apart from a few innocuous voice-overs when I was a presenter, which I checked in advance, I have never read out someone else's words on air. In the BBC I have never been told I can't report something on the grounds that powerful people might not like it. On many, many occasions, on stories that British governments have cared a lot about, the only conversation I have had with a programme editor has been early in the day about the rough theme of what I had in mind, plus how many minutes and seconds he or she had to spare to accommodate it. Very, very often, stories are fed in the last ten or fifteen minutes before they are broadcast. Sometimes, if the pressure of time is particularly bad, they are fed only seconds before they go out, while the opening titles are running and the presenter is reading the headlines. Programme editors at times like that do not have a chance to view the stories before they go out, let alone manipulate their content on the orders of some sinister force.

At times I could have done with a bit more editorial input. Every morning senior news executives at the BBC have a meeting where they talk about the rights and wrongs of the last day's coverage, and what the coming day is likely to bring. I think it is safe to assume that quite a few of my pieces have been discussed over the years; but in all that time, I have only been told about what they were saying about a dozen times, and then usually by a roundabout route. Other correspondents have had similar experiences. So even if they are plotting to manipulate the news, they do not get round to telling the people on the ground who are writing the scripts and going on air with them.

There is a more subtle accusation, about the way that people like me look at stories, and the way we frame our arguments, our questions and our scripts. It boils down to the idea that journalists who work for what our colleagues operating in the blogosphere call the 'mainstream media' do not need to be told what to write by the people who control us because we do so automatically; we censor ourselves, because we share the assumptions of the establishment, or the left, or the Palestinians, or the Israelis, or whoever. The people who make these accusations often have strong views themselves, which shape their own writing; they assume that, subtly or crudely, everyone has an agenda, because they all do. They find it hard to believe that there might be journalists who want to discover what it is going on, and then report it, by giving an account of what happened and why.

Of course, everyone starts from somewhere. No human being can be truly objective. It is impossible because we all have a series of experiences, from parents, from teachers, from what we have seen in the world, that shape the way we think. Every reporter, every morning, has to decide how to cover the story, and those decisions don't come out of nowhere. But that does not make a journalist biased. If they are professional, and not lazy, then they have to recognise their own beliefs and prejudices and then put them to one side.

But the power that global news has these days makes us vulnerable. Everyone wants to influence us, and in a war, the most compelling way to exert influence is to kill. In the connected, non-stop world, journalists have become targets in a way that they never were before. Reporting wars has always been dangerous.

But most journalists who cover wars find it fairly easy to accept – and ignore – the possibility of being killed or wounded by a stray bullet or shell, because they are in the wrong place at the wrong time. But it is very hard to feel as fatalistic about the possibility of being killed or assassinated by ruthless people who want to knock journalists off because of what they do, or because they are seen as representatives of the enemy who need to be removed from the media battlefield. Increasingly the media war is not virtual. It is real, vitally important, and worth shedding blood to win.

Big TV networks like the BBC now spend huge amounts of money on security and safety. It is inconceivable these days for a BBC reporter to drive unburdened by a flak jacket or any training towards the shooting as I did in my first war in El Salvador. Partly that is because much tougher health and safety laws mean that employers have a legal obligation to work harder to protect their staff. But it is also because news teams face a sharper and much more direct threat. The BBC, like all its competitors, employs former military men as 'security advisers'. They look after safety and logistics, and not just abroad. When I went to Regent's Park mosque in London early in 2006 to report on a demonstration against controversial cartoons of the prophet Mohammed, I linked up with a cameraman who was accompanied by a beefy security adviser. Another one was around the corner with the satellite truck. In Iraq, they carry weapons. (One of the Corporation's veteran reporters affably calls them 'TKs' – trained killers.) The news business has come a very long way in a short time from the idea that was still around when I started, that we should not do anything to weaken our claim to be non-combatants. We are still non-combatants. But the danger in the twenty-first century is that not everyone agrees.

5

Don't Dream Dreams

In the early summer of 1992 I was trying to move house and pack to go to Sarajevo on the same day when the phone rang. It was Mahoney, the foreign editor.

'You remember I told you that sometimes you get shot at on the road from the airport into Sarajevo? Well, Martin Bell just rang to say it's much worse. Apparently it's not just sometimes. You get shot at every time you go down it. Well done. Enjoy your trip. Keep pedalling.'

When I put the phone down, I was not sure what I was meant to do with this new piece of information, so I kept on putting books into a box. I had some idea of what to expect in the Balkans. The summer before, in 1991, I had driven into a village in Croatia that was burning. It was very late in the afternoon and the golden light of the setting sun made soft patterns along the faded walls of the cottages and barns that were still standing and on the hull of a tank that rumbled and squealed down the road. It stopped and fired and the sound and force generated by the shell leaving the barrel of the tank made my

126

ears sing and the dust on the road dance. I could not believe what I was seeing. It was a shooting war, full-on, in Europe. It struck me hard that there had been nothing like it since 1945. I was staring at something that looked like a remake of *Kelly's Heroes*. I half expected to see Telly Savalas, chewing a cigar, coming through one of the buildings in a whining, grinding tank. But it was real and no one was there to stop the action. The tanks were trying to kill, real homes were burning and real bodies lay in the streets. In a field behind some destroyed houses in a village close by, pigs snuffled around the shallow graves of people who had been killed in an earlier burst of fighting, worrying away at the soil until they could carry away an arm or a foot to a quiet corner for a decent meal. Perhaps the dead had owned the houses. Perhaps they had owned the pigs, and were feeding them for the last time.

The local Croatians had raided a military museum and towed away a T-34 tank, the kind that the Red Army drove from Stalingrad to Berlin to defeat the Nazis. Its gun still worked and they had the right kind of shells, so they dug the Second World War veteran into the embankment of the motorway of brotherhood and unity that linked Zagreb and Belgrade. Every now and then they fired it at the Serbs, who were about a mile away. A hospital in what had been a spa town was full of wounded men. In the basement, tended by doctors and relatively safe, were the Croatian wounded. In a ward on the ground floor, next to big windows, wounded Serb fighters were tied to their beds during a barrage. The windows had been blown in by the shelling, and the men who lay on the beds had fresh nicks and cuts on their arms and faces from shrapnel and glass, and tortured faces from the thought that the next shell might come in through the roof. They might as well have been pinned out in the sun for the vultures.

The end of the Cold War in 1989 had lifted away the weight of the Second World War from Europe, and gave it a chance to renew itself. We didn't have to worry about being fried in a nuclear holocaust any more. But in the two years since the Berlin Wall had come down, parts of Europe were springing up into another shape. The New Europe could not escape its past, like a son who turns into his father even though he hates him.

A few days after Mahoney's phone call, I was sitting at Zagreb airport in the back of a C-130 transport plane of the Saudi Arabian air force loaded with medical supplies and half a dozen journalists, about to take off for Sarajevo. The moment of leaving for a dangerous place is often the most anxious, and I was feeling jumpy, about sitting next to a window (irrational) and because my flak jacket was in a cargo net at the other end of the aircraft (sensible). The loadmaster, a big, handsome, suntanned Saudi airman, gave a stiff-upper-lip safety talk.

'Gentlemen, you know, I think, where we are going. If we ditch over water there are three or four life rafts. If we're hit, follow what we do, behave as a team, and we'll be all right, *inshallah.*'

The passengers strained to hear him above the noise of engines as the propellers started and the big transport plane started to taxi. A line of canvas seats ran down either side of the aircraft. Everything in between was filled with boxes of bandages, sutures, operating theatre gowns and anything else they could think of that doctors in a war might find useful. During most of the siege of Sarajevo the easiest way in was on a relief flight. As it got more organised, the air crews made the passengers put on their flak jackets and helmets when they entered Bosnian airspace. The German air force made us wear parachutes as well.

'Don't worry. If the plane is crashing you will jump and the parachute opens. There is a barometric pressure device. It is simple.'

Mahoney had promised that the BBC's Martin Bell would give me a good briefing about what was going on when we met. I had never been to Sarajevo before. I knew the story, roughly, but I had no idea where anything was and how to avoid taking the wrong turning and getting killed in a war where the front line went through the middle of the city. The C-130 came in high over Sarajevo then started descending in a steep dive which was supposed to make it harder to shoot us down. We taxied to a halt and the rear ramp came down. I walked out and wondered what to do next. It was very hot. The engines were still running and the flight crew were pushing out the cargo as fast as they could. They did not plan to hang around. A man wearing a white suit and a blue flak jacket came striding towards the plane. It was Martin Bell. Thank God, someone I knew who would give me a bit of information about what was happening.

Martin walked fast up to the aircraft, and then without breaking step shook my hand and said, 'Welcome to Sarajevo. You'll enjoy it – if you live.' Thanks Martin, I tried, but he had disappeared into the back of the C-130. Maybe there was not that much to tell. In the end you have to do the finding out for yourself. I found his crew outside the airport and they drove me into town in a big Vauxhall, right-hand drive with British number plates. It had about a dozen bullet holes in the side, a couple of windows had gone and shrapnel had smashed the locks on the passenger side so the front door was taped shut and you had to climb in through the window. The letters 'TV' were all over it, made from the same gaffer tape that held the door together. It was fast and it had a good stereo and, for a Vauxhall, it was cool. The road into Sarajevo was almost empty except for the occasional white-painted UN armoured personnel carrier. On the right were streets of houses that were badly damaged. A Bosnian tank lay half in a ditch, knocked out or broken down, and abandoned.

Plenty of shooting was going on, but none of it seemed to be directed at us, so I relaxed a little.

Most of the city centre was controlled by the Bosnian government, which was led by Muslims but was also supported by some Serbs and Croats. We were waved through a checkpoint and drove down a broad road with concrete buildings from the 1960s and '70s on either side. Sarajevo is built along the floor and up the slopes of a fairly narrow valley. The high ground to the south was controlled by the Serbs, who could shoot down at will into the city. The Holiday Inn hotel, where most of the journalists were based, was about 200 yards from the front line on the valley floor. But Martin Bell and his team had been staying in a flat that was higher up, which Martin thought gave them a better view of what was happening and was safer because it was further away from the front line.

That first night in the flat the crew still followed the little rituals that had been established by Martin, who is a superstitious man. When they finished work they would play a Willie Nelson tape. When they went into the Holiday Inn, like him, they entered through a broken plate-glass window at the back, like him putting a specific foot through first. I could never remember which one it was supposed to be. The crew had not been with Martin long enough to pick up his other habits, like wearing green socks and carrying a silver dollar in his pocket. The flat was stuffy and uncomfortable and after a night tossing and turning on a dusty couch I decided that my huge respect for Martin did not extend to sharing his sleeping arrangements. I told the crew that they should stay in the flat, playing Willie Nelson and filming the explosions and tracer bullets at night. I checked into the Holiday Inn, which may have been more dangerous but at least gave me some personal space. I also wanted to do the story my way, and the first thing to do was to get out of Martin's shadow, his flat and as far away as possible from Willie Nelson. Later Martin stayed in the Holiday Inn too. Once I took over his room, which had the discarded lower half of one of his white suits folded neatly into the wastepaper basket.

The hotel was a concrete cube coated in brown and bright yellow metal panels, a gaudy left-over from the 1984 Winter Olympics. The best rooms were at the back, facing away from the front line. My room had bullet holes in the window. The city had an almost constant soundtrack of gunfire and explosions. Just after the war finished a film called *Welcome to Sarajevo* gave Hollywood's view of the hotel and the journalists who lived in it. When they weren't rescuing children from the streets they were carousing in the bar, which was well lit and stocked with a great range of wines and spirits. The real Holiday Inn was gloomy, often without electricity and water, and it did not have a bar. The night I checked in for the first time the atmosphere in the dining room was subdued and depressed. Earlier in the day a CNN camerawoman, Margaret Moth, had been shot in the face. Her jaw was badly damaged and she was in hospital being prepared for evacuation. The city was full of danger and it came into the hotel. Bullets fired into the front of the building occasionally penetrated through to the six-storey atrium in the middle of it, smashing the glass panels around it which showered down into the lobby. Before I knew better I got into the lift, which was at the front of the hotel facing the Serb positions. The moment the doors opened at my floor and I stepped out, bang bang – two shots came in and hit the doorframe where I was standing. They missed. A sniper on the Serb side of the front line must have been aiming at the light as the doors opened. After that the lift stopped working most of the time, and I used the stairs at the back.

During most of the years of the war, we had an office at the

Sarajevo TV station, a great concrete block house that had been built for the Winter Olympics. Every evening I would get into my Land Rover and drive back to the Holiday Inn down the long boulevard that ran parallel to the front line. My driving home music was 'Let's Stay Together' by Al Green. Maybe he was my Willie Nelson. I pushed the tape in outside the TV station and if I didn't drive too fast the song ended as I went down into the basement of the hotel, three minutes and fifteen seconds later. With Al singing I was very relaxed about driving down a road where people were often killed by snipers. The TV station workers often used to stand outside to hitch lifts home. We had fuel, they didn't. Once a man asked politely if I could take him to the Holiday Inn. He got in and I put on my tape. The road was empty, no one was around, because the shelling had started again and it was getting heavy. Al finished his song as we pulled up at the Holiday Inn and the hitchhiker said he was going to walk home to the Old Town, at least another mile away. He was fatalistic, said he would be OK, but I felt bad about dropping him in the open in the middle of the shells, so I took him home. The streets of Sarajevo were utterly empty, a very bad sign. At least it meant I could drive fast. I saw a shell going into a roof on the way there, but we were fine.

Going back, I had to pass the Presidency, a battered Hapsburgian edifice that was the headquarters of the Bosnian government. It was a favourite target of the Serbs and at the moment I drove past it a big shell came in. Al wasn't helping me now. Sooty black and blue smoke full of flame burst out of the explosion and came in through the gaps in the bolted-on armour plating; the Land Rover rocked on its suspension and my ears hurt badly from the noise of the shell. The next day I found out that the shell had scored a direct hit on the armoured limousine of the Bosnian president, Alia Izetbegović, and blew heavy sandbags out of the ground-floor windows of the Presidency. I just kept my foot down and drove the last 500 yards or so to the hotel with nothing worse than sore ears and a couple of hours of temporary deafness. I had been a yard or two away from being killed for doing someone a favour, and for being too confident that I could handle what was happening on the streets.

I mentioned what happened to a few people at the hotel but they weren't very interested. Everyone had the same kind of experiences. Strange people washed up at the Holiday Inn, fantasists and desperadoes, soldiers and reporters, often lubricated by the leveller of drink. One evening I sat with Fred Scott, one of the world's top cameramen, and two SAS men, drinking the contents of a bin liner of beer they had brought in. As the cans were emptied one of them drew his pistol, something special he called a SIG-Sauer, which is hard to say if you are drunk, and showed off how he could roll off the sofa and put a couple of bullets into anyone who came in through the door. He made the noises instead of pulling the trigger, trying a couple of times because his timing was off. Then Fred and I both had a go, though he took the magazine out and cleared the chamber first. The two SAS men said they would soon be setting off for one of the besieged Bosnian enclaves in the east of the country, on a complicated route that involved a lot of walking through forests. Fred and I signed up to the mission, and they said they would take us and we'd learn some survival skills on the way. I woke the next day in the ruins of our office. Fred and the two SAS men were sprawled unconscious around the room. They came back to life as I started collecting the empties, thanked Fred and I for an excellent evening and stumbled out of the door. I emerged from my room, which was next to the office, fifteen minutes later, shaved and showered. Our two pathfinders were still wandering around the same floor of the hotel, trying to find the exit. We didn't go walking with them.

War Stories

A French journalist called Paul Marchand used to abseil down buildings when the war got too dull. Paul had many claims to fame. Like many long-term residents of the Holiday Inn he owned a water heater, the element of an immersion tank freed from its copper cylinder, attached to a long lead with a plug. They were like light sabres in *Star Wars*, only more dangerous. As long as the hotel had water and diesel for its generator, you could plunge one into an icy bath, go off to have dinner and a few drinks, and return for a hot soak. Paul claimed he would pick up pretty young Bosnian hitchhikers, tell them about his immersion heater and offer them a bath. The young ladies, by now better scrubbed than they had been for months, would then, he claimed, be so full of gratitude that they would allow him to deploy his skills as a lover. I tried not to believe his Gallic boasting, but he was a tall, thin man with Buddy Holly spectacles who women seemed to like. One day he had his abseiling gear in the hotel, and challenged me to descend from the top of the atrium, about six floors up. He claimed to have learned how to abseil from heli-copters when he was in the French army. I refused because I am scared of heights and I thought that it would be humiliating to be killed in Sarajevo in a climbing accident, like the time I fell through a glass table late at night and thought I would bleed to death on the office carpet.

Marchand said, 'Then you are Mickey.'

'Mickey who?'

'Mickey Murse.'

I had drunk a couple of bottles of 'Sarajevsko Pivo', the local beer. Its wartime recipe was brackish because some of its key ingredients had been replaced with rice brought into Sarajevo by the United Nations refugee agency, the UNHCR, but it was still alcoholic and made me vulnerable to French goading, so I did it. Most of us wrote 'Press' or 'TV' on our cars. Paul had written

134

'Don't waste your bullets, I am immortal.' Maybe he was, because when his car was hit, he wasn't killed, though his arm was damaged badly.

When the airport was closed, because of shelling or bad weather, or because the airlift was suspended usually after a plane had been hit, the only way in or out of Sarajevo was to drive across Mount Igman, the gloomy hill that dominated the southern approaches to Sarajevo. The road went past Serb positions, so the best time to try it was either when it was dark, when hopefully they couldn't see, or in the early morning, when they were supposed to be sleeping off their hangovers and in no mood or condition to fire their guns. Night drives were always without lights. When there was no moon it was very difficult. One dark night it was so bad that I got out and walked ahead of the armoured Land Rover so that the driver had something to follow. Outside was not the best place to be if the Serbs opened fire, but the alternative was driving off the side of a hairpin bend down a steep, rocky slope. Morning drives were not much easier. The last time I left Sarajevo at the end of the war I had spent most of the night drinking and made the mistake of offering a lift to a very serious writer for the *New York Times*. He kept banging on my door, waking me up, and as I was stumbling round trying to pack he shouted, 'Come on motherfucker, we're burning daylight.' One of the CBS guys, a big, cheerful British man called Paul Douglas, made some funny T-shirts commemorating 'The Sarajevo–Igman Rally'. He has had his own commemorations, because he was killed, with his soundman, James Brolan, by a bomb in Baghdad in May 2006.

I stayed in the Holiday Inn a couple of years ago and it felt weird to use the main door. To step that way during the war would have been certain death on most days, because there was a Serb sniper who looked down on it who took his job very seriously.

One strange afternoon – it was 7 June 1993, which I know because the electricity was on and I was watching Jim Courier losing the final of the French Open to Sergi Bruguera – the city was hardly moving, covered in a blanket of heat and inertia. But outside all afternoon I could hear bullets zinging and pinging, hitting the side of the hotel and rattling down to the scrubby ground below, where no one dared to walk. It was just a reminder from the sniper. *I'm here, watch out, I'm looking for you.*

The city outside the hotel was always dangerous, but at first it was mysterious as well. At the beginning of the war, no journalists left the hotel at night unless they had a very good reason. The city had no electricity. Through what was left of my window I could see the headlamps of ambulances making shafts and shadows on the sides of buildings as they moved along the dark, frightening streets. Green and red tracer looped around the sky, and when shells exploded a little way off there would always be the flash first, followed by the sound of the explosion, in the way that thunder always follows lightning. In my first week I went to one of the main hospitals to try to find some stories. Hospitals are good places for journalists in wars. The most interesting stories to get are about what war does to people, and about the easiest places to find them are hospitals. My friend Kurt Schork, who worked for Reuters, used to go to the mortuary at Sarajevo's biggest hospital to count the new corpses that had come in. It was the most accurate way of assessing how much killing was going on. I went with him a few times. There was no refrigeration. The bodies lay on slabs and on the floor, and a strong smell of disinfectant was not enough to cover the smell of rot. It was better once the winter came, when the corpses were frozen solid. Kurt would help himself to the register, a big old book that they filled in by hand, and count the new names. For reporters it is safer and more productive to go to a hospital to find out what is happening than to cruise the streets looking for trouble and hoping to witness bad things, though we did a lot of that too.

There was another hospital, by local standards a fairly tall building, which was very exposed to shellfire from the Serb side. The higher floors had big holes in the wall from tank shells, so most of the patients were either in the corridors, or in the cellars. They could still hear, every few minutes, a dull crash as another shell exploded into the city. In one dark corridor in the basement there was a twenty-year-old woman who had been hit when she was trying with her father to find a safe place away from the shells. She was carrying her dog when a shell came in. Her father took most of the blast and died quickly. Her arm was blown off and her dog was killed too. A little further down the corridor another young woman was lying under a sheet. She had dark, shoulder-length hair, and looked like she should have been sexy. I saw her watching closely as I asked questions. Suddenly she pulled back the sheet and waved the two stumps of her legs in the air. I think one leg had gone above the knee and one below. Her gown rode up above her waist and she was wearing nothing underneath. She shouted something in Bosnian and everyone near her laughed. Our translator, Jasmina Alibegovic, laughed too, and wouldn't tell me what she said until we were out of earshot. 'She said she liked you and even though her legs had gone she could still fuck you . . .' The city had a spirit.

The girl looked oddly familiar. On my way in to Sarajevo the man sitting next to me in a bar in a hotel in Zagreb, who said he was a reporter who had just got out of Sarajevo, showed me pictures of surgeons amputating limbs that had been smashed and torn by shrapnel and high explosive. Croatia's own war was on an uneasy ceasefire, but Zagreb was still one of the few places in Europe where you could get pictures like that developed and printed without being reported to the police. He shuffled repeatedly through the pictures, often stopping and lingering at one that showed a naked young woman with a pretty face and smashed legs that were about to be cut off.

People who have been living in wars for years develop a new mentality. As their memories of peace recede, their lives focus down to a very narrow and important range of priorities, all of which are about survival. But human beings don't have dials on their brains. They cannot just change their settings and click into a new way of thinking. The adjustment is made by time, disappointment, pain, and violent, untimely death. To begin with the people living in Sarajevo could not really believe what was happening to them, despite all the physical evidence. Sarajevo looked like a city at war very quickly after the fighting started. The front line was like a great rip through the centre. Two tall glass office towers, next to the Holiday Inn, were burnt out. The main avenue that ran from the old city centre to the new suburbs to the west, the road from the Holiday Inn to the TV station, was parallel with the front line and was quickly dubbed sniper alley by journalists because anyone using it had to move in clear view of the Serb soldiers, who often opened fire. But for the people who were living in the chaos, peace was much more than just a memory. It was just a couple of months ago; you could almost reach back over your shoulder and touch it. Children emerging in quiet moments from apartment buildings and shelters in that first summer of the war were pale, although the sun was hot. Their parents were not allowing them out until someone pushed the 'off' button to end the appalling horror film that was going on around them. They believed that they would not have to wait too long for the advanced, supposedly civilised countries of Western Europe to step in to stop the killing. Such barbarism was supposed not to happen any more in their continent. By the following summer the children were suntanned again. It was clear that help to stop the war was not coming – as David Owen had said to them, 'Don't dream dreams' – and even when there is killing outside you cannot keep children penned up in a small flat for ever. As a result more of them were killed and maimed.

The oldest hotel in Sarajevo was the Europa. Perhaps it had been grand, but that was a long time ago. It was full of people who had been displaced from the outlying parts of the city by the fighting. One night the Serbs shelled it until it caught fire. When I got there the lobby was hot and full of smoke, and it had that burnt-building smell of wet ash and charred wood and the refugee smell of unwashed bodies and fear. Yet even though part of the hotel was still on fire, people were going back up the stairs and moving back in. They had lost one home and they did not want to lose the rooms they had been given at the Europa. In the middle of the foyer was a woman in her early twenties with dark hair to her shoulders, wearing a grubby grey sweatshirt and sweat-pants. She was looking after some children. She was pretty, with deep shadows under her eyes. She told me her name and said that she was twenty-four and that before the war her ambition had been to get a job as a travel agent. Tears started in her eyes as she told me some of the things that had happened in the ten weeks or so since the war started, friends who had been killed, or maimed. Her father was still in their house, very close to the Serb gun positions. He stayed there because he had to fight and try to protect their home. She was at the Europa with her mother and her two younger sisters.

Every few months after that, when I was in Sarajevo, I went to the Europa to try to find her. I usually gave her family a sack of provisions looted from the BBC stores. Often, she wasn't there, and I left the food with her mother. The war was changing everything for civilians in Sarajevo. As it went on, they started to forget

139

the lives they used to have and the dreams they had about the future. As peace recedes into the past, war takes over and crushes everything. My friend, and I think I shouldn't use her name, went back to her family home to look after her father. It was dangerous but so was sitting around the squalid burnt-out corridors of the Europa hotel. At least she was doing something, and soon she was doing more. She joined her father's army unit as a medic. I did not see her again until the following year, in Sarajevo Old Town near the Europa hotel. The black rings under her eyes were deeper and darker and she was wearing combat fatigues. She said she had become a fighter, and she told a story of deceit and failure.

Her unit was part of something called the 10th Mountain Brigade, which was led by Mušan Topalović, known as Caco (pronounced Zatso). He was a hero to people like my friend and the others who lived in the ruins of the Europa, who had no money to buy black-market food, who queued for water and for bread however bad the weather or the shelling. They saw him as Sarajevo's Robin Hood, because he had busted open one of the government food stores and distributed the riches he found inside. The government saw him as a bandit, dangerous and out of control. Caco was one of a group of tough guys who had been among the first to fight at the beginning of the war, when the government still had no army.

Another of them was Jusuf 'Juka' Prazina, a violent and criminal debt-collector and leg-breaker before the war, who made his gang into paramilitary fighters in the first few months of the conflict. They were in the front line, dressed in black overalls and claimed to have saved Sarajevo. But Juka never stopped his racketeering and was eventually forced out of Sarajevo. He became a follower of a Croat extremist called Mladen 'Tuta' Naletilić, who I gave evidence against at The Hague tribunal when he was tried

BBC News trainees and instructors Alan Perry and George Major, looking into the future in Broadcasting House, 1984.

On the nursery slopes of foreign news: BBC Geneva correspondent, 1987.

El Salvador 1989: first war, first taste of the war drug.

Expelled from Kabul on Ariana Afghan Airlines, 1989. One of its Boeings with seats (except for mine) stripped out for cargo that never turned up.

Voicing a script while editing in a Kabul hotel room in 1989, after a trip to the money-changers with the Afghan equivalent of about £10.

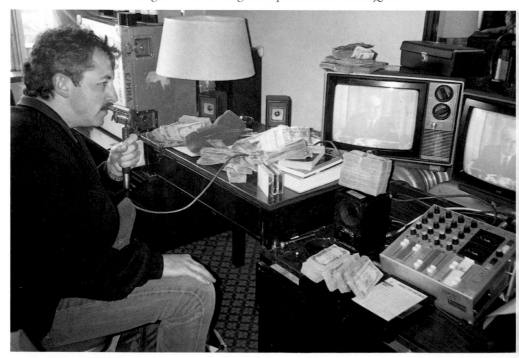

Tiananmen Square in Beijing, 1989, a few weeks after the authorities sent in the troops.

Communist Europe collapsing. Bucharest, January 1990.

Thirtieth birthday celebrations in the Athénée Palace hotel in Bucharest, with the Romanian revolution going on outside.

Rory Peck in the Iraqi desert on the road to Baghdad during the first Gulf war, February 1991. I made the vehicles' owners paint the canvas covers white in the hope that the Americans would not bomb us. Rory was rock-solid in that war. He was killed in Moscow in 1993.

With Kurdish peshmerga fighters in northern Iraq in 1991. The man with the bag took us through a minefield to get there.

Kurt Schork, the Reuters correspondent, in Sarajevo. He set the standard for energy, honesty and rigour until he was killed in Sierra Leone in 2000.

Abandoned Bosnian tank on the airport road to Sarajevo, 1992. The road was often shot at, so a fast drive in from the airport was always nerve-jangling. After he was killed the Bosnian government renamed this stretch after Kurt Schork.

Parliament Square in Grozny, January 1995. Still the most dangerous and violent place I have ever been.

Bosnian soldiers loading the BBC's pack horses for the trek into the besieged east side of Mostar in August 1993. The box with the yellow sticker was the satellite phone. These days a satphone fits into a reasonably sized pocket. Humo, who took us into Mostar, is on the extreme right.

On the trail to Mostar, August 1993. This was the only stream we crossed in a day and half of hard walking, and we didn't have enough water bottles. By the time we got there I was out on my feet from dehydration.

The river Neretva in Mostar after the war. The left side of the river was the heart of the Bosnian government enclave. I testified to the War Crimes tribunal in The Hague about civilians I saw being forced under heavy fire from the Bosnian Croats to cross the river on a pontoon bridge.

Shane McDonald inside besieged east Mostar. The graffiti on the right warns of the sniper who shot at most people who went past that corner, and killed some of them. The people who lived in the house, taking water in on the left, stayed at the back. The sniper made the front rooms uninhabitable.

Chuck Tayman outside the cellar we shared with wounded and dying soldiers in Mostar during the siege. The entrance was to the right of the sandbags behind him. A month or so later the Bosnian Croats put a shell through the roof of the building.

The main street of east Mostar. Early on my helmet was stolen, which made my head feel very exposed.

Above: With Jimmy Michel and Boaz Paldi, at Mar Saba monastery in the Judean desert, 1995. They showed me how to work in Israel and the Occupied Territories, and taught me a lot.

Right: Tel Aviv, November 1995, on the phone. The place where Yitzhak Rabin was shot is just to the left, out of frame. Plenty of Israelis still stop on that stretch of pavement to look at the memorial to Rabin, and to wonder about what might have been.

Ein Karem, Jerusalem, in the snow – our home for five years.

May 1996 in south Lebanon, during Israel's Operation Grapes of Wrath, a major assault on Hezbollah. It failed, and four years later Israel ended its occupation. In 2006, Israel and Hezbollah went to war again.

Paying the bill at the Rashid hotel in Baghdad in 1999. During the years of sanctions the currency became so devalued that the bundles of Iraqi dinars were weighed, not counted.

Our local staff Saddoun al-Janabi and Mohammed Darweesh, on a slow day in Baghdad in the last dead years of Saddam Hussein's rule. During the first Gulf war Saddoun was chief minder at the Ministry of Information, before he was demoted for being too friendly with foreign journalists. Mohammed is Iraq's leading authority on the works of James Joyce, and has translated *Ulysses* into Arabic.

Damascus at the time of the funeral of President Hafez al-Assad, June 2000. The old saying was that the Arabs could not fight a war without Egypt, but could not make peace without Syria.

Miguel Gil filming a Kosovo Liberation Army fighter in 1999. Like many of us who had been in the Balkans, Miguel was getting much more wary about wars by the end of the 1990s. He was killed, with Kurt Schork, in an ambush in Sierra Leone in 2000, the day after Abed Takkoush died in south Lebanon.

Right: Armoured BBC Land Rover in Rafah in the Gaza Strip. Generally they are not marked BBC, because 'TV' is internationally more recognisable, and in any case 'BBC' can attract the unwanted attention of men with guns.

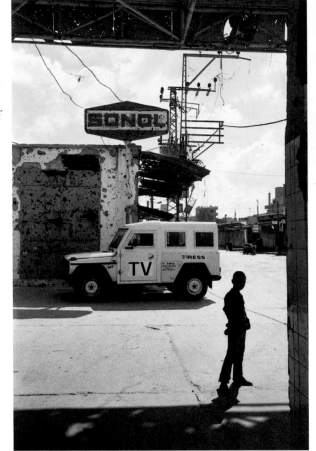

Below: Israeli border police on the edge of Ramallah on the occupied West Bank at the start of the intifada in September 2000. I left my job to return to London eight days before the intifada started, and was in an agony of withdrawal when I was sent back to present *Breakfast* from Jerusalem, which made it worse.

Going live at midnight on Millennium Eve in Bethlehem, a town that was full of optimism then. Years more of occupation have made it one of the saddest places in the Holy Land.

Faster than Schumacher. Abed Takkoush, the top fixer in Lebanon, at the wheel of his Mercedes. Abed was our guide, helper and friend, and the father of three sons. After twenty-five years of covering Lebanon's wars, he was killed by Israel on the last day of their occupation in 2000.

Hezbollah fighters parading through south Lebanon on 23 May 2000, celebrating victory on the day their armed insurgency finally forced Israel to end its occupation. About an hour after this picture was taken, Abed was killed.

Abed's car, a few days after his death. The tank that fired the shell was about a mile away to the left, out of frame. The shell hit the Mercedes at the rear. Malek Kanaan and I hid from Israeli fire behind the building at the top right.

Abed's nephew Ahmed Itani, on the left, chats with a friend on a street in Beirut, 2004. Ahmed took Abed's body back to his family in Beirut after he was killed.

Malek Kanaan, BBC cameraman in Beirut, who was with me on Abed's last day, our worst.

In the southern suburbs of Beirut in July 2006, trying to get out as fast as possible before the Israeli bombers return.

for war crimes. Tuta was convicted. In January 1994 Juka was found dead at a motorway service station in Belgium, shot through the head, some say by his own bodyguards.

Fortunes were made trading food and cigarettes on the black market, which were smuggled into Sarajevo through the front lines and by corrupt UN soldiers and workers. The local mobsters became very powerful. I knew one of them slightly. He was the sort of man who in normal times the police would have arrested, but when the war started he made a reputation for himself as a fighter in what he called a special unit of the military police. He was physically very big, which got him noticed. His head was shaved and his nickname was Celo, which means bald. A year after the war started he had diversified his operations. He drove round in a convertible with a very young girl who was sexy in a tarty way and a couple of bodyguards. All the men were armed. I would see him swaggering into bars with his moll, wearing a silver pendant shaped like a boxing glove, peeling off money from a thick wad of German marks to buy packets of Marlboro cigarettes which he threw back over his head without looking, knowing that his boys would be there to catch them.

The Bosnian government hated Caco, who they saw as a threat, because the 10th Mountain Brigade was his private army. My friend from the Europa hotel told me about an operation she had been on with the Brigade. It was snowing so they were issued with white coveralls to wear over their uniforms, and told that they were going to be part of a joint attack on the Serb lines, to try to break out of the city. Caco's people moved forward, but the support they had been promised on both their flanks never materialised. My friend and her comrades were pinned down in the snow for hours, lying there, not able to go forward or back. Perhaps if they had been a properly trained, even vaguely professional army they might have rallied. But they were not much more than a militia, running on enthusiasm and courage rather than expertise. An attack uphill, without the support they had been expecting, was too much. She had somehow managed to get out alive, but others did not. She was convinced that the government cancelled the orders for their support in order to destroy Caco and the people who followed him, and it was hard to disagree, as he was building himself a state within a state.

I had arranged to meet her near his headquarters. It was close to the Bistric barracks, an old Yugoslav army base that was now in the hands of the Egyptian contingent in UNPROFOR, who did not like to get too involved with what was happening outside their gates. I was warned not to drive in to Caco's part of town in my BBC vehicle, and not to wear the other badge of being a for-eigner, my flak jacket. Caco's people would confiscate flak jackets, or cameras, and I had no reason to suppose that they would let me keep a state-of-the-art Kevlar Land Rover either. So I parked on the other side of the river and walked, unchallenged, into the 10th Mountain Brigade's kingdom.

It felt naked to be without my flak jacket. Jasmina, our trans-lator, who was a surgeon at the hospital when she was not with the BBC, only wore hers when she was working with us, even though she had a long walk to the hospital through the centre of the city.

'I couldn't,' she would always say. 'It would be rude when nobody else has one.'

Some journalists had stopped bothering with them in town and only wore them on the rare occasions that any of us were allowed on to a front line. But a flak jacket really could save your life. All of us had seen people dying or dead, who hadn't had one, with tiny shrapnel wounds in the chest. A piece of shrapnel the size of a pea can kill you if goes into your heart. But you can't discount fashion, even in a war. I think some reporters who left their flak jackets in their rooms did it because not having one made them feel cool. Or maybe that was my imagination, because there were plenty of times when I felt very uncool, in every sense of the word, sweating in my flak jacket when other people wandered around in their shirtsleeves. The other argument against flak jackets was more subtle. It was that flak jackets were a barrier between the journalists and the people we were reporting on. I never bought the idea. Maybe it made them feel better, but the barrier was real, and the flak jacket was just its symbol.

It was impossible not to identify with the people who were caught up in the siege, but we were just visitors. One morning the Serbs managed to bomb the television station, where all the foreign broadcasters had their offices as well as the local programmes. The building was very strong, but people with offices near the windows were hurt. I went to see some of my wounded colleagues in the hospital where we often filmed. One woman, a Bosnian, was terribly traumatised. She cried quietly and without stopping and her hair was matted with blood, and I was shocked that no one had washed it for her.

We shared some of the dangers of the people in Sarajevo, but with important differences. The biggest was that we could leave and they could not. Foreign journalists had a magical piece of laminated plastic, a press card, which allowed us to go in and out and to get seats on UN aid flights. We were also insulated from the worst of it by wads of our employers' cash (literally – it was a war without credit cards) to pay for food and booze, which black marketeers always made sure were available to anyone with enough German marks. At the back door of the Holiday Inn French Foreign Legionnaires would unload cases of the Bordeaux they were issued as part of their rations – a bottle every two days – which were passed on to us in the restaurant for the equivalent of about

£30 each. And it was not our friends and relations who were getting killed and maimed. Our homes weren't being destroyed. It wasn't our city, though it started feeling that way sometimes.

In Caco's domain a line of men in civilian clothes with picks and shovels over their shoulders, like the seven dwarves but without the enthusiasm, had been marched up the hill towards the front line by shaven-headed men in camouflage uniforms. Caco sent his people out into the town to press-gang men who were not wearing uniforms to make them dig trenches. He said that they picked degenerates and shirkers. The men in the line looked terrified. Most were middle-aged and fat. There were a few long-haired younger ones. After the war some of Caco's men were also imprisoned for shooting Serb civilians for no reason other than their ethnicity. They threw the bodies of their victims into a ravine. My friend, who found herself in a world of violence, looked close to breaking, exhausted and pale. She was carrying a loaf of bread that she said was for her mother and sisters. A man in her unit who protected her had been killed. She was not sure what was coming next.

She married one of Caco's men. But then in October 1993, the Bosnian government made its move against Caco and killed him and broke his organisation. Her husband was imprisoned. On 8 January 1994 she left me a note at my hotel. She thanked me for what I had done for her family and said that she was desperate and did not know how to go on. She said she had been locked up too: 'I am a kind of prisoner too. It is so big mess with me. Sometimes I think it is the best to kill myself. What is happening in this world (I mean in Bosnia – is everybody so crazy?) . . .'

Jasmina said she sounded as if she was serious about killing herself. I did not think that my friend would survive the war. But she did, and a year after it ended she telephoned me in my office in Jerusalem. She wanted to say that things were better, her husband was free, she had a job and a child. I went to find her when I was sent back unexpectedly, not long after her phone call, to chase Radovan Karadžić, who was on the run from the war crimes prosecutors in The Hague. I missed the old wartime city, where there were only a couple of dozen foreign civilians, journalists and aid workers. Now it felt like there were hundreds, if not thousands of foreigners, swarms of them, with white four-wheel drives that clogged up the streets. There were traffic lights and traffic jams, and you could walk over the Vrbana bridge between what had been the two front lines, which would have been an act of suicide in my Sarajevo. I met my friend in the place where she had found a job, as a receptionist in one of the big international organisations that had set up shop in Sarajevo since the end of the war. The corridors were full of confident young Westerners with loud voices, dressed in variations of war zone chic. They looked excited to be in Sarajevo, and to be doing their bit to run a country. My friend was not even the receptionist on the front desk. She was in a little cubicle on one of the upper floors, and the smart young people who worked there were not giving their receptionist a second glance. She was still thin and tired, and the black lines under her eyes were dark and deep. I sat and talked to her for an hour or so. A few of the bright young things recognised me from TV, and could not work out what business I could possibly have with their dowdy receptionist, who they never spoke to, though if they had she could have told them everything about war.

Sarajevo felt like just another story for the first few weeks. But it pulled me in, as it did a generation of reporters who wanted to record what was happening in our continent and who shared a sense of bewilderment and anger that the big European countries were ignoring it. It was our war, and it took over the lives of many of the journalists who were there and changed them for good, but not always for the better, and sometimes it ended their lives. Some people kept coming back even though the city had not been kind to them. A French reporter who had lost a leg early in the war sometimes used to stump around the place, struggling up the staircases of the Holiday Inn when the power was out and the lifts were not working. During the three years between 1992 and 1995 when Sarajevo was besieged, when I was not there I was thinking of it. It came into my head every couple of hours for years afterwards. During the war the alternative – 'normal' life – seemed very tame. I had no desire whatsoever to be someone safe in London, commuting to work, knowing what I would be doing and when months in advance. In Sarajevo I felt free. There were no rules, no one to tell you what to do or where to drive. That part of it, the feeling of living on the edge, was fun. The only constraint was making a mistake that could get you wounded or killed, which was straightforward in a way that I liked.

Every morning I decided with my colleagues what we would do that day. Often we had to change all our plans and throw away hours of hard work because a story happened. I liked all of that too. It seemed like the essence of journalism. Every evening we would eat the Holiday Inn's food and get anything from moderately to seriously drunk. I hated the killing and the suffering. But being there stretched me enormously, and all the time, as a person as well as a reporter. I loved that feeling, and being with people who understood what was in my head because the same stuff was in theirs. When I went home after a stint of four or five or six weeks in Bosnia, I was more or less catatonic. I'd sit in my flat and after a couple of days I could probably open the post and go down to the pub for lunch, but I was pretty speechless. I was knackered. I'd watch the TV in the evening and swear or throw beer cans at the screen of anyone whose reports I didn't approve of. I felt more at home in Sarajevo than in London. Sarajevo was normal; London was strange. I didn't have to explain anything to my friends in the Holiday Inn. I could not explain much to my friends in London. It was not good for my personal life. I was spending too much time at a war and the abnormal became routine.

I never stopped being disgusted and angered by the killing, by civilians being shelled or shot dead when they went out to try to earn some money, or find some food or water. But it happened every day and after a while it wasn't even news for the editors back in London, unless it took a particularly vicious twist. War distorts and perverts reality, and it had done that to mine too. One time Julia, my girlfriend, gave me another verbal shaking and told me to get a grip, to realise that London was real and Sarajevo was not. No, I told her, real life for me is not here, it's there, in Bosnia. Now it sounds deluded. But then I believed it.

The irony was that I understood how much most people in Sarajevo wanted their old lives back, and sympathised completely with their yearning for peace. But all I wanted was to keep going to their war. Being a witness to what was happening was everything. I believed in it passionately, certain that a reporter should be prepared to find out what is going on in the bad parts of the world, to see what human beings are doing to their fellow human beings and then to tell their viewers and listeners and readers. Finding out good things does not come up on many reporters' radar. News is about change, about the unexpected, the abnormal, about what's new. Since we have only limited space and time, what's bad is generally going to crowd out what's good. Not always, though.

In 1994, I took a break from Bosnia because I went to Johannesburg to replace the BBC's Southern Africa correspondent, John Harrison, when he was killed in a car accident. Every news organisation believed that South Africa's first democratic election that year was going to end in bloodshed and probably a civil war. They moved news teams en masse out of Bosnia, which was quiet in the first half of the year, to South Africa, to reinforce local journalists who had spent years covering trouble in the townships. One agency produced a T-shirt with a line from David Bowie that said 'South Africa Elections 1994. Take your protein pills and put your helmet on.' In the month before the vote the government declared martial law in KwaZulu Natal. A bar in Durban that night was full of excited and keyed-up TV news people, mainly white South Africans who had rushed in from Johannesburg, drinking beer and expecting a lot of trouble. There were terrible killings, but Nelson Mandela made a deal with the leader of the Zulus, Mangosuthu Buthelezi, and the white diehards were full of talk but not much action. They let off some bombs but could not ruin the poll and sabotage the transfer of power from white minority rule to a democracy under Mandela, the man who was routinely condemned as a terrorist by Margaret Thatcher in the 1980s when he was still in jail.

Some days were full of madness. In a township called Thokoza on the East Rand, about twenty miles outside Johannesburg and on another planet as far as many white South Africans were concerned, an attempt was made in April 1994 to deploy a new peacekeeping force to separate warring factions of Mandela's African National Congress and Buthelezi's Inkatha Freedom Party. I saw a bunch of snappers following an armoured vehicle up the street, crouching down, using it as cover. I was trying to do a piece to camera at the side of the road, and that was mad enough, but I thought they were pushing too hard, asking to get hurt, especially since as far as I could see none of them was wearing a flak jacket. A few minutes later, one of them, Ken Oosterbroek, was killed, and another, Greg Marinovich, who later became a friend, was badly wounded, shot in the chest.

But even though far too many people died, what we were all expecting to be the bad news story of the year turned into a good news story, and not one journalist was disappointed because it was better that way. But it was news not because it was good, but because it was unexpected.

In Sarajevo we specialised in bad news. But we thought that the effect of being there and bearing witness would change things, that our reporting would get the siege lifted and stop the killing. Anyone with half a brain and an ounce of human sensibility could not spend a day in Sarajevo during the siege without asking how and why such barbarity was allowed to continue in a continent whose people considered it the most advanced, democratic and peace-loving place in the world. War is inherently barbaric and the Bosnian government forces carried out their share of atrocities. Serb civilians suffered too, as I saw on the rare occasions when their authorities allowed me to report from their side. But that didn't alter the fundamental truth about what was happening in Sarajevo, that the Serbs were inflicting a deadly siege on an entire city and enforcing it by killing civilians. That truth was recognised after the war by the prosecutors at The Hague war crimes tribunal, who included the siege of Sarajevo in the indictments against Radovan Karadžić, the leader of the Bosnian Serbs; Ratko Mladić, the commander of their army; and against President Slobodan Milošević himself. During the war they had enough firepower to level the place, but that might have jolted bigger countries into stopping them so they chose instead to squeeze the life out of the city with shells and bullets.

I don't think we really changed anything, though I suppose you could say that when the Americans and NATO finally intervened in 1995 it was because three years of stories dripping into the eyes and ears of voters just made it too embarrassing not to do anything any more. But I do not think the fact that journalists do not often right the wrongs that they report matters at all. Being there is important enough on its own. Between us, we at least created a record of what was happening.

I was not trying to write the first draft of the military history of the war, though. Bosnia was a slaughterhouse and when you are up to your knees in blood it is no time to analyse grand strategy. To do that, you need more distance. Anyway, in purely military terms, there was very little movement, except in the first few months in 1992 and at the end in 1995. To report war properly, you need to start with what it does to people. War is all about killing. For a journalist who wants to get on the main television news bulletin most nights of the week, that very often meant finding stories that were so compelling that they could not be ignored, about dead people, how they died, and what that did to the people who were left behind. But reporters in wars also have to remember that editors and viewers get exhausted and bored by stories of unrelenting misery that never change and never get better. So you also need to find stories that can be uplifting, because in wars you can see the best as well as the worst of the human spirit in the same moment and sometimes even in the same person.

It is also vital to remember the wider context, about why we got to where we are, and to explain all of that, or tales of suffering and death just become white noise, a mystifying drone of misery that makes people switch off. Too often during the war in Bosnia we were not clear enough about why the killing was happening, partly because in television, especially, we were frightened of trying to explain things. That taught me a lesson for the future, when after the war I moved on to the Middle East. It also created at times a false equality, a suggestion that the two sides were somehow equal because war's most fundamental truth is that it kills people, and the dead suffer equally: an amputated leg is an amputated leg, whoever lost it.

Reporters should never forget the cruelty of war, but they should also state clearly when crimes are being committed, and, if they can, say who is responsible. We should have been harder on the leaders of the Bosnian Serbs, who were treated by Western governments and their military representatives, until almost the very end, as legitimate people with whom business could be done. But the indictments handed down by the International Criminal Tribunal for the Former Yugoslavia in The Hague show that they were responsible for the majority of the war crimes that were committed.

I did not just see that in Sarajevo. In August 1992 Larry Hollingworth, of the UNHCR, asked if I wanted to join him in an attempt to reach Goražde, a besieged Bosnian government enclave in the east, which was surrounded by Bosnian Serb forces. Larry was probably the most famous aid worker in the world at the time, because he looked unforgettable on television, with a fierce head of hair and a long beard like Father Christmas, and because he had the gift of soundbites. He could come up with terse and memorable gobbets that slotted easily into any news report. Larry also had guts and vision, and always wanted to do the toughest job, which in the summer of 1992 was getting into Goražde. Larry did not want to take many journalists, so he and the BBC producer Vin Ray concocted a story that it could only be the BBC because the trip was very dangerous and we had the only armoured Land Rover which also had room for a couple of writers, one of whom was Kurt Schork.

I drove our heavy Land Rover out of Sarajevo well within the body of Larry's convoy. Had we been taking up the rear, as the press often did, it would have been quite likely that we would have been stopped at Serb checkpoints and pulled out of the convoy. The first summer of the war was a busy time for them; their project to 'cleanse' their territory of Muslims was in full swing, and they did not want cameras or awkward questions. We moved slowly out of Sarajevo with an escort of French armoured personnel carriers, painted white because they were part of the UN protection force, a well-intentioned but under-powered outfit that had a mandate to escort aid convoys and little else. It was a shame because the French were proper fighting soldiers, from the Foreign Legion and the Marines.

The convoy was held up about forty miles outside Sarajevo, in Rogatica, by Bosnian Serb soldiers. I saw a Koran in a ditch, and I knew already that Rogatica's Muslims were being forcibly deported by Serbs, because many of them had turned up in Sarajevo. A French-speaking Serb gave us his view of what was happening. It was simple: in Goražde, the Muslims had killed all the Serbs; all that the Serbs had done in retaliation was to put Muslim women and children in schools for a month before they were expelled to Sarajevo. He said airily that the men of fighting age – older than fifteen – had fled to the mountains. But someone else whispered that the eviction of the Muslims, led by the commander of the Rogatica brigade, Rajko Kušić, had been terrible. 'The leader of the Serbs here is an extremist. He kills everyone. He wants to make the area completely clean.' It was frustrating. We could not leave the convoy; we could not be diverted from our mission of getting to Goražde, but it was clear that the ethnic cleansing of Rogatica was a big story. The Serbs were watching, though, and if we had tried to leave the convoy to film, we would have been arrested instantly.

Since the war, the truth about what was happening in Rogatica has been confirmed. A former Bosnian Serb officer called Dragoje Paunović was given twenty years by Bosnia's war crimes court for, among other things, taking twenty-seven civilians to be used as human shields at a front line, and then giving orders for them to be shot. Rajko Kušić is wanted for war crimes. His men are alleged to have killed more than 349 civilians during the ethnic cleansing of Rogatica. At the end of 2004 reports said that he had turned up in the war in Chechnya, sent there by the Russian secret services at the head of a group of Serbs. Kušić is also alleged to be part of the support system that sustains the former leader of the Bosnian Serbs, Radovan Karadžić, and the former head of their army, Ratko Mladić, who went on the run from the war crimes tribunal when the war ended in 1995. They face sixteen counts of genocide, crimes against humanity and violation of the laws of war in Bosnia–Herzegovina between April 1992 and July 1995. The charges include the unlawful confinement, murder, rape and inhumane treatment of civilians.

Our progress through eastern Bosnia to Goražde was slow. At the last checkpoint before Goražde, the Serbs came up with all sorts of reasons why we could not continue. There were mines ahead; there was shooting around the corner. My notebook says they were 'big men – big boots, big guns, beards, looking tough . . . One very angry man with grey hair shouts "nix" at the camera – then says Serbs won't shoot. Larry asks patiently how come there are mines if the road is [tar]macadamed.' One of the best ways of calming angry Serbs at road blocks and getting their respect was to have a drink with them. The colonel in charge of the French troops handed out bottles of wine. After forty-five minutes a big Serb with a beard and a blue shirt warned that there was more shooting and we should wait another five minutes, which gave him a chance to enlarge on some of the favourite themes of his people. They were fighting our war. Once all the Serbs were killed, Islamic fundamentalism would come to England and France as well. Serbia and Britain had been friends in the past, we had fought the Germans together, we were natural allies. What had gone wrong?

Most Serbs were decent, hospitable people, and I often felt sorry for them. They were led into a catastrophe by Slobodan Milošević,

Radovan Karadžić and the rest, who manipulated their historic insecurity and used nationalism ruthlessly and cynically to secure their own power. State broadcasters rammed home the poisonous message that their enemies were preparing to destroy them; men and women who were often poorly educated country people swallowed the propaganda and were pushed into a war. Many times I would turn up at a Serb checkpoint or in a village to be faced with huge hostility and pointed guns. Like the soldiers at the Goražde checkpoint, the men were often big, physically intimidating and heavily armed. The key to winning their trust was getting inside their dugout, or shelter, or around a kitchen table, and having a drink – often more than one – with them. Once you sat down and they brought out a bottle of the plum brandy called slivovica, for which the highest praise was that it was home-made, and filled up small glasses of it for everyone, and knocked it back, and poured another round, then they would start to relax. Home-cured ham would come out, and slices of air-dried beef, and more slivovica. They could go from hostile to friendly very quickly, and then they would often want to talk about Britain's Second World War alliance with the Serbs, and drink toasts to Winston Churchill.

Once we were through the last checkpoint we had a briefing from Larry. There was a narrow road with hairpin bends going up a wooded slope. After a few of the bends the convoy stopped again. Soldiers in rag-tag uniforms, wearing the fleur-de-lys symbol of the Bosnian government and carrying Kalashnikovs and hunting rifles, shimmered out of the trees and blocked the road. They were very young, with smooth faces and thin shoulders, the opposite of the hairy, muscular men on the other side of the checkpoint, like Peter Pan's lost boys, almost young enough to play soldiers, though they were fighting a real war and later on showed that they could do real killing. Larry and the French officers had negotiated a local ceasefire to let the convoy in, and they hoped the lost boys had taken their mines off the road. The first rows of houses on the edge of Goražde were badly damaged, roofs gone and walls blown out, and looked uninhabited. Then there was a long road that looked just as empty. But as the convoy of 4x4s and lorries moved slowly down it, flying blue United Nations flags and led by the French APCs, people started to emerge, one by one and then all at once, until there were hundreds of them.

The French soldiers started throwing them packets of ciga-rettes, and the people scrabbled in the dirt and started to cheer and to weep. I stopped the car and a woman came to me with a rose. It was like liberating a village in France in 1944, except they did not know yet that the French soldiers were only going to stay for an afternoon. The siege of Goražde lasted another three years, until the end of the war. I was lucky to be working with a young and very tall Australian cameraman called Nik Millard, who went on to be one of the best in the world. I followed him towards the operating room at the hospital, down a corridor that was echoing with the rhythmic screams of a child in terrible pain. In the room, there was no anaesthetic, so they were holding down a three-year-old boy called Amer Djebo while a doctor pulled shrapnel out of his back with a pair of forceps. The boy's screams were unbearable, but the doctor worked grimly to finish the job and the others kept hold of the boy's arms and legs. A few feet away a man grimaced in pain and silently gripped the edge of the operating table as another doctor did the same for him.

Nik worked quickly, making sure that the pictures passed the gore test by focusing on the man's contorted face, and the boy's podgy, bloodied arms. When the doctor, who was called Nusret Popović, finished treating Amer Djebo I spoke to him. He explained how the boy had been wounded by a shell that killed his parents, and how he felt like a torturer for what he had just done, but had no choice. His face was gleaming with sweat and his heart was

155

beating so hard I could see his white coat on the left side of his chest fluttering. In the next room there was a teenage boy lying silently with his mother next to him. After he was wounded by shellfire, the doctors cut off his leg, high above the knee. Surgery in besieged Goražde was not that different from how it had been during the Napoleonic wars. The one concession to modern medicine was a little local anaesthetic that they used where they made the incision to start the amputation. For the rest of the operation, they used brandy. They had no fluids to give the patients, and the teenage boy sat propped in his bed with pale sunken eyes already half-way to being a corpse. We were not able to hang around long enough to see if the medical supplies the UNHCR had brought in would save his life. As we left Goražde, the ceasefire ended and the shelling started again.

The road back to Sarajevo was long and difficult. Just outside the town, some Serbs stopped our Land Rover and tried to load it with their wounded. We persuaded them to take them to a French APC instead. Then the convoy was blocked by mines on the unmade track through the forest going back to Rogatica. We waited a night and a day, listening to fighting close by, while a team of combat engineers worked their way over from Sarajevo to open the road. I slept on the road next to our Land Rover in my flak jacket, and woke up with the front plate digging in and pins and needles from my chest to my toes. I risked finding more mines by slinking off the road into the long grass to take a dump, but the only other way of doing it would have been to dig a hole on the road.

By the time the French engineers blew up the mines to let us through late the next day, the Serbs were full of rage. The Bosnian government forces from Goražde – presumably the young des-peradoes we had seen in the woods on the way in – had attacked, they said, under cover of the presence of the UN convoy. To prove it they took us to a police station and made us film what we saw there. In a room, with gaping, fatal wounds still fresh enough to be wet, were the bodies of around half a dozen soldiers in Serb uniforms, big men with big boots like the ones at the checkpoint as we approached Goražde. This was no time to wait to see if they would offer a glass of slivovica to break the ice. They wanted revenge, and they wanted us to see why they were doing it. Nik Millard filmed them quickly and we left for Sarajevo. It was a hot night, and I was so tired I was hallucinating, imagining animals and people on the road as I followed the lights of the lorry ahead. The air conditioning did not work, and I drove with the armoured door wide open; the risk of getting shot was much less than the risk of falling asleep at the wheel and driving off the side of the road. Very late we crossed the front line into Sarajevo air-port, where the UNHCR staff had a barbecue waiting outside a hangar to welcome us back, and there were cold beers, and I felt like I was home.

In Bosnia, there was not a great deal of reporting from the trenches at the front line. For war reporters, a piece to camera with bullets whistling around your ears is always desirable, because it establishes you in the middle of the story, and makes you think you look cool or brave, but after the very beginning of the war, it was almost impossible to get permission from the Bosnian army to visit sol-diers on the front line. The whole city, anyway, was a front line, because you were never out of range of shells and were often in range of snipers. You didn't need a paper from the army to go to the biggest graveyard in Sarajevo. It was called the Lion Cemetery, after a sad-looking stone lion that surveyed the graves that over-flowed down the hill, across the road and into a football field as more people got killed. The goalposts still stood on the pitch, like drowning men waving, as the graves and the army of the dead marched across the touchline and advanced downfield towards the auditorium and ice rink where Jayne Torville and Christopher Dean had won the gold medal for ice dancing in the Winter Olympics of 1984. During the war, the UN used the ice rink to park some of their armoured vehicles. Most of the graves in the Lion Cemetery were of Muslims, and they all had the same hexagonal wooden grave markers. Christians had wooden crosses. No matter what their religion was, their names and the years they lived were marked with cheap plastic screw-on letters and numbers. The screws would rust and letters would fall out. War cemeteries are usually full of the graves of young men, but in that place there were men, women and children of all ages. What they have in common are the dates of their deaths, between 1992 and 1995.

People were more or less equal in death during the war. Being killed is a pretty fundamental common denominator. But the attention of the international media, especially television, made some dead people stars. In the early 1990s global communications were speeding up, the world was getting connected and the fast new world needed stars, even if they were dead or wounded. Television news needs symbols, microcosms, small stories that illustrate big and complicated truths. They didn't even have to die, at least not immediately, to get star status. I'm not saying it was a bad thing. Some stories just seize the imagination of the viewers, which increases the impact that they have exponentially.

After the war, most of the wooden grave markers in the Lion Cemetery were replaced by permanent memorials. A white marble symphony of hearts and flowers was put up over the grave of two young lovers who were killed together and buried together. They were Bosko Brckic and Admira Ismic. He was twenty-four and she was twenty-five when they had their terrible and frightening deaths. Some journalists called them Sarajevo's 'Romeo and Juliet', only they were double-crossed not star-crossed. Bosko was a Serb and Admira was a Muslim. They were lovers and as the siege went on and the Serbs on the hills killed more and more people in the city who were mainly Muslims, life for the Serbs, even for those who hated what was happening, became more and more difficult. People in mixed relationships, which had been common before the war, came under all kinds of unpleasant pressures.

Bosko and Admira decided to get out by escaping across the front line. Right through the war high-value merchandise like cigarettes, booze and weapons came in and sometimes people went out through the city's perimeter, if the price was right and the right commanders were paid off. Bosko and Admira thought they had paid all the necessary bribes. On 19 May 1993 they crawled out of a trench on the Bosnian side into no man's land and almost immediately were machine-gunned. Admira, severely wounded, crawled across to her lover, who was probably already dead because he was not moving. With her last strength she put her arm over him and then she died too. Their bodies lay embracing in no man's land for days. Both sides blamed the other. For a while it looked as if they would stay there indefinitely. There were other corpses, not far from them, which had been decomposing for months.

But what made their deaths different was that Kurt Schork and Sean McGuire from Reuters heard about the story, reported it, and asked me to do a television version. The story was picked up around the world, which didn't surprise us as they were easy deaths to understand. The Serbs saw a chance to get some good publicity and sent men into no man's land, who attached ropes to the bodies of Admira and Bosko and dragged them to the place they had lost their lives trying to reach. They announced that the two young lovers would be buried at Serb military barracks on the outskirts of Sarajevo and that reporters would be allowed out of Sarajevo through the front line to go to the funeral. Their first burial place was in a small soldiers' graveyard. The coffins were solid-looking, made of carved wood, but they had not been well sealed. Bosko's mother had been brought from Belgrade and as she and the other women from his family wailed, the smell of the two lovers' rotting bodies oozed out of their coffins and hung over the funeral like a shroud. Flies buzzed around the narrow crack between the top and bottom sections of the coffins. Admira's mother and father were on the other side of the front line and had to wait until after the war, when the bodies were moved to their last resting place in the Lion Cemetery, to mourn at the grave of their daughter and the man she wanted to marry.

Bosko and Admira were killed before the internet age started – but a Google search for them still comes back with more than 400 references. Tripadvisor.com suggests a visit to what it calls the 'Romeo and Juliet Bridge'. A tourist has posted a comment with a version of their story, imagining a moment when 'the two lovers embraced, forgetting about the world around them as they kissed, a sniper – with one shot – killed the two youngsters. Instantly, they dropped to the cold, rigid cement where they bled to death in each other's arms; never letting each other go.' There has been a documentary. They are even part of a campaign against sectarianism run by the Scottish Executive, which includes the text of Kurt's original story from Sarajevo, made into a Power-Point presentation to be read out in a school assembly by children who were not born when they were killed: 'In a country mad for war, Bosko and Admira were crazy for each other . . .' It is good that they have not been forgotten, and that they had families who could pay for them to be reburied after the war, and to show their love and sadness with the best gravestone they could afford.

Not far from where they are buried, there is a chipped and stained wooden board, which says 'Vedrana Glavas, 1989–92'. There used to be another, for Roki Sulejmanović, who only lived thirteen months before he was killed, on the same day and probably by the same person that killed Vedrana. He was buried next to her but there is no sign of his grave now. In the first summer of the war they were shot by Serb gunmen who attacked a bus that was supposed to be taking them out of the city to Germany. It was an ordinary city bus, and fifty-three children were on board when it crossed the front line into no man's land. The youngest was six months; the eldest was four years. Not enough adults were there to look after them properly, so the youngest children were tied to their seats with sheets so they would not fall off. They set off, supposedly with promises of safe passage, in mid-afternoon, rush-hour time in the war, when armed men on either side were fully awake and looking for action. Our cameraman filmed the children as the bus drove towards the last Bosnian checkpoint at the edge of town, where he got off. The bus went on into no man's land, where a sniper, presumably a Serb as the bus was coming from the government side, opened fire. Vedrana and Roki were killed. The bus turned back to Sarajevo. A Bosnian soldier who saw the bus moving slowly towards the Serb guns was aghast when I spoke to him. 'They must have been crazy to take them down that road. The Serbs should shoot at me, with a uniform, not at kids.'

The bodies of the two children were taken to a mortuary not far from the place where the bus trip started. Their bodies were left lying there, next to each other. I could tell they had arrived at the mortuary very soon after they were killed, because their bodies were still bleeding and the blood had soaked into the sheets that covered them. Their feet, still wearing little shoes and socks, poked out. I compared the clothes on the bodies with the pictures from the bus, and realised that we had a shot of Roki about fifteen minutes before he was killed. He was sitting with the others, squashed into a seat. So many children on a bus with so few adults looked very wrong.

The children were all supposed to be orphans, but it was not that simple. Roki did not have anybody, as far as we could tell, but Vedrana had a mother and a grandmother who were not able to look after her. They lived in a single tiny room, full of mess and crumpled clothes. No one had bothered to tell them that she was being evacuated to Germany and they were more bewildered than angry. Vedrana's mother, twenty-year-old Svetlana, had learning difficulties, which was why she could not look after her, but she visited her daughter and was proud that she could play with a ball. The grandmother, Ruza, overwhelmed by what life had brought her, did the talking.

'It wasn't right to send children that way. If they'd told us they were doing that we'd have brought her home instead . . .'

On the morning of the children's funeral, with our friends from Reuters, we offered to give them a lift to the cemetery. They had a bunch of wild flowers which they had picked from a piece of ground behind their building and were pleased that they would not have to walk for a few miles, exposed to shellfire, to get to the cemetery. We were happy to make their lives a little easier, and even happier to keep them away from our competitors. If they were with us, they could not speak to anyone else. But a war is made up of thousands of acts of cruelty and another one was heading straight for them.

We arrived at the Lion Cemetery in plenty of time for the funeral, but the two little bodies were already in the ground. The cemetery had been shelled so the gravediggers had decided not to wait. Older boys and girls from the children's home arrived with flowers. They dropped them on the small mounds of earth and ran away, ducking, when the shelling started again. Vedrana's mother and grandmother were walking away from the graves when another shell exploded next to them. The old lady collapsed on the ground and her daughter staggered away, screaming and roaring with fear. Kurt Schork and our translator, Jasmina, who was a surgeon, bandaged her up as more shells came in. I gave them my field dressing, which disappeared completely into the hole in her upper arm. They put another one on top. We took her to hospital in our Vauxhall, which had even more shrapnel holes after the attack.

I was disgusted by what had happened and full of anger against the people who had done it. The deaths of the children were a crime in themselves but then to shell their funeral was another outrage. I was about to vent my anger in a piece to camera that laid into the Serbs for committing war crimes. I was convinced that the Serbs were responsible. A conspiracy theory was put around by some UN people that the Bosnian government was in the habit of shelling their own people to get world sympathy and to make the Serbs look bad. I never saw any proof that it was true. And the graveyard was not just being shelled because the cameras were there; the gravediggers said it was shelled plenty of times when cameras were not there too. Then something in my mind, I suppose the training I had from the BBC, told me to hold on, to calm down, to think hard about what I was going to say and to play it straight. I still think that was the right way to do it. The piece was more powerful because the tone of it was more measured. I laid out the facts and the pictures about what had happened, and let the viewers draw their own conclusions. I didn't need to rant and rave, to say that it was a crime. It was obvious.

Vedrana and Roki never became stars in the way that Bosko and Admira did. Our story was broadcast in the same week as ITN's great TV exclusive on the detention camps the Serbs were running, which included a famous image of a man standing behind a wire fence who was so thin that his ribs were sticking out, like a relic from the Holocaust. When I went back to

163

Sarajevo in 2004, I saw that Vedrana's grave, a grassy hump, was just about marked and Roki's grave had disappeared; the man in charge of the graveyard said that no one had been to visit or to leave flowers.

Perhaps it shouldn't matter who remembers and whether their graves are marked because they are all dead, lives blown away before they were lived. But it bothered me; if no one can recall what happened to the two children, the way they died and what happened at their funeral, or even where they are buried, it will be as if they never lived. Vedrana and Roki died when the Bosnian war was still a novelty. For stories to have a big impact, sometimes they have to feel like the last straw. They have to bring together in the viewers' minds a series of worries and thoughts that were niggling away, which are given a voice and face by what they see on television.

In the third summer of the siege a story about a wounded girl in Sarajevo did all of those things. It touched off a journalistic frenzy that dragged in governments and international organisations. The girl, who was called Irma Hadzimuratovic, was one of the most famous five-year-olds in the world for a few weeks in August 1993. Other children were pulled into the story in supporting roles. The war had a huge impact on Irma and her family, and it changed the lives of other wounded children and their families for ever. But so did the way that the news machine sucked them in after it entered their lives and told their stories. Children and war are a very profitable combination for journalists. The weakness and innocence of childhood and the power and might of warfare together make strong magic, and reporters who spend a lot of time in war zones should only deploy it carefully. Used too often, and on stories that don't include enough horror and pathos, the magic loses its power. But when all the ingredients come together in the right way, as they did in the case of Irma and the other Sarajevo children, the stories get noticed.

It started when a doctor called the BBC office from one of Sarajevo's main hospitals. He was called Edo Jaganjac and he had a little girl, five years old, in his ward. She had been badly wounded by a mortar attack that had killed her mother. Dr Jaganjac wanted publicity for her, because her wounds were too serious to be looked after in Sarajevo. The shell had torn open her abdomen and she had serious internal injuries. It was very straightforward. Unless she was evacuated she would die. There was an official way to organise medical evacuation of the wounded, but it was slow and so painstaking that it was not efficient, and she did not have enough time. When I first saw Irma in the State Hospital in Sarajevo she was lying in a cot, connected up to tubes and pipes and as many monitors as they had. Perhaps because of the pain, or because of the physical effect of her wounds, she had pushed her shoulders back and arched her spine. Her father sat with her, holding her hand, staring at Irma as if the power of his will could save her. He had put her favourite doll in the bed with her. It was all there: a motherless child fighting death, a victim of a war and a siege that showed no signs of stopping and which politicians seemed happy to tolerate as part of Europe's background noise. Television news works best when a small story can symbolise something much bigger, and I knew immediately that I could do a very strong piece about young Irma and her father.

Allan Little, who had the first contact with Dr Jaganjac, wrote a story about Irma for radio and put it out late that night, but I thought I would wait until the next day. I needed a few more ingredients to build it up. However affecting they may be, pictures of a little girl in a bed, badly wounded, are not enough for a TV news report. We needed more variety, more texture, for Irma's story to have the impact it deserved. Her father, who was called Ramiz, was prepared to co-operate; the doctor must have told him that helping us was his daughter's only chance.

'I've lost my best friend already,' he told me. 'If I lost my child, I don't know what I would do.' So we took him back to his wife's grave and filmed him praying, and went to the place where the attack happened. It was a patch of open ground between some tower blocks on one of Sarajevo's many Titoist housing estates. That Sunday, as we assembled the material, I did not think that Irma's terrible experience was particularly exceptional. I had done similar stories in Sarajevo over more than two years about children who were gravely ill and usually they either stayed that way or they died. Telling their stories seemed to have made no difference at all.

This time was very different. Irma's story was broadcast on a Sunday night, which gets the biggest audiences for news of the week. There was an unusually big contingent from Fleet Street in Sarajevo from papers that did not normally staff it full-time, because of rumours that NATO would hit the Serbs in the hills with air strikes. But Western military intervention was still a year away, and they were looking for a story. They picked up on Allan's Saturday night radio piece on the little girl who was fighting for her life in time to get it into Monday's papers. The tone of their coverage must have been a bit too syrupy for some of our bosses at the BBC. At the regular nine o'clock editorial meeting on Monday, when they try to map out the day's agenda, they decided they did not want to hear anything else about Irma. Fighting going on outside Sarajevo was deemed to be more newsworthy.

It was not the right decision. They were simply reacting negatively to what newspapers had done. It was not physically possible to get to the place where the fighting was happening so I ignored the message and got on with the follow-up to the previous night's story about Irma. Then, during the morning, the story grew; Britain's foreign secretary Douglas Hurd announced that the British government would send an air ambulance to evacuate Irma and her father and Medina, her younger sister, who was not hurt in the attack. By the afternoon, there was a journalistic feeding-frenzy around Irma, who was unconscious, and her father, who was praying for her to live. Because the BBC was always in Sarajevo we had better connections at the hospital than most of the visitors, and we had the best access to a girl who was becoming a very hot property. She was flown out that night, with Ramiz and Medina. The British government's surge of humanitarian concern continued. It announced it would be sending a big transport aircraft equipped as a flying hospital. A hunt started through Sarajevo's hospitals for 'the other Irmas', children who needed medical treatment that was not available in a city that was in the third year of a siege.

None of them was in such a desperate condition as she had been, but they would all do better if they were somewhere other than Sarajevo. The RAF sent a doctor in before their aircraft arrived, to choose who to take out. I met him at the airport and offered to take him to the hospital to introduce him to the doctors. I was doing him and me a favour; he had no idea where he was supposed to go and I wanted to keep him out of the hands of other journalists. That morning he made a lot of parents very happy by telling them not only that their sick or wounded children would be evacuated, but also that their partners and other children could go too. Among them was a boy who had lost an eye to shrapnel who needed reconstructive surgery, another boy paralysed by a shrapnel wound in the back, and a girl who was acutely ill with meningitis. I took the doctor to see a baby, a boy called Eldar Kalamujic. He was very sick, bloated and yellow because his liver was failing. His parents were nice people,

desperately worried about their boy, and suddenly full of excitement because he seemed to have been handed a way out.

'Very sad,' the doctor said as we left the room. 'But we can't
take him. He needs a liver transplant. Kids in Britain die because
they don't get livers in time. If I took him he might get a liver that
a British child needs.'

It seemed outrageous to me. What he was saying was logical,
but it also felt wrong. He could not come into a place as miserable
as that hospital, I thought, and invite some children to his party
and not others. So for the only time in my life, I decided to
manipulate a news story, to get Eldar and his family evacuated.
Peter Kessler, the spokesman for the UNHCR, agreed to help,
and provided a soundbite saying that when you come to Sarajevo
to evacuate wounded and sick children, you shouldn't pick and
choose. The lunchtime news ran my story about the baby who
was being left behind and someone in Downing Street must have
been watching. By mid-afternoon Mrs Kalamujic was smiling
again. They were all going to London. The doctor had changed
his mind and her baby had a chance.

There were still spare places on the plane. Some of the most
acute cases needing medical evacuation were not children. They
were adults, very often men who had been soldiers. The British
government had a horror of taking sides and was uncomfortable
at first about evacuating men who had been fighting. Children are
so much less complicated. But even though civilians were targeted
by all sides in the Bosnian war, most of the casualties were still
men of fighting age. There were lots of them in Sarajevo whose
lives were no longer in danger but who were crippled by their
wounds and would stay that way if they did not get months of surgery and rehabilitation. Some of them were flown out too. A
doctor who had been trying to save the lives of children and adults
looked at what was happening with disgust. 'You can't just pick

kids off the shelves and leave others,' he said. 'This isn't a super-market.' A government that, as far as he was concerned, had ignored the grim catalogue of war crimes that had been inflicted on the people of Bosnia-Herzegovina by the Serbs had now sent its people to rummage through the hospitals of its capital as an easy alternative to stopping the fighting that was filling them.

I was deeply suspicious of the British government's motives too. I thought there was one easy way to end the misery and suffering in Sarajevo, and that was to break the siege by attacking the Bosnian Serbs on their hills. But the government of John Major was urging caution, not action. I didn't report my own belief that they had stumbled on a tremendous, face-saving way to make themselves look good. I had no proof and BBC foreign correspondents are trained to keep thoughts like that off the air. But it was logical, it might have been justifiable as legitimate comment, and I should have said something. Lack of action by European governments to stop the killing in Bosnia made them complicit in what was happening. Douglas Hurd, the foreign secretary, dismissed journalists like me as 'the something-must-be-done club'. But the fact remained that a festival of medical evacuation created a rosy glow, gave an impression of progress, and meant that the press would not be writing so much about the West's failure, once again, to end the killing.

Journalists' motives are never pure in these matters either. We also intervene in people's lives, telling ourselves that the upshot of it all will be positive. What right had I to play God when I decided to use my platform on BBC News to make sure that Eldar Kalamujic, the boy with liver failure, was evacuated? The answer is that I thought I was doing good, that I was righting a wrong. But actions have consequences. Eldar was evacuated to King's College Hospital, where his condition was stabilised. His mother and older brother started a new life in south London, with a nice house from a housing association and furniture from well-wishers. They spent a lot of time with Eldar in hospital, and I visited them as soon as I got back from Bosnia. Eldar was still in intensive care and it was taking time to get him a liver. We stood outside one of the entrances where people go for a smoke and talked, while red London buses went up Denmark Hill and people pushed by to see their sick friends and relations with flowers and fruit and chocolates. It was like any other visiting time at a National Health Service hospital. Eldar's big brother Kenan angrily kicked a football against a wall. His mother was very grateful for everything that the NHS was doing for her son but she looked lost, removed from her family and friends and transplanted in a day from her home to a great faceless city.

It got better after a while. Eldar's father was allowed to leave Sarajevo to join them, and eventually Eldar had a liver transplant. But by the time he had the operation Eldar's condition had deteriorated to the point where his brain was damaged. He died in 1999. They have a new baby now, and Eldar's father is a station manager on the Underground. They are doing well and are very glad they had some extra years with Eldar, because he would have died in Sarajevo. But maybe what the RAF doctor said when he first saw Eldar in Sarajevo was true. Perhaps a British child with a better chance of survival died because Eldar Kalamujic had a transplant instead of him. I hope not, but I cannot forget his mother's face in Sarajevo when she thought he would not be evacuated, and I would do the same again.

Irma, whose horrific wounds started it all, never really left Great Ormond Street Hospital. She was paralysed from the neck down and for the rest of her life needed help to breathe. The first time I saw her in London, a few months after she was evacuated, Irma was still very ill, and in a lot of distress, wearing some kind of gum shield because she was chewing her lips. I was horrified, and even wondered whether it would have been better that she had died in Sarajevo. But the following year she was smiling and laughing and I could see that the staff loved her and that her father and sister were overjoyed that she was still with them. She died in Great Ormond Street in April 1995 because of complications that came from her wounds. The coroner said she was a victim of war, and I joined the mourners in Regent's Park mosque who lined up to see her for the last time before they closed the coffin. At least we helped to buy them all a little more time together.

6

Mostar

A lot of times reporting in a war zone means that you have to choose a road, take a deep breath and then drive down it. Moving along an empty, quiet road chews your nerves. When Yugoslavia was breaking up, the wrong road could lead to big trouble. This time the houses on either side were badly damaged – roofs destroyed, walls blown out – trees hung down blocking the way in places, hedges and gardens were overgrown and advancing out into the road. The whole time I was half-expecting someone to start shooting, for the hedges to be ripped apart, to feel the bullets hitting the armoured Land Rover. But nobody was around. The place was abandoned; man's bad nature had emptied it, and Mother Nature was now taking it back. I drove slowly, further down a narrow lane, but after about half a mile there was a UN checkpoint, which meant it was the right way. Thank Christ for that. I was trying to leave the area of Sarajevo controlled by the Bosnian government, cross the airport which was patrolled by UN troops, and then enter more Bosnian government territory at the village of Hrasnica on the other side. The route was rarely taken by journalists, because it was hard to get permission to go to Hrasnica. Bosnians tried to cross the airport every night without the right papers and French Foreign Legion troops with blue UN helmets played a game with them, arresting them and sending them back so that they could try again, until the Bosnians dug a tunnel under the airfield to avoid the French and to connect their two enclaves.

One war per country is usually enough, but in 1993 Bosnia had two on the go. Around Sarajevo and in the north and east, the Bosnian government was fighting the Serbs, who had pushed hundreds of thousands of Muslims out of their homes, killing tens of thousands in the process. The Serbs wanted to cut chunks off Bosnia to make their own ethnically pure Serb state. Sarajevo was under siege and so were a handful of other enclaves loyal to the Bosnian government. Then the Bosnian Croats, in Herzegovina to the south and in the mountains and valleys of central Bosnia, decided that good ideas were worth copying. Aided and abetted by the Croatian government in Zagreb, they started dismembering the other half of Bosnia's corpse, in the west and south, to make a Frankenstein state of their own, which would be ethnically pure. Mostar was going to be its capital. The Croats' problem was that 30,000 people, mostly Muslims, were surrounded in the east of Mostar and were fighting like hell.

All sides in Bosnia's wars claimed that they faced extinction. Some of the Croats and Serbs believed it, because their leaders told them it was true and pushed propaganda down their throats until they could not doubt it. But the ones who really did face genocide were the Bosnians who supported the Muslim-led government in Sarajevo. The 30,000 who were fighting in Mostar were fighting because they had a good idea what would happen to them if they didn't. In the Balkan wars the losers lost everything – men had a strong chance of being shot; women, if they weren't killed too, could be raped and then kicked out over the front line to become refugees. The fighting in Mostar was hard, and the civilians were in a very bad way. They had almost no food and were getting sniper fire when they took water from the river Neretva that cut the town in two.

Bosnia was back in the news that summer because once again the European powers were hinting that they might intervene and deciding not to, and because of the evacuations of Irma and the other wounded children. Journalists were still trawling the shelves of the baby supermarket that was open for business in Sarajevo, looking for more Irmas, but Mostar was the biggest unreported story in the Balkans. Even better, as far as I knew, no foreign reporters were in the east side of Mostar. Information trickled out from Spanish UN troops who mounted occasional patrols and from aid organisations who were struggling to get supplies into the besieged part of the city.

Hot summer, hot war – it felt very interesting. It was the biggest story around, but also the hardest to get at. When Peter Kessler, the spokesman for the UNHCR in Sarajevo, said there was a 'Ho Chi Minh trail' going into east Mostar, all I wanted to do was walk down it. I thought I would be trampled in the rush to get details from him. But to my amazement, not many other reporters were very interested. For some of them, Mostar felt even harder to explain than the siege of Sarajevo. One American TV producer told me that they were not going to touch the story because there was a new set of bad guys and that would just be too hard for anyone watching back home to understand. But there was another reason for not wanting to leave Sarajevo, and it hit me as we were getting ready for the Mostar trip. Sarajevo was one of the most dangerous places in the world. But after a year of war it was also comfortable and familiar. The child evacuation stories, and the baseless speculation about foreign intervention, kept journalists busy enough. There was water in the hotel most of the time. If you had the money and the logistics you could get enough beer and wine to get as drunk as you wanted every night. And everyone else was there, so it couldn't be the wrong place, could it?

I had long discussions with colleagues about the best way to get to besieged Mostar.

'Quite simple,' a cameraman who had been some sort of special forces soldier in an earlier life said unhelpfully. 'For us it would be a standard infiltrate/exfiltrate job . . . maybe with a HALO [high altitude low opening] jump to get in.'

But since we did not have an air force, or parachutes, he had no idea how to do it as a journalist, and no one else did either. It was just a question of getting in the car and pushing down the road. As we packed gear and supplies into the armoured Land Rover, I felt apprehensive about what we could be getting into, and lonely at the thought of leaving familiar territory. I knew where the shells came from in Sarajevo, where the snipers were, where to eat dinner and I was getting on television most nights. Somewhere inside a voice was telling me that I was bloody mad to do it, but it was too late for that. Even getting the right pieces of paper to get through the checkpoints to leave Sarajevo was not easy. To cross the front lines we had to get permission from the Bosnian army headquarters in Sarajevo and from their enemies, the Bosnian Serbs, in Pale, a dingy village in the mountains outside the city that they had made their capital. Any trip to Pale had a highlight and a lowlight. The good bit was the chance of some Serbian beer and a veal steak at one of the places near the ski slopes. At the height of the war some of the lifts were still working, for the Bosnian Serb army's ski championships. The low point was an encounter with Sonia Karadžić, the moody daughter of Radovan, the wild-haired leader of the Bosnian Serbs. He had given his little girl the Bosnian Serb press office to look after. She rarely arrived before lunchtime, and was a master of obstruction. But we got the right pieces of paper in the end. We did not even know if the journey from Sarajevo to Mostar – about sixty miles – was possible. These days it is an easy two-hour car ride, maybe less. In the summer of 1993, with the war going on all around, it took us three days.

We loaded the Land Rover with as little TV equipment as we thought we would need, plus a generator and a satellite telephone. In 1993 satphones were still very new – and very big. Now they can look almost like ordinary mobiles. But the one we packed came in a big steel box, weighed so much that it took two strong men to pick it up, and needed lots of electricity (which, along with the need to charge batteries, was why we had the generator). We had some ration packs, cartons of water and a case of beer. With me were two great cameramen, Shane McDonald, an Australian, and an American called Chuck Tayman, who learned how to shoot pictures in the US Navy. I first met Shane in Baghdad before the 1991 war. His party piece, jumping out of a high window as if he had a death wish, was notorious. Instead of falling he would grab the concrete window sill and hang there until he felt like hauling himself back in. But Chuck and Shane were very good at their jobs, and I suppose they must have trusted me too. At the last minute a French photographer called Alexandra Boulat asked if she could come too. We had room in the Land Rover so I said yes.

I drove across the Sarajevo airport tarmac, through another checkpoint and into more wrecked, empty streets. Gradually the houses ended and we were surrounded by fields and a landscape that was bizarre because it looked so peaceful. It was like discovering a lost kingdom, separated from the city by a mountain and virtually untouched by the war. The sun was golden and the children were out playing in it, and people worked in the fields and strolled around in a way that is only possible when there aren't any shells or snipers, when they do not have to live with the possibility that their lives could be snuffed out at any time. No one was moving like they did in Sarajevo, doing a fast walk mixed up with bursts of running and ducking. We bowled down what had been the main Sarajevo–Mostar road and what I could see through the Land Rover's bulletproof glass looked like peace. It was an illusion, of course. The people in that part of Bosnia had enough to eat and were not in range of anybody's guns, but they were trapped. Bosnia's wars were all around them and they could not get out, and not much further down the road was a corner of the killing that was more vicious than anything anyone had seen in Sarajevo.

My spin through the little golden Shangri-La I had discovered behind Sarajevo's mountains ended at a roadblock. Bosnian soldiers said the next front line with the Serbs started a mile or so down the road. We had to turn off, to find a track through a forest that would take us round the spur of land the Serbs held and bring us out near Jablanica, a town about half-way to Mostar. It was starting to get dark but we pushed on into the forest. In wars you have to think about all the things that people in peaceful countries can ignore. If it gets dark when you are driving from London to Manchester, or Brussels to Paris, it does not matter; the street lights come on, and so do the car headlights. But when there are people around with guns who are used to killing, who do not like strangers, all the primal fears of the night that our ancestors left somewhere in us come flooding back.

The track narrowed as we moved higher, away from the valley floor and up through the fields towards the trees. The golden sunlight faded away, along with my fantasies about peace. I started remembering reports, not made up, about bandits. There was no law in the forest. If we got into trouble we had no way of telling anyone, and not much chance of being rescued. UN troops, who were stretched very thin, tended to stay near the main supply routes. We did not expect to see any friendly faces among the trees that looked thicker as it got darker. The part of *The Wind in the Willows* where Mole gets lost in the Wild Wood was in my head. There were human stoats and weasels somewhere ahead of us, and we had to have a plan; think about the bad things before they happen, and you may be able to deal with them when they do. I couldn't think of much. I told Chuck, Shane and Alexandra that we should close the steel bolts that were fixed on the inside of the Land Rover's doors, presumably put there for moments just like this. If we drove into men with guns we had to assume that they wanted to rob us or kill us or both. I was going to put my foot down and drive like hell. Our Land Rover was supposed to stop Kalashnikov bullets. But if they had physically blocked the road, we would have to stop and try to talk our way out. We agreed we wouldn't have much choice. Looking back on it, I don't think we would have had much of a chance either way.

Around midnight we saw a light somewhere in the distance. It was a small cottage, belonging to some local people who seemed to have spent most of the lives in the forest. They said we could stay the night and then drank all our beer and I was as relieved as Mole was when he found Badger's den. We slept on the floor of their kitchen. The next morning the empty beer cans, Boddingtons that had been bought from the British army, had been arranged on a shelf in a neat line, shiny souvenirs of their encounter with the outside world. They put us on the road to Jablanica, the town where the trail into Mostar started. In daylight the forest was not frightening, and the road opened out of the trees towards the valley of the river Neretva that leads to Mostar. We bumped over the river on a railway bridge and entered

Jablanica by mid–afternoon. It was the Wild West, a place that had run out of sympathy for anyone a long time ago, and it made Sarajevo seem genteel. Men had breath that stank of booze, bad food and tobacco, most carried guns and wore bits and pieces of military uniforms with a black sheen of dirt and grease on the camouflage. Filthy children ebbed and flowed around the gates of the heavily protected Spanish UN base. The soldiers inside, who were almost as dirty as the people outside their stockade, warned us that anything we left in Jablanica's only hotel would be stolen. They said we should leave our armoured Land Rover inside their base or it would go too. Shane had already run out of clean underwear. He bought all they had at the base shop – khaki bikini-style briefs with the Spanish army logo.

Like the rest of Jablanica's buildings – or the rest of the country – the hotel was a scruffy relic of a Titoist dream. Jablanica was one of the favourite places of Josef Tito, who led the partisans in their fight against the Germans in the Second World War, created the communist republic of Yugoslavia after 1945, and dominated it until he died of cancer in 1980. Tito liked Jablanica because his partisans had secured a famous victory there over the Germans in 1943, when they blew up the railway bridge, which still hangs down into the river, and then escaped across the Neretva.

In the Jablanica hotel they were serving lunch. A man called Vlado was hanging about in the restaurant. He had come back to Sarajevo from Germany to volunteer for the 10th Mountain Brigade, the Bosnian army's most controversial unit. Now he was wounded and half-starved, begging for food, giving off waves of disillusion and despair. Most men between fifteen or sixteen and about sixty were not allowed out of Sarajevo because they were needed to fight. Vlado had only been allowed to leave because of his wounds. The first time he tried to cross the French Foreign Legion's tarmac at Sarajevo airport was with a friend who had one leg. They were caught and sent back, but the next time they tried they made it. Vlado's father, who was forty-nine years old, was still in Sarajevo, still fighting. Vlado's eyes could not focus, as if he were drunk, though he did not seem to be. His mind was wandering and his sanity was slipping away. He looked enviously at the meat, four small pieces that we had been given because the waiter had worked in a London hotel.

'We don't get that. Not that I care.'

It was lucky Vlado did not care that we had some food and he did not, because he didn't get any of it. The mean Jablanica atmosphere was getting to us.

I still had no idea how we were going to get to Mostar. Then someone in the hotel put me in touch with a man called Humo, who introduced himself as the second-in-command of the Bosnian fighters in Mostar. He said he would take us the next day. Humo (he had a first name, but nobody used it) was on the way back in from Sarajevo, where he had been trying to get a TV team to bring back to Mostar. They had decided that they needed some publicity. He said he had not found anyone who would do it. He had never made it to the BBC office. Humo was a lean man who looked like a fighter, with deep-set dark eyes and hair that was shaved close to his skull.

Around eight the next morning, 23 August 1993, we were at Glogosnica, a village a couple of miles away, where the trail to Mostar started. The high mountains were all around, and it was like a scene from the Spanish Civil War, or the partisans' fight against the Germans. The pack horses which took weapons and ammunition into Mostar were tied up in long lines next to the turquoise waters of the Neretva. Wild men with guns and tattered uniforms were everywhere. Women were shaking out blankets. Dirty kids with rotten teeth ran around, eyeing our bags. We had been there since before dawn but now the sun was well up and the caravan of horses that we were to join still was not ready. The horses had old pack saddles, with wooden frames and leather straps and ties. They stood stoically as they were loaded, eating hay and corn from ammo boxes. A few displaced people sat around, unwashed and miserable. One old woman started to moan when she saw me opening a tin of herrings and cutting bread. She cheered up when I made her a sandwich. Perhaps I felt guilty about not giving Vlado any food the day before. Hairy soldiers were talking to the animals, whispering into their ears, pushing the straps of pack saddles under their tails, protesting and shouting at a few who start to kick each other. It was casual, everything was taking a very long time and I was getting irritated. I wanted to get at the story, and I knew the journey was going to be long and hard and dangerous and we had to get going. At this rate, I thought, we'll be walking for two days. Only one man seemed capable of balancing the loads on the horses. He was tall with shaggy hair and a beard and a faded camouflage tunic with the badge of the blue and white fleur-de-lys of the Bosnian army on his sleeve.

I negotiated over the horses, not very effectively, shelling out a couple of thousand German marks to rent three to carry our gear. When the shaggy man loaded them, it looked as if the horse with the heaviest load was going to have its back broken. On one side he strapped on our massive, steel-encased satellite phone. On the other side, balancing it, were four heavy flak jackets. The poor beast's back held but its knees buckled as it took the strain and its hooves slipped on the stones. It seemed to compose itself, take a breath, and then we started. The caravan was of more than twenty horses. All the others apart from ours were carrying boxes of bullets and mortar bombs. We walked next to them. Humo said they had a generator in Mostar, so ours was left behind, locked up in the armoured Land Rover. Neither the vehicle nor its contents were ever seen again, at least not in BBC colours. The Corporation decided not to send a rescue party to retrieve it, presumably because it was considered too dangerous to dispatch another team into the badlands of Jablanica. It was spotted a few months later decorated with the colours of the Bosnian army and carrying a gun.

The path to Mostar started with a steep climb of about three hours up a wooded hill until, covered in sweat, we reached a wide mountain plateau, surrounded by the high mountains whose flanks rattled down into slopes of scree. The horses moved across open grassland. The August sun was very strong. We took it in turns to carry the camera. Later in the day when Alexandra the snapper got very tired, we carried her cameras too. We stopped once in the morning and once in the afternoon at springs where the horses were rested and where we could refill our water bottles. But we were ludicrously badly equipped and we did not have enough bottles to carry the water we needed. At one of the springs were dozens of exhausted-looking women, children and old men, who were on their way out of Mostar and already in their second day of walking. Men of fighting age were all going in the opposite direction. We walked fast, with very few breaks.

I felt good, until I saw the only thing that could make me unhappy. A CNN camera crew was coming towards us, on the way out of Mostar. Brent Sadler, my old ITN opponent now transported to CNN, had already been there. Mark Biello, the cameraman, told me that they had not shot for very long, just enough for one piece which Sadler had taken out. That wasn't so bad. It was irritating, but I wasn't too worried because we were planning to dig in there, and Mostar did not sound like the kind of place you could do quickly. In 1993 the BBC's global television service was still minute, and not a priority for us, so officially

CNN were not even the competition – though in my competitive mind, they certainly were. Biello was more interested in swearing at Sadler, who had hitched a lift with an aid worker and taken the tapes out to Croatia, which meant he got his story out sooner, but also hot water, good hotels, decent food and no war, leaving them to walk back to Jablanica with the gear on horses. Biello was a nice guy, a big drinker who called himself Mad Dog and did everything he could to become a journalistic legend. On his arm he had a tattoo of a television camera with flames coming out of its sides attached to a parachute.

In the mountains there were no roads. Walking fast was hard work so we did not say much, and the dehydration made it worse. We left the plateau and started moving through thick woodland. It was quiet, except for occasional and frightening bursts of gun-fire. As the sun was going down we reached an area Humo said was very dangerous, because it was in direct sight of a Croat gun position and they often opened fire. The trail bent round to the left, and went up an open escarpment on one side of a broad valley. Humo walked fast up the path, shouting over his shoulder that this was no place to stop. But there were also bushes full of blackberries and we were out of water. I slowed down to tear off a few handfuls of ripe black fruit and stuffed them into my mouth. Suddenly a line of bullets kicked up the dust about a yard from me. The Croats were firing a heavy machine-gun at us. It thumped again and kept on thumping and I threw myself into the blackberry thicket. I lay there and found I still had a handful of blackberries, so I ate them, and picked off all the others I could reach from my hiding place. I was too hot, hungry, thirsty and tired to care much about the machine-gun. After a while they lost interest in us and the shooting stopped. We shouted to each other to check we were OK. Chuck was sitting behind a thick tree; everyone else was in the bushes. We stayed there, not moving. I lay thinking it would not have been cool or dignified to have been killed for a handful of blackberries and dozed until it was dark and safe enough to get back on to the trail.

In the blackness we walked another few miles to the place where the horses' heavy loads were taken off them and put on to a truck. I was falling asleep on my feet, literally, so dehydrated that only the fear of a humiliating collapse kept me going. I lay on the ground as soldiers transferred the cases of mortars and ammunition, and our gear, on to the back of the truck. We sat on top of the ammo boxes with a couple of dozen soldiers who had also come in from Jablanica. Humo warned us that this could be the most dangerous part of the journey because the truck had to drive through the Croat front line. No one seemed very bothered. By then we were up to our necks in it and the only way out was forward. We raced into town. For a while, for some unexplained reason, the truck stopped outside a building. The driver and whoever was in charge went in. We just sat on the ammo, packed in like sardines with the Bosnian soldiers. Every now and then green and red tracer rounds went over our heads, as lazy and harmless-looking as ever. We made jokes about what would happen if one of the bullets hit the truck.

That night we slept in the military headquarters, a former bank in the centre of the town's east side. I was woken up by the sound of heavy shelling. The building was shaking. We were exhausted, still dehydrated, because getting good water in Mostar was a problem – and now we had to find some stories to film and find a way to get them on the air – in a city that, judging by the noise that morning, was suffering fighting many times more intense than Sarajevo. It was also a hundred times more dangerous for us because we did not know our way around. The same thing seemed to have occurred to the rest of our little team as they woke up. Just getting there had taken all our energy, and it felt depressing and anti-climactic to have arrived. I left Shane and Chuck trying to heat up a tin of Toulouse sausages with lentils – the best meal in the French army ration packs – and went outside, with a vague idea of finding the hospital, which could not be far off. Hospitals were relatively safe places to film and doctors often spoke English.

The main street that ran through the enclave was deserted. Every minute or so shells were exploding, but far enough away not to be too alarming. I walked along from doorway to doorway until the road opened up into a T-junction. I was about to cross it when a man shouted from another doorway and told me not to try it. Later I found out that it was about the most toxic place in the city, where snipers had an easy shot and had killed many people. The man came towards me and we ran to the opposite side of the road along an alleyway and up some steps into a flat. It was fitted out as a hairdressing salon. A middle-aged stylist in a blue nylon overall was cutting the hair of a woman of about the same age. They were chatting, ignoring the shelling outside and hardly looked up as we trooped in through one door and out of the other. It turned out that the whole town was taking a short cut through the hairdresser's shop to avoid the sniper junction – at least when they were feeling cautious, or if the sniper had announced himself with bullets that day. Life in Mostar was so dangerous that on other days it seemed to be a perfectly accept- able risk to run across the dangerous junction rather than to waste a few minutes at the hairdresser's, and we started doing it too.

Muslims from villages in Mostar's hinterland had been forced over the front line. Some were drifting, lost, with no idea about what to do next. I saw two women sitting in a doorway, both with babies. They were sisters: Daria, twenty years old and Srdana, thirty. Their babies were both six months old and had been suffering from diarrhoea for three days, since they had been forced out of their homes by Croat gunmen. They had been expelled from Capljina, about thirty kilometres to the south, and had just arrived in Mostar, pushed over the front line at gunpoint by the Croats. Srdana's husband had been taken by the Croats and was in a prison camp. Daria's husband had been killed in the fighting. When the two women were captured they were raped five or six times each. So was their mother, who was fifty-nine. They were vague about where she had gone. After they were raped they were taken to a place where they thought they were going to be shot. They were saved because their mother told the men who had raped them that her mother had been a Catholic.

After about a week, the first UN convoy managed to get in. With the convoy came a dozen or more journalists. Most of them only stayed a couple of hours. By then we knew the places to go, how to move around without being too exposed. We were also more dirty and smelly than civilians who had been there for months. They had all worked out some sort of water-gathering infrastructure. We just stank. But the invasion of rampaging, day-tripping reporters, still nicely washed and shaved from the hotels they had woken up in, showed how alienating it can be when the press suddenly descend. It was funny and made me feel smug to see a well-dressed gang of about a dozen of them trotting over the sniper junction in the lee of an UNPROFOR armoured personnel carrier. They were just being sensible but I had left sensible a long way behind by then. We were all relieved when they went. Chuck was exhausted and left with them. Shane and I stayed a few more days, though it felt longer than that. I was prepared to stay weeks more, but we left because the BBC lost interest in the story.

Edit gear was big, heavy and expensive then (now it is the opposite) and the Corporation had only one set in Bosnia at the time, which had been moved to a place outside Mostar where we could sometimes send out tapes with aid workers. But Kate Adie had arrived in central Bosnia to cover the British army, and needed the edit gear, so it was moved away. When we heard what had happened, and that they had done it without even discussing it with us, Shane and I were disgusted and pulled out. If the BBC decided that the activities of a couple of hundred British soldiers were more important than the lives and deaths of 30,000 civilians trapped in a few overcrowded square miles, then we saw no point in risking our lives further. Later, one of the bosses apologised for not supporting us properly. We hitched a lift out of Mostar with an aid worker and drove out across the front line, through Herzegovina to Medjugorje, a Bosnian Croat stronghold. It is place of pilgrimage for Catholics since some children announced in 1991 that the Virgin Mary had appeared to them in a vision. One of them now has a website listing his speaking engagements in the United States, offering a 'personal prayer experience' with his family. It was bizarre that even at the height of the war there were overweight American pilgrims in the town, spending their money in the sinister Bosnian Croat statelet, which had called itself Herzeg-Bosna. I went back to Mostar with a documentary team about a month later to make a film about the siege. In 2001 it was admitted as evidence at the war crimes tribunal in The Hague, during testimony I gave against two Bosnian Croats who were on trial for besieging Mostar. Unlike some other journalists, who refused to go to the tribunal on the grounds that it compromised their independence, I had no hesitation about testifying. I told the court about what I had reported. It was already in the public domain, and I was prepared to be cross-examined about it because I was confident that what had been broadcast was accurate, and because I was glad to see men who had persecuted innocent people being brought to justice.

I made three trips to Mostar during the siege. With my colleagues, I was befriended by a delightful family who shared their food and even insisted that we stayed in their flat. But every moment in Mostar was dangerous. One day a woman who took her washing down to the river was shot dead by a sniper. Her thin, lifeless body was left slumped on the river bank next to her family's dirty washing, bunched up and baggy in clothes that had become too big for her, like another pile of laundry. On another night dozens of civilians, including many children, were forced to cross the Neretva under heavy fire from the Croat side. They were Muslims who were being expelled from their homes in the west of the city. Bullets zinged around their heads as they struggled over a rickety pontoon bridge, and the soundtrack of our pictures picked up the whimpering of the children as they were helped up the opposite bank.

Everyone was permanently dehydrated. There was no running water and very little food in east Mostar during the siege. The soldiers had one good meal a day, of fresh bread and thick bean soup with some small pieces of meat in it. Civilians had less, but at least everyone got something. The war economy was well organised; everything was rationed, and unlike Sarajevo there was almost nothing available on the black market, except booze. Mostar had one of Yugoslavia's biggest commercial wineries, and the Bosnian government forces captured it intact early in the war. Once I had become familiar with east Mostar's back alleys, I found places to buy loza, a fierce drink a bit like Italian grappa. Nothing was easy. One night, making terrible whooshing noises like demented fireworks, shells started hitting the houses around me when I was trotting back with a vat of firewater under my arm. The woman who sold it looked at me keenly. 'Now we'll see how fast you can move,' she said, unsympathetically.

We took a gallon or so of the loza to a party with one of east Mostar's 'special units', called the Tigers. Lots of units in all of the Balkan wars of the 1990s called themselves special forces. They were nothing like special forces in professional armies, but the Tigers were hospitable young men who had done some tough fighting. Their leader told terrible stories of how the Croats had attacked using Bosnian prisoners as human shields, forcing them at gunpoint out into no man's land and then advancing behind them. So he had given the order to open fire, even though it would kill their own people, friends they had grown up with, to get at the Croats behind them. As the Tigers got drunker they kept on singing their song, which included hand gestures pointing at the horizon, towards a future that a lot of them did not expect to have. I stayed extra late, drinking more loza. When almost everyone had collapsed one of the fighters, as drunk as anyone else, offered the two of us who were left a lift back to where were staying. In his tiny car, we raced down a road that was sometimes under fire during the day, but it was too late, and too wet for the Croats to be manning their guns, and besides we were too drunk to care. We stopped in sheeting rain in east Mostar's main street. He wanted money in return for the lift. Just to show he was serious he pulled out a big handgun from the holster on his belt and put the end of the barrel against my temple. So I pulled some German marks out of my pocket, and with his gun still an inch from my right eye shuffled them close to the car's headlights to see if there was enough. I gave him a soggy handful, about the same as I would have paid for a taxi in London, which seemed to make him happy. He put the gun in his holster, shook hands and drove off. I was too drunk to be alarmed, but I can still feel the heavy clunk of the gun barrel as he pushed it against my head.

Mostar is surrounded by hills and high buildings. I discovered there were plenty of places where snipers could get you, sometimes from three or four angles simultaneously. It was hard to know which way to run. The people who made the wrong choice were taken to the hospital. It had been built from scratch in an old Turkish building in the three months since the siege started. Beds were crammed into the cellar, and there was an operating theatre and a place for the doctors and nurses to rest. They worked hard to keep the cellar clean but the nature of the work they did and the wounds they saw meant that it smelled of blood and was splattered with it, and piles of sodden bandages built up on the floor. The blood smell never went away. One of the first times I went to the cellar four young soldiers lay there with hideous burns. Their girlfriends, probably no older than eighteen, stood over them, fanning them, trying to cheer them up and to be brave. After a while one of the young women gave the piece of card she was using as a fan to her boyfriend's mother and dragged herself up the stairs for some air. Her eyes were wet but she still looked as if she had not yet realised what was going on; she was still at the stage where she could dream about waking up to a world as it used to be. Perhaps peace was still too fresh in her memory.

War brings sudden and terrible changes. No one expects that they will suddenly become widows, or amputees, or blind, or paralysed, burned or dead. But then they are, and it takes time to understand what has happened to their lives. The girl leaned, exhausted, with her cheek against the cool stone wall at the top of the steps. In the stuffy, foetid cellar, her boyfriend was staring straight in front of him, hardly blinking, entirely conscious and acutely aware in his pain of how badly he was hurt, and how little the doctors could do. They expected him to get an infection, and probably to die of it. His wounds were oozing through the bandages and soaking the sheets of his bed. One of the doctors, Amila – in my notebook I called her the elegant anaesthesiologist – looked around, and said to me, 'At least you have the chance of getting out.' The radio was playing the old Engelbert Humperdinck song, 'Please release me, let me go . . .' Amila noticed from a piece of tape stuck to the back of my flak jacket that I had the same blood group as one of the wounded boys. She asked me for some blood and I gave them some.

Mostar had a modern general hospital, but it was on the Croat side. At the improvised war hospital the pharmacist took pity on me when I first visited because I looked so dehydrated. He made me drink infusions he had produced from a herb that was growing wild behind the hospital. On the other side of the road they had put beds into the basement of a half-finished building. It wasn't being used and at first they let Shane and Chuck and me sleep there. But after the first night it started to fill up with wounded soldiers. A young man with a bad wound in his chest retched blood constantly. A tube came out of his chest and drained blood and muck into a bucket. A nurse sat next to his bed, trying to comfort him, wiping the blood away from his mouth. I don't think he lived. While I was sleeping someone stole my helmet, which was one of the latest American carbon-fibre types. I suppose it was my fault for not looking after it properly, but my head felt very big and naked afterwards. After another day or so, more wounded were coming in and they needed our beds, so we moved into a house next door. I was sorry to leave the cellar, even though we were sleeping next to men who were dying, because it was well sandbagged and seemed to be safe. But a few weeks later a shell came in through the roof, blew out the sandbags and the place was abandoned.

The area around the hospital would have been a pleasant district, without the war. The houses had roomy front gardens. There were tables under trees, as there always are in the former Yugoslavia, and it was easy to think of families sitting together on hot days before the war, talking and laughing and eating. Some of the gardens had weeping willows, and when the shelling was not too loud, I could hear the hot wind that roasts Mostar all summer stirring their branches. The wind never took away the smell of rotting bodies that hung around the streets, the gardens and the hospital. It was the kind of smell that gets into your clothes and into your hair and which you can taste in your mouth with your food. It was the first thing anyone smelled in the morning and the last thing you smelled at night. It came from a skip a little way down the road, where the rubbish was mixed with rotting limbs and flesh that doctors had cut away from the bodies that had been ripped up by high explosive and shrapnel. Occasionally, half-heartedly, because there was no petrol to waste, people tried to set fire to the stinking mess inside the skip. All that did was to add another layer of odour, of smoke and ash, to the smell of putrefaction.

The local residents who were left were trying hard to stay respectable. One woman said to me, with dignity, 'We wish all your children the best. We wish our children only the minimum.' In east Mostar that summer, that meant surviving. Some of them were being driven crazy. One man became fixated with keeping the street clean. He would work through bombardments, sweeping the gutters and loading his garden wheelbarrow with dust and rubble and broken glass. He was a charming man, who was trying to protect himself by forming a bubble of tidiness and order around himself and his family, sweeping and shovelling to make the street look normal to help him forget that everything that was certain had gone. His wife was as delightful and distracted as he was. She insisted on making me coffee, which was the rarest and greatest delicacy in the city, and gave me a small medal of Our Lady of Medjugorje, even though the Croats who were bombing her went there to be blessed before battle. She said the medal would bring me luck. I still have it. Their son, about twelve years old, was deeply disturbed by the shelling and the killing, smiling nervously and cowering at the noise of explosions. The siege was unhinging them all.

Mostar

On days when the shelling made it too dangerous to get to the graveyard, the corpses decayed gently into their plastic sheets in a pastry shop that had been turned into a mortuary. Outside, the undertaker always kept one or two coffins handy. They were made of roughly planed planks of wood, and he propped them up against the wall, ready for the next customer, like the undertaker in the shoot-out at the OK Corral. He was a small, cheerful man. The first time I saw him, on a hot day in August, he was supervising Bosnian Croat prisoners – emaciated, bearded men who spent most of their time locked in another set of cellars – as they dug up the bodies of some of the men who were killed when they were captured. They wrapped their shirts around their faces as they disinterred the half-decayed corpses of their friends, which were going to be exchanged for the bodies of some soldiers from the east side of the town. A few weeks later the cheerful undertaker was killed outside the former pastry shop by a shell.

The graveyard was in full view of the Bosnian Croat positions. They had a big anti-aircraft gun mounted on top of the hill that dominated the whole city. But it was not there for aircraft. They would depress the gun and fire it into the east side. It produced a huge crack every time it was fired that echoed around the hills and the streets. Sometimes it hit the graveyard, disturbing the dead and killing the people who were mourning them. That made funerals into businesslike, hurried affairs, always held at night.

One night they were working particularly fast. The forces of nature, as well as the power of their enemies, were against them. Shells were exploding during a storm full of thunder and lightning. They picked up the bodies from the mortuary as it was getting dark, then staggered with them through the rain and the noise and loaded them on to the back of a truck. They drove, as fast as they could, down the main street, accelerating through the big sniper intersection, carrying the remains of two people who had been

193

killed trying to drive across the same junction in daylight a couple of days before. Their coffins were taken to a bombed-out building that looked as if it had once been a shop. Inside, in almost complete darkness, they held a short Muslim service. The imam chanted prayers for the dead over the coffins, which were draped with blue and white Bosnian flags. The mourners were just black silhouettes. Several hundred of them walked in silence through the dark streets to the cemetery. Lightning flashed across the dome of the mosque. They ran to the sides of the graves, without a sound that would attract the Croat gunners. In a few minutes, it was all over. The bodies were buried and the mourners melted into the night.

Reporters enter people's lives at their worst moments and intrude deeply into them. The only way to justify it is with the story that comes out of the intrusion, by showing that it was worth doing because something has been exposed that was hidden. Intrusion produces very strong stories. Many of the best ones I have done would have been impossible without poking my nose into someone else's life when events have stripped them bare of every protection. I am not cynical about the suffering of people, and I have never faked sympathy, or wanted to; I have often had to fight my own emotions when I hear people's stories. As far as I know, all the colleagues I have respected are the same. My friend Allan Little – and there is no better journalist – told me that there were times when moving in on people at their worst moments made him feel like a pornographer, or a predatory animal. Scores, maybe hundreds of brief encounters with abject misery have left a nagging, uncomfortable feeling behind in me too. I am not a bad person, or a voyeur. But I know what makes a good story, and how to get it. In the end, that was why I was there, talking to them at their worst moments and persuading them to share their misery with my television camera.

194

Mostar

Some strong stories do not make it to air. A girl called Belma, who was seventeen in 1993, was sitting at home with her family one morning in east Mostar having breakfast. In the middle of a war doing something that normal sounded strange. Then someone on the Croat side of the lines fired a tank shell into their building and Belma was badly hurt. They took her to the basement of east Mostar's war hospital, in the operating theatre that used to be a store room, where blood would run off the narrow table to the floor so it was sticky under the clogs of the surgeons and the nurses. Both her arms were amputated very close to the shoulder. The next day she was conscious, lying in a room that had been an office before the war and still looked like one, with the beds shoved between bookcases of dusty reports. We thought her story might be a powerful moment in the documentary we were making, and Belma and her mother and her two younger sisters who were at her bedside agreed to co-operate. With the camera running, Belma's sister helped her to sit up and a nurse pulled back the sheet. Her stumps were bandaged neatly and she was also naked. It did not take very long to film the tableau of the mutilated girl, surrounded and supported by her sisters, her mother and the nurses. The scene was horrific because of what had happened to her, but they were caring for her with such love it was also tender. Later that day, the surgeon who had operated on her, who was still trembling about what he had been forced to do, lost his temper when I asked him, not very tactfully, whether he was the one who had amputated the girl's arms. 'No, I did not,' he said angrily. 'The Croats destroyed her arms, and I just did what I could to tidy up the mess.'

A month later in the edit room in London, we discussed what to do with the pictures. They told a story about the way that war maims the innocent, but the producer, Eamonn Matthews, was concerned that they could also give anyone who gets a kick out of powerless young women a sexual charge. I thought he was probably right, and we did not use the pictures. Perhaps we should have. Belma was prepared to reveal her injuries to show what happened to her and what was being done to civilians. Our decision to protect her because her breasts were exposed may have been condescending, considering what she had suffered and what she faced for the rest of her life. Belma and her family were evacuated to Texas where she was eventually fitted with electronic prostheses and given the chance to continue her education.

A few days later a man called Franjo Pavlović was killed in front of our cameras. Until you see it happening, it's hard to realise how quickly life can end. In less time than it takes to snap your fingers, a shell can land, explode, maim and kill. That morning the streets were almost empty – on the orders of the authorities, who imposed a curfew – because it was the time of day when there was usually shelling. But we were roaming about and heard a loud explosion very close by and then a woman yelling. She staggered out of a cloud of smoke and dust, screaming her husband's name. He was a big man in late middle age, lying on the ground next to a pile of rubble. I had done some first-aid training, and I was convinced, long before I even got to him, that he had a sucking chest wound, which people often get when their chest has been penetrated by shrapnel or a bullet.

I opened a field dressing as we ran towards him, ready to find the entry and exit wounds to try to stop any bleeding, but there were none. I was so convinced that he had a sucking chest wound that I forgot to do the basic stuff, like checking his airway. It was too late for that anyway. The couple had been trying to fix their wall, which had been damaged by another shell, and a wheelbarrow was next to him. I helped two other men lift him into the wheelbarrow – he was very heavy – and we pushed him about ten yards to east Mostar's only fire engine, which by some chance was very close by. At first we tried to lift him up to the cab door in the wheelbarrow. Perhaps we sensed he was already dead and for some primitive reason did not want to touch him. Perhaps it just seemed easier that way, because his heavy limbs were flopping about and his big, weighty body was difficult even for three men to lift. We did it second time round, by taking him out of the wheelbarrow and pushing him into the cab of the fire engine. His wife Rehema and the cameraman Brian Hulls jumped in too. Mr Pavlović lay over the seat, very still, during the ride to the hospital, which took only a couple of minutes. They put his body on one of the bloodstained olive-green army stretchers that were always propped against the doorway and carried him down the stairs to the cellar.

One of the medical staff tried, half-heartedly, to do some heart massage, more for the sake of Franjo's wife than as a way of saving him. But when he pulled open his shirt there was a tiny puncture, made by shrapnel, over his heart. The medic looked at her and took her hand. She wailed her husband's name and put her head on his chest and sobbed. She clutched his spectacles, which she must have picked up from the ground as we tried to put him into the fire engine. We filmed everything, and used it. It made a very powerful beginning to our documentary. But once again we had come on the scene at the worst moment of her life and the last of his.

She signed a release form, like all the interviewees, giving permission for what was filmed to be transmitted. In her state she probably would have signed anything. Of course, I was sympathetic and so were the crew. Whenever they went back to Mostar they used to take Mrs Pavlović and her son presents. But it bothered me for a long time that I had exploited ruthlessly the death of her husband and her grief for our own ends. Newly bereaved people are usually in a daze and they tend to get carried along by what is happening to them. Sometimes it takes time for the reality of what has happened to sink in, and it is easy to get them to talk and co-operate. If you treat people who are at the worst moment of their lives with decency and respect, they are often even grateful, as if they want to be reminded that not every human being in the world is brutal.

In 2004, eleven years after the death of her husband, I had the chance to visit Mrs Pavlović. It was a hot day and she made lemonade, squeezing fresh lemons into a jug and adding sugar and water. She looked well and was glad to talk about what had happened that day. Her husband's death had terrible consequences for her. When he was killed they had already been displaced from their home on the west side of the city by Croat gunmen because she was a Muslim. He was a Croat, but had chosen to go with her to the east side of the city. But after the war, Mostar was effectively divided into a Muslim side to the east and a Croat side to the west, and because she was a Muslim she could not get their original home on the Croat side of the city back. She lived with her son in a couple of rooms in the cellar of a block of flats. She had made it homely and it was scrupulously clean and tidy, but very cramped.

She seemed almost surprised when I told her I was uneasy about how we had come into her life at such a bad time, filmed her husband's death and broadcast it. She said she was glad that we had filmed his death and used it in a documentary which described the misery and the brutality of the war for the people on the east side of the city. It stopped him being a statistic. The people who had seen it knew his name and knew how he had been killed. His death had some meaning. Our film was popular on the east side of Mostar because people there thought it was a true story of what happened to them. Some shops even sold bootlegged copies to tourists. Her answer gave me some absolution.

I did not get it from the family of another dead person we had filmed, a small girl, also called Belma, who died over a few days in the hospital from a head wound. Her father agreed to meet. He was tragic and broken, destroyed by the war and the death of his daughter, with eyes that were distracted and full of pain. He said he would speak to us, but his surviving daughter would not. He had a message from her. She did not trust my motives for being there, eleven years after the death of her sister, who had been exploited enough already. Was I going to use it again to make me look like a hero? He apologised uncomfortably. Because I could not meet her, I never knew whether she was angry with what I had done with her sister's death during the war, or whether she was angry with all the outsiders from the luckier parts of Europe who had been in Bosnia to watch them die. I can defend the way the images of her sister were used, and would have, had we met. The pictures were used not to shock or to exploit the death of a child, but to make a point about what the people who were besieging east Mostar were doing to children. I would also have told her that journalists are not heroes, that they have all sorts of motivations for going to wars, from finding out the truth and telling it, to giving the poor and dispossessed a voice, to building their careers, or because they like being in a place with no rules. And I would have said that the same person can have all of that going on inside him at the same time, though I can also understand why she might not have wanted to listen.

Did filming her sister when she was dying make things any better for them? Mrs Pavlović believed that filming her husband gave his death some meaning. But he was a man in his fifties, who had some good times before the war. She showed me black and white pictures, of outings to the sea and to the mountains in the 1960s and '70s, when Yugoslavia was peaceful and even rich. The death of a child in a war leaves only a sense of loss and waste.

7

Grozny and Glamour

K urt Schork's eyes were shining with excitement.
'It's wild, Jeremy, it's like a movie. Do you want to go
downtown? There are buildings exploding and park benches
flying through the air.'

I said I was planning to go there that day.

'You gotta run over the bridge to get to the parliament. In
daylight. You don't get the tie if you haven't run over the bridge.'

Grozny is still the most violent, dangerous place I have ever
been. For Kurt it was like some kind of high-octane fuel. He was
hyperactive and even wore a flak jacket, which most of the time
he had given up in Sarajevo. We were standing in Minutka
Square, one of the hotspots of the first Chechen war in January
1995. It was at one end of the main boulevard that ran up from
the dead centre of town. There was constant gunfire and the crash
and crump of shells.

We all got into the armoured BBC Land Rover. I did the
driving. It was a classic Soviet avenue, the kind which probably
used to have a special lane in the middle for important party

apparatchiks to swish down in their big cars. But after a couple of weeks of bombardment you could not exactly follow the white lines. The road was covered with lumps of concrete that had been blown off the buildings, branches that had been blown off trees, smashed cars, and shell holes. I decided that the best thing would be to drive as fast as possible down the middle of the road. The only people moving were cheerful groups of Chechen fighters, happy at the thought of dying that day, and journalists. The Land Rover spluttered. It had a V8 engine and was not enjoying the gritty, watery Dagestani petrol we were feeding it. I revved a bit more and its tubes seemed to clear. We set off. Out of the corner of my eye I saw shells exploding into some of the solid old buildings that lined the avenue. In a couple of weeks, the Russian army had gone a long way to turning a steel, stone and concrete city into rubble.

Steve Lidgerwood, the cameraman, was filming out of the front windscreen. In the back the rest of the BBC team were trying to stare past us, to see what was coming for them. It can't have been a good feeling to be in someone else's hands, chugging towards what was probably at that moment the most dangerous patch of ground in the world. As the Land Rover accelerated ponderously down the road, I saw a bunch of photographers running out of an underpass, led by James Nachtwey, about the most famous of them all these days. It felt better to be inside a Kevlar car than on foot. The armour would not save us if we had a direct hit from a shell, but against anything else it should (I guessed and hoped) be fine.

Kurt was joking about the tie; we were not going to try to get anywhere near the parliament, which was the centre of a cauldron of destruction. In broad daylight, the idea was suicidal. Instead we were heading for a block of flats that looked down into the danger zone. It sounded like a good place for top shots and I hoped we might find some people still living in it. I pulled up in front of the building and we piled out. Most of one side of the block, which was about eight storeys high, had been ripped off. Cross-sections of rooms and lives had been opened up like a dolls' house. Another shell hit the opposite side of the road. We raced for a doorway where some Chechen fighters were standing, as casually fatalistic as usual. In one hand I was carrying a small backpack of camera batteries that felt like it was full of rocks. We ran into the side of the building via the shortest route, which meant jumping over a small wall. My backpack hit the wall and so did I. I was clumsy in my heavy flak jacket, helmet and winter clothes and I slipped on some broken glass and gashed my hand.

One of the Chechens gestured at the Land Rover. He was saying the Chechen equivalent of you can't park there, not because he was unfriendly, but because it was exposed to shellfire and might not be there when we came back. 'I'll move it,' said Kurt. He grabbed the keys out of my bloody hand and dashed out to where the car was sitting. A few more shells hit the buildings opposite. He brought it round to the side, where I should have left it in the first place, and came back grinning. 'Took care of your car, Mr Bowen, and now I better take care of your hand.' I gave him a long bandage which he started wrapping around the place where the glass had cut me. He was having a great day. We all were.

Even though Grozny was dangerous, appalling and brutal, most of the time I was not frightened. Neither was Kurt and I doubt many of the other journalists there were either. It sounds strange, or paradoxical, or boastful, but it was none of those things. I do not think of myself as a brave person. I am not physically aggressive. Raging motorists at traffic lights in London worry me more than most of the shellfire I have experienced. In all the wars I have ever seen I have had moments of abject terror. But they were just moments, or a few minutes at least. You cannot be frightened the whole time, even if the place you are in is dangerous all the time, because if you were, you would not be able to function. Human beings are adaptable. You can learn to absorb and ignore a lot of what is going on around you.

Minutka Square was a meeting place for the news people in Grozny. Getting to the square was an achievement, but much harder was getting back to it in one piece from the streets heading down to the parliament building. Minutka Square was a big, windy, open space, bleak and desolate. On the day I came closest to dying there, some of the buildings around it were on fire when we arrived. The Chechen fighters who were always in and around the square said that Russian warplanes had been attacking, as part of their relentless campaign to stop the southern republic from seceding from the Russian Federation. I knew it was not a good place to stay but we did not have a choice. We had an appointment to meet Nigel Chandler, a freelance cameraman who was selling his pictures to the BBC. He had been living in cellars and shell holes with Chechen fighters for days and was relying on us for a lift out. I did not want to abandon him – and we needed his material.

We got busy. There was plenty to do, Chechens to interview, burning buildings to film. The sound of shelling was constant, but every now and then a shell landed a little too close to ignore, whooshing in and exploding with a great crash. I stayed talking to a group of Chechen fighters while the crew moved a couple of hundred yards to the other side of the square, where fighters were warming themselves at a ruptured overground gas main that was on fire. It was giving off enough heat to melt the snow around it. It is not safe to spend too long next to ignited gas belching from a broken pipe. If a gas main was flaring in London they would evacuate the street, and the one next to it. But Minutka Square was so dangerous that day that a gas leak just wasn't worrying about.

As well as being a meeting place for journalists, Minutka Square was also the place where Chechen fighters formed up into little groups, tramping through the snow, or racing around in pock-marked Ladas with smashed windscreens. That made it a target. It was not a place to just hang around, but Nigel still hadn't turned up and we could not leave without him. I started to wonder what the crew were doing. They took it in turns to take the pictures. That day Steve Lidgerwood was filming and Scott Hillier was doing sound. They were both expert cameramen, Australians who were great company. When the bridge on the way into Grozny between Dagestan and Chechnya was blown up, the only way around was to take a long drive along the muddy bank of a river in a slow-moving line of Ladas to get to another crossing. But Steve had another idea.

'Mate, we'll just drive through it.'

'The river? You're joking.'

I didn't like the thought of £100,000 worth of armoured Land Rover drowning in a Chechen river, with us in it. I got out and walked doubtfully down to the water, which was only about thirty feet wide but looked dark, freezing and deep. I picked up some stones and lobbed them in, wondering irrationally if I could tell whether we could make it from the plop they made. Steve leaned out of the driver's door.

'For fuck's sake, just get in.'

As I slammed the door he reversed a couple of yards back, gunned the engine and drove straight into the river. The water covered the bonnet and broke over the windscreen. But by then we were through.

'Piece of cake, mate,' Steve said nonchalantly. 'Go hard or go home. What kind of pommy stuff were you doing with those stones?'

In Minutka Square it was freezing cold. A thick coat, heavy

boots and thermal underwear were not helping much. I left the Chechen fighters I had been talking to and jogged across the square towards the flaming gas main, looking for Steve and Scott and wanting to get warm next to the fire. Something in my brain was thinking about the danger, although I was calm. I looked at the street and tried to work out what to do if there was another air strike. A low wall nearby, a bit higher than a kerbstone, looked like the best cover. It wasn't much. The Grozny city planners who had laid out the square in the Soviet days had created a nice flat expanse of concrete.

I could see the crew filming the Chechens who were squatting and standing cheerily around the fiery gas main, stamping their feet and rubbing their hands, and then I heard the scream of jet engines. I jerked my head to the left and saw two Russian warplanes, very close to each other, skimming over the rooftops around the square. I threw myself down flat next to the wall I had spotted, which was about a foot high, and pressed my body into the hard, cold concrete. Explosions pumped across the square. I pushed my nose into the snow and put my hands behind my head, trying to cover the space between the bottom of my helmet and the collar of my flak jacket. It only went on for a few seconds but there seemed to be a lot of time to think. *This time it's really happening, Jeremy. This is it. You've really done it this time. Any second now you're going to be dead or badly hurt.* I forced myself down flatter on the ground and braced myself, lying there, waiting for fragments of the bombs to rip into me. The explosions were very loud. I hoped the shrapnel would hit my flak jacket, which had heavy plates made of carbon fibre. The front one, with all my weight on it, was cutting into my chest, but the back plate suddenly did not feel wide enough.

Then the explosions stopped. To my amazement, I wasn't hurt. I ran towards Steve and Scott, who had got up from where they had thrown themselves and were coming back to me, shouting something about getting under cover. The nearest building was a ruined shop. I grabbed the tripod and followed them. Scott is an athletic little guy and he was the fastest. He ran straight at the remains of a plate-glass window and threw himself at it. He chested away the shards of glass with the front of his flak jacket as he went through and he rolled over back on to his feet on the other side. His move was very impressive. Steve and I had a Keystone Cops moment trying to get in through the door at the same time. I got the tripod tangled up with both of us.

My heart was beating very hard. All three of us were shaken, because we knew how close we had come to being killed. Apart from a cut on my leg, where I had landed on the ground, we were fine. Scott didn't even have a scratch from his heroic dive through the window. After a few minutes panting and swearing we went down to a cellar next door. We waited for the planes to come back. My mouth felt like it had something dead inside it so I kept spitting. We kept saying fuck that was close. Fuck. Bastards. Fuck. Ten minutes or so later the planes hadn't reappeared so we went outside. On the other side of the square, where I had been talking to the Chechens, a small group of them had gathered round a body. They were tying a green martyr's ribbon around the head of one the younger ones, who was dead. I remembered him talking and smiling before the raid. They were calm and full of resolve about their war.

A little while later Nigel turned up. He smelled like a fox after his time in smoky, foetid basements. He was a driven man, who I had met the year before, during the siege of Mostar. We had used some of his pictures then. He seemed to have no fear at all, and would push right up into the hardest places, but this time he had been rocked by what he had seen. He told me he had been in a building right in the centre of Grozny with Chechen fighters as

Russian troops fought their way into the floor upstairs. He thought he was about to get killed or captured, so he cut up his credit cards, presumably to stop the Russians making a profit out of his death. When he ran across the big open square near the parliament with some of the Chechen fighters the man in front of him was hit and fell down dead. Nigel was subdued and very tired. The rest of us, Grozny day-trippers, were elated and out of control. We swigged from a bottle of whisky – Laphroaig – as we limped out of Grozny in the armoured Land Rover. It had dozens of small pieces of shrapnel in it from the air strike. None of them had got through the carbon fibre armour – like the flak jackets, only thicker – around the passenger compartment or through the armoured glass in the windows. But the metal covering the engine was not reinforced and the radiator was pierced. A couple of miles outside the city centre, with the engine boiling up nicely, we found a garage that was open. They patched us up and we went back to Dagestan, fording the river again, merry and hysterical.

We were sharing tapes with ITN, an idea that was supposed to maximise safety and minimise competition. Steve's camera had been running throughout the attack so we had some frightening video of what had happened. From the series of rapid explosions over a couple of seconds we deduced that the square had been attacked with cluster bombs. I passed on the dub of the tape to the ITN correspondent Julian Manyon, who did not have much to show for his day's labours, and looked to me a bit jealous that we had been in an air strike and he hadn't. The BBC version of the story was perhaps too low-key. Maybe I was trying too hard to demonstrate that the people of Grozny, not the reporters, were the story. But Manyon's version made the most of every crash, bang and wallop on the tape. His script was not complimentary: 'A BBC crew caught in a cluster bomb attack in Grozny . . . The result . . . sheer panic,' he gloated over pictures of us running like hell.

'Nice piece, Jeremy,' said the foreign editor Jenny Baxter over the phone from London. 'But Manyon's was great. Where did he get his video? Couldn't you make it more like Manyon's? More dramatic?'

I explained where the pictures came from and on the main news that night we tarted it up, wallowing in our own drama.

Some newspaper journalists and stills photographers had found places to stay in Grozny, but TV people with daily dead-lines were commuting to the war every morning from a muddy, slushy town called Khasavyurt in Dagestan, the republic next door to Chechnya, along a single road that the Russians had left open. In January 1995 satellite dishes were still expensive and not very portable, and the owners of the one that we were using did not even contemplate taking it into a city that was being pounded by the Russians. Anyway, it probably would not have worked there, even if they had wanted to risk it. It needed a big generator, a couple of engineers and spare parts. Live shots, where the reporter is asked questions by a presenter back in a warm studio some-where peaceful, needed to be lit because the days were short in the Caucasus in January, and I would not have fancied standing in the open in Grozny in the middle of the evening in a pool of the only electric light for miles around, a living invitation for anyone who felt like opening fire. I thought at the time that the journal-ists who were camping in Grozny had the purer, more intense experience – after being in Mostar during the siege in 1993 I was convinced that you get better material by living in the battle zone – but driving in every day through the Russian lines meant that we could get the pictures on the satellite, out to London and on to the news, which was the reason, after all, for being there. And we could get a hot meal, a shower, and a few drinks. Driving into Grozny every day was risky, but staying there was much worse. Every minute in Grozny was another minute that could get you killed. It happened to an American, Cynthia Elbaum, who was photographing civilians who had been in an air strike when another bomb killed her. At least six journalists died in Grozny in the first year of the Chechen war, along with thousands of its residents.

In Khasavyurt the dish had been set up in the garden of a state kindergarten. Most of it was being used to shelter people who had been displaced from Chechnya, but TV journalists who needed the dish stayed there too. Everything was miniaturised for the children, whose paintings were still on the walls. I put four tiny beds side by side and slept across them. Nigel Chandler established himself at the end of our dormitory. He wore a long parka which he didn't take off, and his smoky, foxy smell rapidly impregnated the room. One of the room-mates was smoking a joint and its herbal smell mingled with Chandler's scent. It was becoming intolerable. No one wanted to give Nigel a hard time after what he had done in Grozny, but I had to say something.

'Nigel . . . There's no easy way to put this . . . but do you feel like taking a shower? There's hot water at the Muslim boys' school next door. Sorry, but you smell of dugouts.'

Chandler looked at me uncomprehendingly.

'I'm going back in, Jeremy, and I am not going to change my clothes until I finish with Grozny for good.'

He lay down on his row of miniature beds in his filthy trousers and went to sleep. I think he was superstitious rather than scared of hot water. He certainly was not scared of the Russians and what they were doing, which was very violent and deadly. He did some outstanding work in Grozny, closer to the action than any other Western cameraman.

The next day Scott Hillier came up to me with something

else that could not have been easy to say, in the supercharged macho atmosphere of kindergarten number 5 in Khasavyurt. He had recently become a father for the first time and had decided that one air strike was one too many. He was going to go home to Paris. Scott had guts. He was a tough character and had worked in Bosnia and Somalia and other nasty places and did not have to prove himself. But he had just discovered something that it was going to take me a few more years to find out – that once you have children, it becomes much harder to solve the equation about risking your life in pursuit of news.

Although I admired Scott's strength of character – it must have been more difficult to go than to stay – he had still left us in a jam. I did not want to ask Steve to go into Grozny without a sound-man but we had to go back because that was why we were there. Scott said he would do one last trip, and we agreed that we would take it very easy and stay away from Minutka Square. We found a hill overlooking the centre of Grozny. It seemed like a good place to start. Buildings around the city were on fire. There were some shots to get. Scott went to work busily. Then it felt as if the world was shaking. The centre of Grozny erupted into smoke and fire. We saw it before we heard it. It took a second or two for a horrible, churning rumble to reach us. At first I thought it was carpet bombing from the air, then we worked out that the Russians had hit Grozny with a massive artillery and rocket attack. Shells exploded and rockets slammed into the city centre. It was terrifying, even from the safe place where we were, and hard to see how anyone could have survived it, though if they were in cellars I suppose they might have had a chance.

Scott left the camera running on the tripod and took cover behind a stone wall. It was enough for one day. We headed back to the kindergarten in a hurry. But even after the strike the day before that could have killed us, and even though Grozny was by far the most violent place I had ever been, I was still happy to go back in. I sympathised with Scott, and respected him for having the courage to admit his fear when he was in a very macho world. But as yet I still did not share it. That day I was more worried about the fact that I had lost my Brooks Brothers sheepskin gloves, the warmest ones I'd ever had. I was cautious, did not see myself as a risk-taker, and was dedicated to reporting the news. But doing stories around shells and bullets was so familiar to me by then that explosions felt like background noise. In a strange way, they were even reassuring, and so was the first sight of smoke on the horizon on the way into the city, or the first distant noises of shooting and explosions that got louder as you went closer, because they were all signs that this was the right place to get at the story. That didn't stop it being nerve-wracking. About the time that the noise of shells was getting louder and the smoke was big through the windscreen of the armoured Land Rover, when it felt like the big test was approaching, we used to stop to get our flak jackets on and to have a nervous piss at the side of the road. Getting closer always put my stomach into knots. It felt better when we started working.

In a place like Grozny, I would never go in with a predetermined idea of what the story of the day would be, unless we already knew that something big had happened and were trying to find it. I would be aware of the stories that had already been done, and since the mid-1990s was a violent time with plenty of wars going on, just being somewhere dangerous was not going to get us on the news. You had to keep pushing to keep it fresh. Civilians usually provide the best kind of stories in wars, and plenty were left behind in Grozny with the war going on around them. The city's long avenues were lined with apartment buildings. Most of them were empty, and badly damaged, but the place to look was in the cellars, where life had been transferred

211

underground. In places lit by candles and daylight trickling down the stairs there would be scores of people, usually old or very young, or very poor, who had not been able to get out of the city in time, or had nowhere else to go. The cellars stank of unwashed bodies and fear. They had a lot be scared about in Grozny that winter. One group in a cellar had to go into the yard outside to get to the nearest tap, which must have been put there in another life, to water plants, or to spray the paving stones, or to wash cars. The problem was that it was exposed to the shelling, so getting water could get them killed, and sometimes did, but they still had to do it.

A story about civilians trapped in the cellars would do for one night only. The next day we would be back, doing the same three-hour drive to get in, looking for something different. Russian prisoners, locked in another cellar, provided it on another day. The Chechens, looking gleeful about what they had, led us down some steps and undid a padlock on a door. Inside, kept in total darkness, were about a dozen miserable and terrified Russian conscripts, skinny adolescents who blinked and covered their eyes when the doors opened and the camera light came on to film them. The Chechens behaved like the owners of unusual pets who were showing them off to the neighbours. They relocked the doors, leaving the boys inside back in the dark while they decided what to do with them.

But something like that visit to the prisoners would not be enough on its own. It was a sequence, but it was not a story. A decent, medium-sized news report from a hot spot on the BBC is usually between two minutes and two minutes fifteen seconds. One forty-five is about the minimum you need to make sense and stay coherent. Anything getting close to three minutes or longer has to be memorable. So to be able to make an average-sized two and a quarter minutes of news television, it is best to have three

212

sequences when you sit down to edit, though two will do at a push if they are strong and there are some other good elements – powerful soundbites, or a piece to camera that is well-phrased or dramatic or, best of all, both. You also need what the Americans call 'B-roll' and the British call 'GVs', which stands for general views; in Grozny that meant long shots down wrecked boulevards, or shells hitting buildings, or fighters running through the snow – the sort of images known, a bit dismissively, as 'bang-bang'. Some people in the television news business sniff at it because it does not do anything to explain what is happening and because the only story attached to it when you see it on news agency feeds is something like 'Fighting continued in downtown Grozny today'. It can look samey – but if you haven't got it a report from a war can look meagre and unconvincing. On the other hand if all you have is bang-bang, it can look thin and repetitive. Many bang-bang pictures in Grozny were shot by local stringers, who had cheap video cameras and took huge risks often for not much money.

To flesh a piece out, to make it into a story, to give people an idea about what it is like to be a human being in a place like Grozny at that particular moment on a miserable, dark day, you need the other elements too – civilians, prisoners, soldiers – characters that the viewers can get to know, and even if they cannot identify with them, they can start to understand the human impulses and experiences that have brought them to that second in their lives.

When I started in TV news, I was surprised to find out that reporters and crews did not shoot everything that is broadcast in their names. Sometimes all they have done themselves is the piece to camera. That is not ideal, but it is not uncommon, especially when the team have just parachuted into the country. In quite a few places I have landed somewhere, done a piece to camera in the dark, on the airport tarmac or near the local TV station, gone inside to hoover up all the local and news agency pictures I could find, dashed something together and fed it to London. It is not great, but it was better than nothing for a first go, and the next day I was able to start doing some proper journalism. Every TV news network has formal and informal alliances with colleagues from other countries, with whom they don't compete, to share video. There are also television news agencies that have commercial contracts with organisations like the BBC to sell them pictures. Agency material gets distributed every day by satellite around the world. The informal alliances are done in the field, and usually involve a producer or a picture editor going from room to room around a hotel – or in Dagestan around the kindergarten – getting copies, known as 'dubs', of other people's stories. It makes sense. Even on a well-resourced operation, with two or three crews, you can't be everywhere at once.

But I always find it easier to script and cut pictures that have been shot by a crew I was with, or one that I deployed. You have a better feel for what the pictures show, and for the best way to use them to reflect what is true. In Grozny in the first month of 1995 there was so much violence and killing that we were never short of strong material. But in other places, on other days, it can go quiet. What if someone then comes in with a picture of a tank rolling down the street? It looks dramatic and could lift the story. But was it the only tank there that day? Or were they all over the place? Would it be right to start the piece with the shot? Or would that give a false impression of what was really happening? It could be that the real story is less dramatic, that because it was quiet for the first time in weeks civilians were able to get out to buy food and get water. As long as the journalists providing the material are trustworthy, and if you know them that is easy to judge, then it is fine to use dubs of what they have shot. I have done it plenty of times. But if you don't know enough about the material, mistakes can happen.

Putting together a piece of television news is pretty straightforward, as long as you have a story and the pictures to illustrate it. A reporter sits down with an editor, and often, though not always, the person who has shot the pictures. Usually in big TV networks a producer is there too. If there is time, and even if there isn't quite enough, it is wise to view all the pictures and to note down the time codes so you can find them again in a hurry. Then you work out a pictorial structure, deciding where everything goes and in what order, and start writing. The opening is very important, and often takes the longest time to do well. Even though TV journalists cannot live without pictures, the words are vital. All writing for television should enhance the images and the sound. If reporters end up just describing what the viewers can see with their own eyes then they are wasting everyone's time. Don't tell people what they're seeing – instead tell them *about* the events on the screen, things that they didn't know. The script needs to touch the pictures, to keep a sense of time and place, but it also has to amplify and explain. For example, if there is an image of fighters in a bunker blazing away with their Kalashnikovs, there is not much point in saying something like, 'The fighters opened fire.' Better to say something like, 'They've been doing this for nearly a week.' If, as a viewer, you can have the TV news on while you are doing something else, listening to the sound but not needing the pictures, then it is probably not a very good bulletin. But if you are forced to stop what you are doing because the report is a good mixture of words, sounds and images, and you don't want to miss any of them, then the programme-makers are doing a good job.

The mechanics of making a television report about a war are only part of it. There are other things to think about, that are to

215

do with the power of the medium and the nature of the violence itself. In a twisted way, war is glamorous. War zones can be attractive to people who have never experienced them – and also to some of the people who have. In the 1990s a lot of soldiers I met, like the Tigers in Mostar, tried to be cool by imitating films they had seen, especially the Rambo series, with bandanas instead of helmets and bandoliers of ammunition crossed over oily muscles. Rambo was a fantasy. But his imitators were trying to be him, to make him real. The deep, fundamental reality of war is absolutely not glamorous. War is about destruction and killing, about tearing people apart with high explosive, about corpses rotting in the sun until they stink and swell and their bellies burst. But the bits that look like Hollywood films or advertisements or even war comics, tanks moving in the dust at sunset, or warplanes taking off from the deck of an aircraft-carrier, can give an illusion of glamour, and if they are not countered by a big dose of brutal realism they can even make war look desirable.

In 2004, after the American military had flattened large parts of the Iraqi town of Fallujah, someone took a picture of a twenty-year-old Marine called James Blake Miller. He was photographed looking exhausted and handsome, his face covered in camouflage paint, with a cut on his nose and a lit cigarette hanging from his mouth. His portrait appeared in newspapers across America: to many of their readers he looked like an actor in a war film, like an advertisement, like a hero (except to those who thought that a soldier with a cigarette sent the wrong message to American youth). Philip Morris, makers of Marlboro cigarettes, offered him money to use his image. The anchor of CBS News, Dan Rather, said about the picture of Miller: 'For me, this one's personal. This is a warrior with his eyes on the far horizon, scanning for danger. See it. Study it. Absorb it. Think about it. Then take a deep breath of pride. And if your eyes don't dampen, you're a better man or woman than I.' But Miller himself knows how unglamorous war really is; a year after he fought at Fallujah, he attacked a sailor who had made a noise that sounded like an incoming shell. Miller was discharged from the US Marine Corps with post-traumatic stress disorder.

I never thought that what I did as a reporter in a war zone was glamorous. I did fancy myself, in a shallow sort of way, because I could operate in an environment that was hostile, knowing where to drive in somewhere like Sarajevo or the West Bank, being comfortable moving around in a place where taking a wrong turning could kill you. The problem is getting over-confident, and that kills too. On the way home from Grozny some businessmen on the flight to London were toasting each other with champagne because they had survived a trip to Moscow. They were telling each other war stories about their encounters with taxi drivers who tried to rip them off and with aggressive beggars or drunks. I sat back thinking, Christ, if only you guys had any idea of what real life is, and felt very superior, and that was not good.

The best antidote to the idea that war is glamorous is seeing what it is really like. The more soldiers know about war and killing, about taking life and losing their friends, the less willing they become to dress up like movie characters. If any Americans thought that there was any glamour in the lead-up to the invasion of Iraq in 2003, as their country assembled its armadas and its armies, then they don't think it now, after the terrible, flesh-grinding business of invading Iraq and occupying it.

But deglamorising war on television can mean showing pictures of horrific events and telling stories that are hard to take. In Britain the editors of news programmes are less squeamish now than they were in the 1990s. Once during the Croatian war in 1991, a released prisoner told me in an interview how he had been tortured, and went into some of the gory details. One programme editor asked me to cut it because what he was saying was 'too shocking'. We were not seeing it, just hearing his story, but she wanted a report that danced around what had happened but didn't show it and hardly described it. That probably would not happen now. There has been a lot of bad and violent news in the last fifteen years, and there is a recognition that if we are there to cover it, we have to see at least part of it, too.

Even so, viewers of the aftermath of a bomb will get a much better idea about what it really looks like – pools of blood, lumps of flesh, disconnected limbs and heads – if they watch, for instance, one of the Arabic satellite channels. They argue that if they don't show death in all its horror, they are covering up the truth. In the West, the argument is that we ought to spare the feelings of our viewers.

But strong stories involving death get on air, even if we don't always show the reality of what that means. A traditional British newsroom follows a terrible arithmetic. Generally speaking, the further away from London, and the poorer the people, the more deaths it takes to qualify as a big story. In 1991 a cyclone hit Bangladesh. The first reports said that around 10,000 people had been killed. I was put on standby to go, if it turned out that more people were dead. By the afternoon the reported toll was over 50,000, but that was still not enough. A day or two later I was on my way to Heathrow airport on another mission when I heard on the *Today* programme that Bangladeshi authorities were saying that more than 100,000 had died. A couple of hours later I was at Gatwick, on a plane for Dhaka. Six figures had done the trick. The arithmetic is changing now, because round-the-clock news services have much more airtime to fill, and because technology makes it easier to cover stories in remote parts of the world. Within a week of the Asian tsunami in 2005 (newsrooms reacted relatively slowly because it was Christmas) satellite uplinks had been flown in and set up on obscure beaches right around the Indian Ocean.

I had arguments during that trip to Bangladesh with programme editors who did not want any pictures – not even one, distant shot – of dead people in my reports. I pointed out, more and more loudly, that the only reason I was in the country was the body count. It didn't make much difference. Reporters in the field had – and to some degree still have – a running dialogue with London about the portrayal of death. The issue is important, because there is so much violent and untimely death about, and so many stories concern it. Much more of the horror was shown after the tsunami. The custom now is that corpses can be shown in moderation if they are filmed 'tastefully', usually after nine o'clock when children are officially deemed to have gone to bed. That means close-ups of hands or feet, and long shots of what looked like bundles of clothes lying face down. The images do almost nothing to show what high explosive, or high-velocity bullets, or hunger or disease, can do to the human body, but they show that life is extinct.

In January 1994 in Sarajevo, a shell fired from the Serb side exploded among a group of children who were tobogganing in the snow. Six were killed. Whenever it was quiet, children came out to play. Parents discovered that however much they would like to, it was impossible to keep children indoors for the entire war. Sometimes that meant they died when the shelling started again. The children were in Alipashnopolje, a concrete enclave of high-rise flats. The bodies had been taken away by the time we got there, but their blood was still on the snow. We filmed the blood, and talked to the neighbours and families of the dead and wounded. It all made a strong story. It got on air because our editors decided that even people who were put off by the complexities of the Balkans would understand the idea of children playing in the snow.

It helped too, in an awful way, that so many children were killed. One or two would not have done it, but six was plenty.

A few years after I did the story of the dead children in the snow in Sarajevo, I was bemused to see excerpts from my report in an internal BBC training video about the portrayal of violence. Apparently my report about the dead children had done it the wrong way. They did not like showing blood in the snow. I would have said, had they asked me, that the way I did it may not have been nice, but it was accurate, and it was powerful, and a lot less shocking than showing dead children. We are allowed to show 'bang-bang', but if we cannot show the consequences of shooting or bombing, then news programmes are reduced to Cowboys and Indians.

8

Jerusalem, City of War

I heard a rustling in my garden one morning just before we moved back to London from Jerusalem in 2000. Was it the breeze in the palm trees? I listened again. No, something, somebody, was moving around. It was an old lady, bent almost double, wearing a traditional Palestinian embroidered dress, working hard to harvest prickly pears from the great bush of cactus down by the limestone wall at the bottom of the garden. She did not stop when she saw me. The late summer is the time to eat the fruit of the cactus, which Israelis call sabras. They like them so much that they have nicknamed native Israelis after the fruit – prickly on the outside, soft and sweet inside. Palestinians never really get the joke. The old lady said it was her cactus, and that she always came to take its prickly pears. She pulled up handfuls of grass, which was long and dry, and yellow like straw after six months of hot sun. She rubbed the fruit with the dry grass and packed them in an old milk crate. Still bent double, she tied string around the crate when it was full and dragged it away.

This was not a chance encounter with a neighbour. I knew

my neighbours, and none of them were Palestinians. They were all Israelis. We lived in a village called Ein Karem on the western edge of Jerusalem, where the mountains on which the holy city is built start falling away towards the Mediterranean. Ein Karem is built around two wadis, river valleys which are wet in winter and dry in summer. Christians believe it is the birthplace of John the Baptist. There are beautiful old houses made of white and pink Jerusalem stone, fig and cypress trees, Moroccan synagogues, church bells and quiet lanes. Until July 1948, two months after Israel declared itself independent, Ein Karem was a Palestinian village. It still has a mosque; disused, because the Palestinians who lived in Ein Karem ran away, or were driven out by the advancing Israeli army. Ein Karem also has lots of cactus, which Palestinians used to use as hedgerows. More than four hundred villages that were Palestinian were either populated by Jews or destroyed after Israel was established in 1948. Sometimes the only evidence that a village was there once are clumps of cactus.

When we moved to Jerusalem and I signed a contract to rent a house in Ein Karem in 1995, I felt uncomfortable about the history of the village. I had just spent the best part of four years in the Balkans, and I had seen plenty of places whose inhabitants had been forced to leave in a hurry as the war ate their lives, and I had seen refugees dreaming of the homes and the people that they had lost. It looked to me as if something very similar had happened almost half a century earlier in Ein Karem. I did not want to take sides, but wasn't I doing that by living in a place with that sort of history? I used to say, look, the house is great, the village is lovely, and this is not my war. It always sounded a bit hollow, and not just to my ears. Once a Palestinian colleague, who was eating dinner in our house, offered, somewhat acidly, to take me to Balata refugee camp near Nablus on the West Bank, to see some of Ein Karem's original residents. I wish I had taken up her offer. Ein

Karem is one of the most beautiful parts of Jerusalem. In the Holy Land paradise and hell are never far apart, and if Ein Karem is paradise, Balata is hell – overcrowded, impoverished and violent.

The first time I went to Jerusalem was in the summer of 1991. I flew in from Zagreb in Croatia, where I had been covering the first few battles in the break-up of Yugoslavia. John Mahoney, the foreign editor, growled into the phone that it was 'time you did it'. I can see now what he was getting at. It felt like joining the grown-ups. Reporting the Israelis and the Palestinians is not for beginners. The Holy Land is complicated, dramatic and bloody, which makes it a very demanding story, and a theme park for reporters. So is the rest of the Middle East, which for generations has been the most consistent exporter of high-quality news in the world. Any young journalist with dreams of being a foreign correspondent would be mad not to want to go there. But it is full of traps that can leave journalists belly-up and helpless in the face of those who are always lurking, waiting to pounce on anyone who does not share their views. And the traps never disappear, as journalists foolish enough to believe that they do not have anything else left to learn will soon find out. Many of them are to do with language. Like everything in Jerusalem it is highly politicised, and loaded with hidden as well as obvious meanings. In no other part of international journalism is there as little room for error as there is with the Israelis and the Palestinians, especially if you work for a big broadcaster like the BBC, which tries to be fair.

I found out very early on what happens if language gets sloppy. After every bomb in Israel bearded, religious Jews appear to mop up every last piece of flesh and drop of blood. They even keep the tissues they use to collect the blood. They are members of Jewish burial societies and they do it to give the human remains a proper burial. But when I first saw them after a bomb I made the mistake of calling them 'zealots'. It was a sloppy use of the

223

word, suggesting they were fanatics, which they are not, as I discovered before the news was off the air, when the faxes started to
come in from enraged viewers. I didn't know about the burial
societies before I did the report. Afterwards I knew a lot.

When Julia and I moved to Jerusalem in 1995, I thought it
was repellent. Sucking in so much intolerance and hatred was
exhausting. I had done a biggish handful of trips to the Middle
East, but visiting the holy city is no preparation for living there.
Even when it looked calm, its beautiful stones oozed tension and
hatred. The shops that sell souvenirs to Christian pilgrims, including crowns made of real thorns which, worn correctly, draw real
blood, also stock religious greetings cards describing the place as
the city of peace. They always made me laugh. Jerusalem is a city
of war, and it always has been. It is a few square miles of rock,
sacred ground for Jews, Muslims and Christians, and it has been
washed with blood. Jerusalem has been conquered or overrun
thirty-seven times, according to Uzi Narkis, the Israeli who was
the last general to capture the holiest parts of Jerusalem, inside the
walls in 1967. Thirty years after the war, not long before he died,
I stood with him in the Old City, just inside St Stephen's Gate,
which his troops had stormed on their way to victory. He was
small and quiet, looking back happily on what he had done for
the Jewish people and certain that Jerusalem, all of it, was theirs
for ever.

Jerusalem stands on the rocky spine of mountains that stretch
right along the Levantine coast of the Middle East, through
Lebanon and southern Syria and down to Israel and the West
Bank. To the west, past our old village, is the Mediterranean. The
Judean desert and the great rift valley of the River Jordan lie to
the east. Jerusalem's Christian, Jewish and Muslim heartbeats
come from inside the walls of the Old City. The Muslims have
two great mosques, the Dome of the Rock and al-Aqsa. They

believe that they mark the place where Mohammed ascended to the seventh heaven and beyond after his night journey from Mecca on a winged white beast called al-Buraq. The mosques stand on the site of the ancient Jewish temple that was destroyed by the Romans in AD 70. The remains of the temple are the centre of the Jewish claim to Jerusalem. The only part that is still standing is the western part of the wall that ran around it. For centuries it was known as the Wailing Wall, because devout Jews would go there to weep for the temple. Modern, muscular Israel does not do wailing, so it calls it the Western Wall; it is still a centre of prayer, but it is also a national symbol, where paratroopers take their oath of allegiance. A short walk away, through the covered alleys of the Old City, is the church of the Holy Sepulchre, which Christians believe was built over the quarry where Jesus was crucified and his body entombed until he rose from the dead.

Jerusalem's special place in the hearts and beliefs of Christians, Jews and Muslims is the reason why so much blood has been spilled on its stones. People want it too much. The conflict (it always takes the definite article; no one in the city doubts which one is being discussed) is part of everything in Jerusalem. It is never just at the back of people's minds and it is very often right at the front. It infects the smallest details of everyday life. Once I heard a foreign woman trying to buy fish in Mahane Yehuda, the raucous, teeming Jewish market in west Jerusalem. The fishmonger told her off when she made the mistake of using the Arabic word for the fish instead of the Hebrew one. 'No, this is not an Arab, it is a Jewish fish . . .' He wasn't joking.

An Israeli writer once said that Jerusalem is the only city where the dead are more important than the living. Some of its people are not content with fighting their own generation's wars;

they want to fight their ancestors' enemies too. History is everywhere, and they are conscious that there is history still to be made. An Israeli immigrant, originally from Latin America, told me with great passion about his attachment to the biblical land of Israel and to Jerusalem, its capital. I asked him where the Palestinians fitted in. After all, they had been there for many generations, also believed that Jerusalem was their capital, were at least as attached to the land as he was, and hadn't he grown up somewhere else? His answer was full of triumph, as if he had been expecting the question and was ready with the killer fact. 'A-ha, but the Romans threw me out. If it wasn't for the Romans, I would still have been here!' He talked about it as if it had happened last year.

History is full of killer facts for Palestinians too. When Israel was celebrating fifty years of independence in 1998, Palestinians would sometimes sit back and declare that anniversaries didn't mean much. The Crusaders, they would say, were a great military power too. But they lasted only a century, and so would the Israelis. These days I know the Israelis and the Palestinians and their histories, recognise their preoccupations and even share some of them, so I am no longer surprised by people who believe that actions taken a thousand or two thousand years ago are still having a direct impact on their lives. But in the mid-1990s, even though I was fresh from wars in the Balkans and Chechnya and hardly naïve about power and violence and history, it seemed just a little insane.

Reporters in Jerusalem have to master a whole range of emotional, political and historical vocabularies and narratives, not just the ones used by my Latin American Israeli, and by the Palestinians who consoled themselves by thinking of the Crusaders. In Jerusalem, across Israel and in the occupied territories, there are many shades of opinion. Our job is to try to decode them all, not easy when phrases that sound innocent and straight-forward can carry a rich variety of meanings. The Israeli who had come from Latin America pointed the way into the first part of the puzzle facing reporters who want to explain what is happening between Israel and the Palestinians. Where do you start? Do you link today's news story to last week's atrocity? Or to years of occupation? Or to a war a generation ago? Where does Israel's memory of the Holocaust fit in? What about the promises that Britain made to both sides while it was the colonial power? Who owned the land first? If you want it to, the argument then jerks back through a couple of millennia, to the Ottomans, the Crusaders, the Romans, the Jews, the Canaanites and the Bible. Scholars have written dozens, hundreds, of books over centuries on every detail of each of those subjects. Every reporter can be pretty sure that at some time the version of events they present will alienate big chunks of the population there. Plenty of people, on both sides, believe that if you don't buy their version, if you are not their cheerleader, then you must be their enemy.

It happened to me plenty of times. In the mid-1990s BBC News was carried by one of the Israeli cable providers. One morning I had been covering some clashes in Hebron, the Palestinian town on the occupied West Bank that has a settlement of aggressive and highly nationalistic Jews in its centre. I had just filed the Hebron report for the lunchtime news, when we heard that a Palestinian had attacked Israeli civilians in Tel Aviv, and children were among the casualties. We drove down to Tel Aviv, and a crowd gathered as I did my piece to camera, listening hard to what I was saying; almost everyone in Tel Aviv speaks at least a bit of English and a lot of people are fluent. They were hostile. A man with an Australian accent who had seen my report from Hebron, and decided the fact that I was standing with the Palestinians meant that I was too sympathetic towards them, started shouting, getting close to blaming

227

the BBC, or me, for the attack on the Israeli civilians in Tel Aviv. Other times, people hung out of windows to shout, or came up to me in the street, sometimes in a friendly way, sometimes not.

'You're from the BBC?' one woman yelled, who sounded as if she had grown up somewhere in north London.

'Bloody British Crap, that's what it stands for. Crap! I don't let my kids anywhere near it.'

Pressure came from the Palestinian side too. When I did a detailed documentary about the failings and corruption in Yasser Arafat's Palestinian Authority, I was summoned by the minister of information, Yasser Abed Rabbo, to his office in Ramallah for a carpeting. He expressed his outrage and demanded that the BBC withdraw the film from its own networks and from any distribution worldwide, or we would be hearing from the Authority's lawyers. We stood firm and that was the last we heard of it.

Complaints from both sides are not necessarily a sign of good journalism, but in the Middle East being an honest journalist is not a particularly good way of making friends. Journalists have to get used to a little flak; if they just describe what has happened, on anything but the most straight-up-and-down stories, they can end up raising more questions than they answer. A bit of explanation is helpful in any piece of journalism, but it is vital with the Israelis and the Palestinians, otherwise most people who pick up the paper, or the remote control, or look at the news on the web, will go away baffled. The trouble with trying to explain things, though, is that it can get you into trouble, because it involves making choices and assessments. Even if you work so hard to be fair that people cannot tell what your real or imagined views are, they still try to deduce things from that. A British Jew, a supporter of Israel, congratulated me on something that I had written. He could not tell, he said, which side I was backing, but he assumed it must be the

Israelis, because I sounded reasonable and only Israel's supporters were reasonable.

How can a journalist make sense of it all in a few hundred words or in a couple of minutes of airtime? The depressing answer to that question is that it is very difficult; the best reporters who try the hardest do not always succeed, and the clueless get lost very quickly.

If you do not have the time or the inclination to dig deep into history – and plenty of Israelis and Palestinians will say that if you don't, you will never grasp their unholy land – one way of understanding some of today's big issues is to take a good look at their failure to make peace in the 1990s. When I arrived in Jerusalem in 1995 most of the world thought that there was a good chance that the Palestinians and the Israelis were going to make peace, or at least find a way to live alongside each other. A Spanish TV reporter I knew in Bosnia was amazed when I said I was going to cover the Middle East. 'Why? Jeremy, are you mad? The story's over in that place, everyone knows that.' The world in the mid-1990s had a lot less obvious trouble in it than it did ten years later. In 1992, the American academic Francis Fukuyama had come up with the idea of calling his book about the new world that was emerging *The End of History*. A calm time, a chance to build better things, looked as if it might be possible. In the Middle East, the end of the Cold War opened up the chance for a deal; the region was no longer a cockpit for Moscow and Washington. It was also important that the first President Bush built a coalition that included Arab states in the 1991 war against Saddam Hussein, and that the war ended without a Western occupation of Iraq.

What they tried to do in the 1990s was to unravel the consequences of the 1967 Middle East war. That is still the only hope for peace for the Palestinians and Israel. In six days in June that year Israel destroyed the armed forces of Egypt, Syria and Jordan.

It captured Gaza and the Sinai Desert from Egypt; the Golan Heights from Syria; and the West Bank, including east Jerusalem from Jordan. The Sinai went back to Egypt after it signed a peace deal with Israel in 1978 (the Egyptians did not want Gaza, a narrow, overcrowded strip of land that is a hotbed of Palestinian nationalism).

The idea in the 1990s was to do a similar 'land for peace' deal with the Palestinians, settling their differences by coming up with a territorial compromise. The Norwegian diplomats who brought the two sides together in Oslo, secretly at first, were deliberately vague about what the compromise was going to be. They had to be, because the biggest issues – the future of Jerusalem, of Jewish settlers on occupied land and the right to return of Palestinian refugees – were politically radioactive. But the key to any deal was Israel pulling out of some or all of Gaza, the West Bank and east Jerusalem, allowing the Palestinians to establish a state of their own. The idea behind the Oslo process was that they would make deals on small things first, like who runs Jericho, and get so used to talking that they would be able to tackle the big issues later on. Nice idea, but it didn't work. It turned out they couldn't make the small things work properly, so by the time they were supposed to discuss the big ones, there was a mountain of distrust between them – built higher by the constant expansion of Jewish settlements in the occupied territories, and by Palestinian attacks on Israeli civilians.

But that was still not apparent to the people who gathered on the lawn of the White House in 1993, invited by a beaming President Bill Clinton to watch the signing of what they hoped would be a historic agreement that would lead to peace. The emotional highlight of a euphoric day was when Israel's Prime Minister, the former general, Yitzhak Rabin, shook hands with Yasser Arafat, the Palestinian leader. Arafat had been as reluctant to accept Israel's existence as Rabin had been to accept that Arafat was not dripping with Jewish blood. Both men still had doubts about what was possible, but had decided to try to find a peaceful way to end their war.

Arafat was the living symbol of the Palestinian fight for a state. After the Arab armies had been defeated in 1967 he was at the forefront of a specifically Palestinian armed struggle: he was a ruthless enemy of Israel who now seemed ready to look for a political solution. Rabin had been at the centre of Israeli military and then political life since the creation of the Jewish state. In 1948 he had been one of the leaders of the Palmach, the shock troops of the Jewish army that won the war of independence; he became chief of staff of the Israel Defence Forces and architect of their victory in 1967, and then Ambassador to Washington. By 1995 he was three years into his second term as Prime Minister. A peace process was under way, and the conventional wisdom was that it was not going to be easy, but they were going to get there, not least because Arafat and Rabin had been leaders in war, so the assumption was that they had the credibility with their followers to have a better chance than anyone else of making peace.

A minority of Palestinians were unhappy about the peace process because they thought that it gave too many concessions to the Israelis; some of the objectors were secular nationalists, others believed that God intended Muslims to control the entire land of Palestine. Arafat used his unique position as the embodiment of Palestinian nationalism to ignore, isolate, placate and occasionally lock up the dissenters. In Israel, Rabin became an object of hate for right-wingers. Some made up posters of him dressed in an SS uniform, or in Yasser Arafat's Palestinian headscarf. Most Israelis had trusted Rabin with their security, but when he started to make concessions to the Palestinians many turned on him, accusing him of selling their birthright and endangering their lives. And just as religious Palestinians were the fiercest opponents of Arafat's decision to negotiate, Rabin's biggest opponents in Israel were also convinced that they were doing the will of God. They believed that Gaza, the West Bank and Jerusalem were Israel's for ever, a gift from God in biblical times that Israel had regained because in 1967 he had granted them victory through a miracle.

Rabin was the general who had captured the land, but they hated him because he was prepared to give some of it up. He had allowed the Palestinians to administer the small oasis town of Jericho in the Jordan Valley and the parts of Gaza on the Mediterranean that were not occupied by Jewish settlements, and by the autumn of 1995 he was about to start pulling Israeli troops out of some of the big towns on the West Bank. Rabin's supporters on the left had been passive during the summer, letting the extreme right seize control of the political debate in Israel. But on a Saturday night, 4 November, they had arranged a peace rally in the biggest square in Tel Aviv, outside the City Hall, a place where major demonstrations were traditionally held.

The day before I stopped my car at some traffic lights near the Prime Minister's office in Jerusalem. A young peace activist shoved a pamphlet advertising the rally through my car window. Boaz Paldi, the BBC's soundman, was with me, and we discussed whether it was worth covering. It was the last frantic few hours before the beginning of the Jewish Sabbath, when observant Jews in west Jerusalem rush to buy food, flowers for their wives and mothers and to get home, so the traffic was heavy and there was time to talk. Boaz had strong views about peace. He was an Israeli conscientious objector who used to tell me not to halt or show any documents when the army in which he had refused to serve tried to stop us at one of its checkpoints in the West Bank. 'Jeremy, keep going . . . I said don't stop . . . [then, as we stopped] Poor bastards,' he would rage, 'don't they realise they're being corrupted by an illegal occupation?' His advice about checkpoints should be ignored, by the way. I gave up even reaching quickly for my papers after a few checkpoint experiences where the red dot of a sniper's laser sight played around my chest.

Boaz and I agreed that the only way the rally would be a story would be if the Prime Minister got shot. We joked about it because it seemed impossible, even though there had been threats to Rabin's life, which the Shin Bet, Israel's internal security service, had told Israeli journalists to take seriously a few days earlier. Boaz and I thought that because the Shin Bet knew about the threat, no one would be allowed close enough to Rabin to kill him, and surely the Israelis would be watching the high places around the square where he was speaking to stop a sniper. We decided to leave it to the television news agencies, the wholesalers who have contracts with the big broadcasters to provide raw tape of news events. In Israel there are probably more news crews per head of population than in any other country, so it is not possible to miss a story. The only issue is whether you go yourself, to get your own pictures, interviews and a piece to camera. In 1995, twenty-four-hour news was not something I had to worry about yet, and since bulletins on BBC1 are very short on Saturday nights, and the peace process had started to bore editors, it was not a hard decision to make. And on Saturday night I was going to be busy. We were having a dinner at our house in Ein Karem, and if I didn't cover the rally it wasn't much of a risk because my opponent, the ITN correspondent Robert Moore, was one of the guests. On Saturdays, Jewish Jerusalem is very quiet, with almost every shop closed, so in the morning I went shopping in the Palestinian streets of east Jerusalem, the occupied side of the city.

That evening I made a casserole with some very special sausages I had imported illegally from London. All our guests were expatriate journalists. Jerusalem is a city of tribes, and though we tried hard to make friends with some of the local ones, sometimes it was easier to stay within your own. Then the bleepers and phones around the table erupted. ITN's beat the BBC's by a couple of seconds; to his credit, because news is a competitive business, Robert Moore showed me what it said: 'Rabin shot. Ring office.' Our dinner broke up in about ten seconds. When we got home about three days later, the food was still on the table. The ITN fork, loaded with the next mouthful, was lying there abandoned. At another journalists' dinner party across Jerusalem one of the American TV correspondents tried to leave in a hurry when his message came through, without saying why. Keith Graves, the man from Sky, and before that the BBC, blocked his way and wrestled his bleeper from him.

Rabin was killed by a Jewish extremist because he had decided that if Israel was going to have a chance of peace, it was going to have to pay a price in territory. His assassin, Yigal Amir, thought he was rescuing Israel from a man who was going to kill its hopes and deny its destiny. Security was lax around the Prime Minister, for the last time in Israeli history. Rabin and the other leaders of the left had been speaking from a big terrace that runs round the front of the Tel Aviv City Hall, overlooking the square. Rabin had been moving towards his car, which had been brought round to the back of the building, and there were plenty of people around, who were allowed to get very close. Yigal Amir pretended to be a well-wisher, and when he was a foot or so away, perhaps even less, he shot Rabin in the back. His bodyguards bundled him into his limousine and sped off to Tel Aviv's main hospital, which is very close by, but the doctors could not save him.

I was on air, live on the main evening news, a couple of hours after we abandoned our dinner, when the announcement came on Israeli radio that Rabin had died. The cameraman was listening through one of his headphones, and passed the news on to Boaz, who was standing next to him. I could see they were talking, and then Boaz started advancing towards me. 'He's dead, tell them he's dead,' he hissed, getting closer and closer. I hesitated. 'Tell them he's dead,' he said again, so loud I thought the microphones were going to pick it up. So I told them, saying reports were coming through that Rabin had died in hospital. The news came back on the air an hour or so later, with a special programme, and I just about had time to put together a decent report. Pictures were being fed in from Tel Aviv; there were even shots of the scene immediately after Amir pulled the trigger, as he was hustled away in the middle of a big crowd of security men. Ironically, if I had gone to Tel Aviv, I might not have got back to Jerusalem in time to put the piece together.

Rabin's assassination was a turning-point in the history of Israel and the Palestinians. He had been able to persuade a majority of Israeli people to put aside their existential fears, to make them feel safe in a way that nobody else could. He had the guts to take difficult decisions and the vision to see that they were necessary. One of the hardest was to deal with Yasser Arafat. Whatever he thought about Arafat's past, he accepted that he had a unique position as the leader of the Palestinians, and if there was to be a solution he was going to have to be part of it. Making peace would still have been slow and difficult. But I think that had Rabin lived, the two sides would have got further, faster. Perhaps because he had seen so much war close up, he seemed to have made a decision, in his head and his heart, that there was no military solution to the conflict, that Israel had to make peace with the Palestinians, and if it was going to happen it would have to give up a lot of the land that his men had captured in 1967.

After he was killed the Israeli left went into mourning, wracked by guilt and grief that they had not supported him enough against right-wingers who had waited outside his flat to yell abuse every night as he returned home. For a while there were calls for Israelis to take some of the poison out of their politics, which didn't work. Within a few weeks, it was back.

The Palestinians, and their leader Yasser Arafat, were making mistakes of their own. He squandered a chance in the mid-1990s to build a state in waiting. If he had created or allowed others to create institutions that worked – an independent judiciary, a credible legal system, an honest police force and a proper parliament – he might not have lost so many allies in the West. Arafat also did not want to risk alienating Palestinians by pushing ideas, like a compromise on territory or on the future of Palestinian refugees, when Israel was confiscating land to build settlements for Jews in the occupied territories.

Many Israelis argue that Arafat's actions would have destroyed the chance for peace even if Rabin had lived, and believe that he played a hypocritical double game, claiming he wanted peace when he met Westerners but inciting terrorism when he spoke to his own people. Maybe – this is hypothetical, after all – but there are other questions too. Would Rabin have ordered the assassinations of senior members of the Palestinian militant groups Islamic Jihad and Hamas at the end of 1995 and early in 1996, which were followed by a wave of suicide bombings? Labour under Shimon Peres lost the elections later that year to the right, under the hard-liner Binyamin Netanyahu. What if Rabin had won in 1996? Tackling the big questions, the radioactive issues like Jerusalem, Jewish settlements and Palestinian refugees, would still have been appallingly difficult and could have killed the whole process. But Rabin and Arafat had a partnership, and there has been nothing like it since. Their relationship had deep flaws, but they realised they needed each other to deliver the future. And since Bill Clinton was so committed to what they were doing, it might have worked.

In many ways, everything that has happened between the Israelis and the Arabs since can be traced back to the assassination of Rabin. It was one of the most effective political killings of the century, because in my view Yigal Amir succeeded in his objective of stopping a territorial compromise between Israel and the Palestinians. The Oslo peace process did not die on 4 November 1995, but it developed a terminal illness that crippled it and finally did it in by creating so much poison that a low-intensity war started between the two sides in September 2000.

But even though it failed, the attempt to make peace in the 1990s did one vital thing: if Israel and the Palestinians ever want to have another go, they know the price that they will have to pay, and the risks of trying. Both sides always say they want peace, but a lot of the time what they really mean is that they want their enemies to surrender. That is not going to happen. Neither side is going to go away, so if they want a chance of ending their war, if they don't want to condemn their people to another hundred years and more of hatred and fear, they will, at some point, have to make a deal. It needs to be a deal that is fair to both sides, because any deal that is not fair will not work.

Palestinians and Israelis carry a lot of scar tissue. Some of the original wounds were inflicted by each other; some of it was left by others. A lot of the complications come from the fact that the scar tissue is regularly reopened. The struggle is unequal. Palestinians feel its consequences in their daily lives much more than Israelis, but Israel feels its losses just as keenly – and can do more to hit back. Both sides believe they are victims, and both in many ways are correct. They hate the events that make them feel like victims; but both sides also recognise, instinctively, that being a victim is politically useful. Makers and consumers of news broadcasts from Jerusalem should never forget that both sides – for different reasons, though often at the same time – want to be portrayed as victims. If they are, they believe they are more likely to get international sympathy, it is easier for them and their supporters to believe in the actions that they take to gain redress or revenge. Victims have legitimacy.

Both sides have drawn their own conclusions from the twentieth century. After Israel was created in 1948, three-quarters of a million Palestinians lost their homes to the Israelis and became refugees. After that, hundreds of thousands of Middle Eastern Jews had no choice other than to leave their homes and possessions in Arab countries and go to Israel. The bitterness has been deepened by the obduracy of the Palestinians and the stamina, determination and strategic vision of the Israelis.

History has left many, perhaps most, Israelis with the uncomfortable feeling that even though they are strong, they are also weak. The first time I saw this for myself was on a Monday afternoon in the spring of 1996, when there was a suicide attack in the centre of Tel Aviv. It was the last in a series of bombs that had killed fifty-nine Israelis in eight days. As I drove into Tel Aviv, still a couple of miles from the bomb site, men were yelling and sprinting down the road. Cars raced around sounding their horns. People were panicking. But by the evening Israelis were pulling themselves together and the next morning they got back on the buses to go to work. The bomb had exposed their sense of weakness, but also their biggest strength, which is the ability to absorb terrible shocks, and then to regroup quickly to face what is coming next. Israelis can lurch from panic to resolve in a day.

Israeli insecurity comes from two main sources. First, the fact that they took much of their land by force and have had to fight to keep it. That will not go away until they make peace with the Arabs. Much more deeply, their insecurity comes from Jewish history. Israel has an intimate connection with the Nazi Holocaust that killed six million Jews, as well as the centuries of persecution in Europe that led up to it. When I am in Jerusalem and have the time and energy I go running in the forest near Ein Karem. I always pass the iron gates of Yad Vashem, Israel's monument to the

Holocaust. From the track through the forest where I run you can see one of the railway cattle trucks that the Nazis used to transport Jews to the camps. When the survivors of the Holocaust started coming to Palestine after 1945, they were not treated well by the Jews who had spent their lives fighting the Arabs and the British and, on at least one occasion, each other. They saw themselves as strong, virile, independent; and for many of them the Holocaust survivors were just the opposite. Some of the traumatised new immigrants were even taunted with the nickname 'Soapy' because of the myth that the Nazis had tried to turn their victims into soap.

Israelis are very sympathetic now, and the Holocaust casts a big shadow. The whole country comes to a halt when the sirens sound on Holocaust Day. People get out of their cars and stand to attention in the street. Buses pull over, the passengers get out of their seats, and the country halts for two minutes. When the sirens stop, Israelis drive off and pick up their incessant mobile phone conversations as if they had never been interrupted.

Politicians sometimes feed shamelessly on the past. Yitzhak Shamir, Prime Minister in the 1980s, did not believe in any kind of deal with the Arabs. He justified it by playing on the fear that Israelis could end up being pushed back to the beaches and expelled, by remarking that the Arabs are the same Arabs and the sea is still the same sea. But their state is strong. Though it won't admit it, Israel has nuclear weapons. It has the most advanced economy in the region and a relationship of unconditional love with the United States. Yet despite all of that, there is still an existential insecurity in many Israeli minds.

The stern, secular European immigrants who created Israel wanted its people to be a new sort of Jew, who would not be persecuted like the ones back in Europe. They would build their country with their own hands and fight for what they had created. They had to have no illusions about how hard it would be. Their vanguard came from the people who lived on collective agricultural settlements called *kibbutzim*, which as they became more established increased the size of the Jewish footprint in Palestine. On the kibbutz the collective was everything; children were not brought up by their parents, but by the community. Only a minority of Israelis ever lived on a kibbutz. But they were an elite; fathers and sons who had been raised to put the community first and their own desires and needs second made excellent soldiers. These Jewish aristocrats fought and died in disproportionate numbers in their country's wars, just like the Christian ruling classes in Europe, and were often among those who asked the survivors of the European Holocaust why they did not fight, why they went like lambs to the slaughter. The Holocaust deepened Israel's conviction that they had to face their enemies and destroy them, because no one else would do it for them.

But there was another, deeper reason why the new Jews who had been born in Palestine were so suspicious and fearful of the way that the diaspora was pursuing them to the Middle East. The Holocaust and its survivors tarnished the armour they had created for themselves and their new country. Israel was exposed to the virus not just of fear – anyone who had been in a war knew what it was like to be afraid – but of weakness. The virus flares up at bad times. In the weeks leading to war in 1967 many Israelis believed Egyptian propaganda about the impending destruction of their state. And when Israel's high-tech armed forces were not able to stop suicide bombers in the early years of the twenty-first century, old fears, however irrational, about the perpetual threat of extinction were stirred again.

The Palestinians learned from the twentieth century that however hard it gets, they should not leave. In 1948 up to three-quarters of a million had fled for all the reasons that civilians run away from wars. Some of them were forced out by direct threats to their lives, at the point of a gun or because they heard reports and rumours of massacres and wanted to get out before it happened to them. A few had money or connections in the Arab world, in Europe or America, and built new lives. Most were poor farmers who lost their land and spent the rest of their lives dreaming about it in refugee camps in Gaza, the West Bank, Jordan, Syria, and Lebanon, where their grandchildren still have a very hard existence.

Another 400,000 Palestinians lost their homes when Israel occupied the West Bank and Gaza in the 1967 war. Of course, the pressure of the occupation means that some Palestinians still come to the painful conclusion that the only way to get a better life is to get out. Ironically, once the decision is made, they find it difficult to go because many countries will not accept them. It is not easy even for the well-educated. For the poor majority, whose educations were wrecked by the Israeli occupation and the fight against it, getting a visa to live and work somewhere else is almost impossible. Until they were allowed to cross into Egypt on foot in 2005, hundreds of thousands of Palestinians grew up in Gaza without ever being able to leave. Once I managed to get permission from the Israeli authorities to take a Palestinian grandmother from Gaza back to Jaffa, the town next to Tel Aviv from which she had fled in 1948. Her grandson, a boy of about ten, came too. I asked her if he had travelled before.

'Of course,' she said indignantly, 'he's been to Khan Younis.' It is a town about five miles from Gaza City. It was his first time outside the Gaza strip, where more than one million people live on a piece of land that is about twenty-three miles long and between four and seven miles wide. Our journey back to her birthplace just made her sad; she could not find the place where her house had stood. On the road between Jaffa and the checkpoint that leads into Gaza her grandson asked her to identify the iron machine racing alongside us through the fields. It was a train; he had never seen one before. At the end of the day, the old lady looked glad to disappear back through the wire into the place she called a prison.

When Israel captured east Jerusalem from the Jordanians, it knocked down the concrete and wire barriers that divided the city. Physically there was nothing to stop Jerusalem's residents, Jewish, Muslim or Christian, from going wherever they wanted. But the walls still stood in people's minds, and when Palestinians started their first mass uprising against the occupation in the late 1980s, Israelis, with a few exceptions, stopped going to Palestinian areas. Perhaps they were just being sensible, but if they are honest they will admit that the Palestinian quarters of Jerusalem had always felt like a foreign land. In times of trouble, after bombs or riots, Israeli police and soldiers set up checkpoints on the roads that link Palestinian districts to Jewish ones. Understandable behaviour, perhaps, but also a sign that the capital Israel calls indivisible can be divided. The boundaries between the communities already exist. They just need to be ratified.

When people talk about Jerusalem they mean different things. Until 1967, the municipal area of Jerusalem was fairly small. But after 1967, Israel annexed not just the Old City and the Palestinian suburbs that had been administered by Jordan since 1948, but also a big chunk of the West Bank. Since then, according to B'Tselem, the human rights group, Israel has built more than 44,000 homes in which more than 176,000 people live, on land it has expropriated inside the expanded boundaries of Jerusalem. Israel considers it all part of its eternal and indivisible capital; but it was outside the city limits before 1967.

In the newly reunited and expanded city, nothing escaped the conflict. Everything, even the water they drank and the drains below them, was politicised. Palestinians and Israelis had separate bus routes, used separate buses. In Israel gas does not come through the mains but in cylinders. When the man came round to deliver more gas for our cooker I asked him also to replace the cylinder for a gas heater. He took one look at it and said patiently that he couldn't do it, because 'I sell Jewish gas, not Arab gas.' I had bought the heater on the Palestinian side of Jerusalem, one Saturday afternoon when all the shops in west Jerusalem were closed for the Sabbath. Because Jordan controlled east Jerusalem and the West Bank until 1967, the cylinders had different valves from the ones in Israel. The gas refueller in Jerusalem was closed, so I had to take the cylinder through the Israeli checkpoints into the occupied West Bank to get it filled. On my way back, inside Israel, I overtook a police jeep. The officers inside saw that I had a gas cylinder, gave chase and pulled me over. They thought the cylinder could be wired to explode and that I could be a bomber wanting to kill Jews.

Town planning is also used by Israel to strengthen its hold on the city. Israel does everything it can to make it easier for Jews to live in Jerusalem. It makes it extremely difficult for Palestinians to get permission to build, so much of what they construct is illegal, and can, if the Israeli city council wants, be bulldozed. Even so, Meron Benvenisti, who spent years as the Israeli deputy mayor of Jerusalem, stood with me once on the Mount of Olives over-looking the ancient Jewish graveyard, the walls of the Old City and the gleaming gold of the Dome of the Rock and admitted that despite everything they had done, the ratio of Jews to Arabs in Jerusalem was the same as it had been in 1967. The full resources of the Israeli state, directed at vast expense at increasing the Jewish population of the city, had only been able to keep pace with the natural growth of the Palestinian population.

The weapon that Palestinians have that scares the Israelis most is their determination to stay put and to have children – lots of them. The birth rate in the Palestinian territories is one of the

highest on the planet. Half the Palestinian population is under fifteen. Childbirth has been turned into an offensive weapon. Ariel
Sharon, the man who devoted his life to making Israel stronger
regardless of the cost to the Arabs who got in the way, was always
confident that with the right troops and generals Israel would win
any war. But by the end of his career what alarmed him most
were Palestinian mothers and their babies.

From the time that Israel captured the West Bank in 1967, he
was convinced that it was not just Israel's right and privilege to
colonise it; moving Jews into the occupied land was strategically
necessary too, to make Israel bigger and stronger, with borders that
were easier to defend. He set up military bases that became settlements for civilians, made speeches saying that every Palestinian
town should have Jews living around it, and when he went into
politics put the power of the state behind the drive to build Jewish
settlements. But after he became Prime Minister in 2001 he started
to change his mind. Partly the reason was the violent Palestinian
uprising. At first, he responded to it as he always had: he set about
killing the people who were prepared to kill Jews. But as time
went by he realised that while Israel was strong enough to crush
its Palestinian enemies, it couldn't make them go away.

Israelis were not matching the Palestinian birth rate. Sharon,
like many others, realised that if Israel annexed all the land
between the River Jordan and the Mediterranean it would face a
baby nightmare. The Palestinians would be the majority, and Israel
would have a hard choice. Either it could refuse to give
Palestinians the vote, and turn its country into an apartheid state,
or it could stay democratic, give them the vote, and watch as
Arabs outvoted Jews in an Israeli election. Decades of armed
Palestinian resistance to the Israeli occupation of the West Bank
and Gaza had, if anything, strengthened the resolve of Sharon to
hang on to the land, to show by building for Jews and by fighting

back that Israel could not be scared away from what it considered to be its own. But when he saw the sheer weight of numbers in Palestinian maternity wards and schools, even Sharon, the king of the settlements, knew that Israel could not keep all the land. So he broke what had been the biggest taboo in Israeli politics: he pulled Jewish soldiers and settlers out of Gaza and started the process of dismantling at least part of what he had built on the West Bank.

It took a few years, but Jerusalem started to get under my skin. Jerusalem's indigenous tribes ignore any foolish ideas about loving their neighbour and are indifferent about temporary foreign residents. It is not an easy city, because of its intolerant heartbeat, but by the time I left, I loved the place. Its history and politics are addictive, and there's also the light. In the middle of a summer day it can feel oppressive, bright and white, but in the evenings it softens everything and turns it into gold. And then there are the smells, of the pine trees in Ein Karem on a winter day, and the herbs sold by Palestinian women just inside Damascus Gate in the Old City: mint, basil and za'tar, a blend of local herbs and sesame. A Palestinian market trader in Hebron once showed me the authentic West Bank way to eat it. You wet a piece of bread with olive oil, and then dip it in the za'tar. It is good way to start a cold day on the West Bank, though if you overdo the oil, it runs down your fingers. Za'tar is a bit like thyme, but more pungent, and it works well with chicken, if you sprinkle it on before it is roasted. When I unscrew the lid of a jar of greenish and coarse ground za'tar in London, I get transported back to Jerusalem and to the rocky highlands of the Holy Land. Their arid beauty is an acquired taste for most of the year, but the hills and valleys that have not disappeared under concrete or tarmac yet are perfumed and green in the spring, with new leaves growing on the olive trees and clumps of herbs growing wild.

I liked a lot about the Israelis. Foreigners from more polite societies often have problems with them. For British people who are more comfortable beating about the bush it can be disconcerting to meet people who say what they mean. But in the end, when my skin grew a few more layers, it felt like a better way to do business. Israelis are also informal. In the smart sections of Lebanon, the Italy of the east, it is impossible to be over-dressed. In Israel it is still almost impossible to under-dress. When Yitzhak Rabin, as a young man, first went to a set of international talks, someone had to show him how to knot a tie. Once at the aftermath of a bomb, I saw Raphael Eitan, a famous commander of Israel's paratroops, by then a Cabinet minister, inspecting the damage. He was wearing a bad pair of jeans, training shoes and a purple T-shirt that showed his belly off well. Funerals happen so fast after someone has died, almost straight away, that people go in what they wore to work that day. There were plenty of funerals to go to.

Palestinians have a lot of funerals too, and they don't have time to dress up for them either. Despite everything they have suffered, and still suffer, the vast majority of them have kept their dignity, still welcome strangers and can even make jokes about their own difficult lives. The one single thing that would improve them is an end to Israel's occupation of land they want for their own state. The occupation is still, so many years after the 1967 war that created it, the sharpest, hardest feature in their world.

While I was based in Jerusalem I stopped feeling defensive about living in a village that had been Palestinian until 1948 and since then has been part of Israeli Jerusalem. I decided that if Israelis and Palestinians wanted the peace their leaders talked about so much, there were some parts of history that they simply could not unpick. One of them, give or take bits and pieces here and there, is the boundary that ran between Israel and the Palestinians between 1948 and 1967. A division of the land, more or less along that line, is still the best chance of creating two states.

It will be much more difficult to pull off now even than it was in the 1990s, when Rabin and Arafat were trying. Both sides have been radicalised by the bloodshed of the second intifada, which started in 2000. Israel's settlements in the occupied territories are much bigger, and a new generation of settlers have expanded on to more hilltops in the West Bank. Israel started building a separation barrier – a concrete wall in some places, a high-tech complex of fence and sensors in others – that it said was to protect its people, and also consumed more Palestinian land. On the other side, when Palestinians had a chance to vote in democratic elections, they punished the failure of Fatah, Yasser Arafat's faction, to improve their lives by handing victory to Hamas, the Islamic resistance movement.

I think that a two-state solution is still the only one with any chance of working. The fundamentals of the challenge are reasonably simple. There is one piece of land between the Mediterranean and the River Jordan, which is made up of Israel, the West Bank and the Gaza Strip. For much of the twentieth century both the Palestinians and the Israelis wanted all of it. By the end of the century most of them, though not all, realised that they would have to find a way to share it. Sharing it means a mutual recognition that a Palestinian state will have to stand as equal alongside Israel. That means that the big question for the first part of the twenty-first century is how they divide the land up.

That is where it starts getting complicated. Dividing the land, deciding who gets what, is the heart of the problem; doing it gets us back to that question of price. Neither set of leaders has yet dared to be really truthful about what its people would have to pay – or what they would have to lose. Israel would have to give up occupied territory that it wants for itself, or compensate the Palestinians with other land on a one-to-one basis. It would have to accept Palestinian sovereignty over its own land, not some sort of imitation independence. Palestinians would have to drop the dream that their refugees will be able to return to their original homes in what has been Israel since 1948. They would have to accept Israel's rights to its land – and to its share of Jerusalem.

Creating a Palestinian state that is acceptable to a majority of its would-be citizens, that Israel can live alongside, is the only way to start making real peace. It will not of itself end the hatred, but in the long run it is the only way to make peace possible. The alternative is for Palestinians and Israelis to let the hatred deepen and to condemn their children and grandchildren to more misery. That would be bad enough. But their conflict is hardwired into the rest of the region. Because it has been allowed to fester, it exports instability and hatred. If that is allowed to continue, the rest of the Middle East will continue to pass on instability and hatred to the rest of the world.

9

Cold Turkey

On 23 May 2000, after Abed Takkoush was killed, the smoke from the burnt-out remains of his Mercedes faded away until it was thin and wispy. His body lay on the road near the driver's door, where it had fallen after he had used his last strength to writhe and kick his way out of the open window. Malek Kanaan and I were about 100 or 150 yards away, sheltering behind a building that came between us and the Israeli border wire, and the soldiers who had fired the shell that killed him. When I moved a few yards into the open they shot at me with their heavy machine-gun. After that I did not try to go near Abed's body again. Malek and I did not speak much. We were not able to tell anyone about what had happened, as our phones had been in the car when it was hit. We did not want to move, in case the Israelis were still waiting to kill us. Once or twice cars came to the top of the hill on the far side of Abed's car, took a look down at the wreckage and at his body lying on the road, on the edge of the village of Mays al-Jabal, and at the Israeli border wire beyond that, and then turned and went back the way they had come.

The drivers must have told someone about what they had seen, because after about another hour, a small car with a Lebanese newspaper reporter and a photographer arrived from the direction that we had taken that morning. They had heard that something had happened. We told them about Abed and how he had been killed. Once they heard how the Israelis had opened fire on us when we tried to move towards his body and the wreckage of the car, they did not go any further. One of them had a phone, a pay-as-you-go mobile that was almost out of units. Malek borrowed it and called the Reuters office in Beirut. He managed a couple of minutes before the credit ran out, enough time to tell them what had happened to Abed but not long enough for any details about us. He had seemed calm but when he got through to his friends in Beirut, he spoke fast and with a lot of passion. By the time the phone cut out, he had not got round to mentioning my name.

I was trying to work out where we had gone wrong, conscious the whole time that Abed's body was lying on the road close by. In war zones you know when you are pushing your luck, moving too far down a road, talking your way through a checkpoint that should have been the place where you turned back. But it hadn't been one of those mornings. We weren't trying to catch up with the Israelis as they retreated, or even to see any action. For me, the story that day was about Lebanese people repossessing territory that Israel had occupied for a generation. Perhaps Abed, Malek and I were too relaxed as we followed the Israelis back to the border. We thought we were doing all the right things, stopping and talking to local people, asking them if they had heard shelling or shooting or seen the Israelis.

About the same time that we were sitting there watching the smoke from Abed's car fading away, a report from Lebanese intelligence came into the office of the United Nations peace-keepers in Tyre. It was almost correct. It said that a car had been destroyed near the border and that two bodies were on the road. When that was combined with what Reuters knew, that Abed was dead and that Malek was alive because he had phoned, it suggested that I could be dead. Malek had not said that I was, but also had not said I wasn't. For a while that is all that the BBC team there, which was led by my partner Julia Williams, had to work with. They stayed close to the UN team in Tyre, who were feeding them whatever information came in.

The journalists gave us a lift away from the place where we had been hiding to the next village. I felt very bad about leaving Abed's dead body on the road, but we had to get help. Based on what Malek had told them, Reuters had put the report of Abed's death on the wire, and the news was spreading around Beirut. I managed to get a call out from the post office, so at least Julia, who was expecting our first child, knew exactly what had happened, but Abed's body still had not been recovered. A Lebanese Red Crescent crew went to get him, but decided it was too dangerous to approach the area because the Israelis were still too close. It was hours before a civil defence team managed to pick up his body and take it to the hospital in Tibnin, a small town on a crossroads. By the time I got there, Abed's nephew Ahmed had arrived. As soon as he heard what had happened he drove an ambulance down from Beirut to take Abed's body home; as well as working in the family business, guiding journalists around Lebanon, he had been an ambulance driver during Lebanon's wars. The first thing I said to Ahmed was sorry. I was blaming myself, so I thought Abed's family would be blaming me. He said that they were not.

We walked round to the back of the hospital, past Ahmed's ambulance towards the open door of the mortuary. Abed's body was inside, in a refrigerated stainless-steel drawer. Ahmed told me that his body had not been badly burned or broken by the shell that hit his car. I thought there were unasked questions in what he said, like, how did he die? And how come you survived? Couldn't you have done something to save him? In fact the questions were in my mind, not his.

I tried hard to give it to him straight. I told him what had happened, all the details. Ahmed and I stood talking outside the mortuary where Abed lay in his steel drawer. I had seen many dead bodies, at least hundreds, probably thousands, since the first one in El Salvador in 1989 that was burnt and half-buried in a pit, but never the body of a friend. They would have let me see Abed's body. I sensed that Ahmed was waiting for me to ask as we stood outside the open door of the mortuary at the back of Tibnin hospital, talking about what had happened, staring in at the closed front of the polished stainless-steel drawer where Abed lay. I wish now that I had seen him, but I did not have the courage. I did not kill him but it was my decision to stop the car. If I had not wanted to do a piece to camera there, he might still be alive. I did not kill Abed – an Israeli soldier did – but I will always bear a share of the responsibility, and I will always carry the guilt. Not having the guts to see him dead just makes it worse.

He was buried in Beirut the next day. The mourners gathered at his home, an apartment building in Hamra, in the centre of the city. The women were in the Takkoush family's flat, which takes up the whole of the top floor. The men were downstairs, sitting in white plastic chairs that had been placed in lines around the courtyard behind the building. Neighbours and friends would come, a few of them talking quietly, but mainly sitting in silence, as they do in the Middle East, to show their respects. I had seen gatherings like that dozens of times, filmed them, interviewed the people, accepted their offer of bitter coffee, but the difference this time was that I was not a visitor with a camera and a few questions, but one of the men sitting on the white plastic chairs, and we were there to mourn and bury our friend.

I felt very separate from the rest of them, because I had been there when he was killed and in my own mind I was implicated in what had happened. I felt that they thought I was too, even though they were polite and welcoming. A message came down that Abed's widow Hana would like me to join her upstairs in the flat, where she was sitting with the women, so I could tell them what had happened. It was an invitation I had been expecting and dreading and my stomach was in knots as I got into the lift. Hana and the other women listened as I went through everything with them. She was calm and attentive, asking questions and asking me to repeat some parts of it. Once another woman interrupted, with a cry of pain, asking why I had taken him to such a dangerous place. Hana told her to be quiet. She is a pious Muslim, who has the comfort of her religion's teaching that God decides when we die, and that we cannot change our fate. I envy that belief. Then it was time to bury him.

It was not the first time that I had been to the funeral of a friend and colleague who had been killed. The first one was the BBC's Croatian cameraman Tihomir Tunuković, always called Tuna, who was buried in Zagreb after he was killed in central Bosnia on 1 November 1992. He had been filming Bosnians who had been pushed over the front line by the Serbs, after they had been expelled from their homes. He was on his own when his Land Rover was hit by a round that went straight through its armour and into him. Tuna was a 24-year-old student at film school when he had been hired the previous summer, during the war in Croatia, as a translator. It was not long before he picked up a camera, and he made his name when he drove into a besieged village with Croatian soldiers in a lorry that had been covered in steel plates and turned into a home-made armoured vehicle. Too often in the news business risking your life is a good way to build a reputation. We have all done it. When I joined up with the BBC team in the Intercontinental Hotel in Zagreb less than a year and a half before Tuna was killed, Martin Bell gave me the tape of Tuna's rushes.

'Take a look at that. Incredible.'

The pictures were so vivid that the fear and the adrenaline surged out of them as the soldiers blazed away from firing holes in the armour plating. His microphone distorted at times because it couldn't handle the noise of the firing, but it picked up the sound of bullets thudding into the armour, and of the spent cartridges rattling and bouncing off the steel floor as they poured out of the assault rifles of the men inside. I could imagine being there, the rifle smoke burning my eyes and my ears hurting from the clatter of so many guns firing in a steel box. The pictures made me want to work with Tuna and a bit jealous that I had not been in the lorry too. He survived his own country's war, and decided not to get mixed up in the fighting when it started in Bosnia the following year. He spent the money he had earned from the BBC on a steadicam and decided to make his fortune shooting advertisements and directing films. But then he was tempted back for a guest appearance in Bosnia because the BBC needed someone, and he wanted to see a few old friends. And perhaps he had been infected by the virus of reporting wars too, and found that jobs that can't kill you are easier and safer but not always as beguiling. I saw him in Split, when he was on his way into Bosnia and I was on my way out. He was on good form.

Tuna was popular and charming so there was a big crowd in the bar of the Intercontinental in Zagreb the night before he was buried. We were there for only one reason, but the atmosphere was not sad, at least not among those of us who were still young enough to think that we were indestructible. Instead it was cheerful and raucous and as we got drunker and drunker, there was some madness in the room. How could it have been any other way? We were not prepared to accept what had happened. We felt bulletproof, but here was hard evidence that we were not, that it was just as easy to kill a journalist as it was to kill the people in the Balkans whose bodies we were seeing every day. But I was not ready to face up to the fact that what I was doing could get me killed. I felt detached from what was happening at times in Zagreb that night, as if I was hovering somewhere near the ceiling and watching, and it wasn't the drink, as I felt the same the next day when Tuna was buried.

It only sunk in properly that he had been killed the next morning when I arrived at the cemetery in Zagreb and saw a cross with the name, Tihomir Tunuković, and the dates when he was born and died propped up against a wall and then being carried in front of his coffin to his grave. He was buried in the section that was reserved for national heroes, patriots who were killed in the war of Croatia's independence.

Eight years later, in 2000 in Beirut, Abed Takkoush was given a martyr's funeral in the mosque around the corner from where he lived. I stood outside with Malek as the rest of the male mourners prayed inside. Afterwards, the coffin was carried down the steps and out into the streets of Hamra. A tarboush, the brimless, tasselled hat that used to be worn by men in the Middle East, was put on top of the coffin. Walking fast, they took his coffin down the road and past his home, where the women had come down to the entrance hall and on to the pavement outside. A terrible wailing came from the women at the door and joined up with the men's chant of God is great and bounced and echoed around the narrow canyons of the streets. At the graveyard his three sons, all teenagers, the youngest only just, waited after he was buried to receive the condolences of the mourners. It was a beautiful, breezy spring day, but the air felt clogged. No women were at the burial. The men lined up, shook the boys' hands and kissed their wet cheeks.

I went back to work in south Lebanon. I saw no point in going home to Jerusalem, though the BBC asked me if I wanted to. The Israelis were out of the south. The last man locked the gate behind him. The new flashpoint was around another gate, called Fatima, in a border village that was hard up against the wire. During the occupation, the Israeli army used the Fatima Gate as one of their entry points to the south. I travelled through it with them once, in a convoy of specially converted Mercedes with Lebanese plates that they used to move around commanders, visitors like me and men who were on much more shadowy missions. The cars were mainly from the 1970s, like Abed's old green one, and had what looked like luggage lashed on to roof racks. In fact the cases contained sophisticated electronic equipment, designed to neutralise or detonate Hezbollah's roadside bombs before they could explode. The car moved fast, and inside the driver's door there was a rack to take a short-barrelled M-16 assault rifle. But now that the Israelis had gone, the Lebanese could come right to the gate to throw rocks at the Israeli positions on the other side. The American Palestinian academic Edward Said was photographed throwing a symbolic stone over the wire, embarrassing some of his friends in the chattering classes of New York and London who saw him as the cultivated face of Palestinian liberation. As the days went by the IDF brought in concrete blocks and tons of earth to stop the stones doing any damage. It became a place for day-trippers to bring their children and their parents at the weekends to stare over at Israel, and throw a few stones if they felt defiant. Hezbollah put up a tent where they played liberation songs at deafening volume and sold their own version of snakes and ladders, where bearded men in uniforms went up if they knocked out Israeli tanks, and down again if they were wounded by a bullet from the Zionist hordes.

In the first few days after Israel pulled out, Hezbollah and the Israeli soldiers were eye to eye; when the stone-throwers got too adventurous, the soldiers fired over their heads. It was a good picture story and I went there straight away to do a piece. I was pretty sure that the Israelis were not trying to kill anyone, because if that is what they wanted they could have done so easily, so I wasn't too worried when they opened fire, which they did a couple of times an hour. I also had a strong desire to do a piece to camera with plenty of gunfire in it, which I did. In the standupper I look . . . normal. I made good contact with the camera, and what I said made sense. But I think I can detect now that I was in a dangerous mood. I didn't care what happened at that moment. I felt detached again; neither frightened nor reckless or even angry. Perhaps by exposing myself I wanted to show the BBC management that what had happened to Abed had not stopped me doing my job. Perhaps I wanted to show the Israelis that I wasn't scared of them. Or to show myself that I was still capable of working. God knows. Probably all of them.

After the standupper was done I sat down on a wall to wait to see what happened next, and got talking to a journalist from the Associated Press. He commiserated with me about Abed, and said that for a couple of hours in their office they had thought that I had been killed too. Then, in passing, as if it was old news that I must have heard, he added that it had been a bad few days because of what happened to Kurt and Miguel as well. I knew he must be talking about Kurt Schork and Miguel Gil, two journalist friends I had known in various wars.

'What about them?'

'Christ, you haven't heard. They were killed in Sierra Leone yesterday.'

Miguel was a cameraman for Associated Press TV. When I first met him in Sarajevo he was a freelance, who had given up a career as a lawyer to go to Bosnia, doing some writing, taking pictures and trying to break into television news. He drove round on a motorcycle, with video and stills cameras hanging round his neck. He was a tall, wiry man, very intense, even tortured by his desire to cover the news the right way. Miguel never spoke to me about religion, but he was a devout Catholic, a member of Opus Dei. At his memorial service in London, one of the priests told me that Miguel believed that reporting war was work he could do for God.

A few years after the fighting ended in Bosnia, the next Yugoslav war was in Kosovo. Miguel developed very good contacts with the ethnic Albanian fighters in the Kosovo Liberation Army, who wanted to make their province independent. Once he was with a small group of KLA fighters as they tried to get away from a unit of Serbs that was after them. He came away with the kind of pictures that are only possible in the most dangerous places, as true to what war is like and as exceptional as the ones that Tuna had shot in Croatia in 1991, more claustrophobic than dramatic, showing the men's fear and their desperation as they struggled to catch their breath, to stop the panic rising, to try to find a way out. The Serbs were closing in, and they knew they could expect a bullet if they were captured, and Miguel might have got one too.

About a year before he was killed, I had the chance to join him on a trip over the mountains into Kosovo from northern Albania to link up with the Kosovo Liberation Army. NATO was bombing the Serbs and as far as we knew no journalists were operating behind the lines. But I was doing strong stories with the refugees who were coming out of Kosovo into Albania, and although

I didn't want to recognise it I was already losing my appetite for danger. I decided not to go, though I would still have taken the risk if I hadn't had a better alternative. Vaughan Smith, the cameraman I was working with, was not put off. He had fixed up our part of the trip as, like Miguel, he had good connections with the KLA. We had all based ourselves in Kukës, a flyblown town in the wild mountains of northern Albania of 25,000 or so people, which had been overwhelmed by hundreds of thousands of ethnic Albanian refugees from Kosovo. We hired some of the former Yugoslavs from Kosovo as translators. They were not impressed by their ethnic brothers in poor, primitive northern Albania.

'These people,' one of them shuddered. 'We used to dream about being together with them, but they horrify me. If we ever get home and get a state, we'll build a wall and keep them out. None of them will get in. Not even as folk-dancers.'

But as the sun grew strong, public health experts brought in by aid organisations announced with grim relish that the refugees had brought their own little gift for their hosts: 'faecal dust' from the drying-out human shit in the refugee camps, that was blowing around the town. The experts warned that since nobody in Kukës could avoid breathing in the faecal dust, we should at least try to stop it settling on our food.

I drove Vaughan slowly through the dirty streets that were clogged with refugees to the café where he was meeting Miguel, and his producer and girlfriend Elida Ramadani. Miguel couldn't believe I was not going to join them. I tried to explain how it was not a good use of my time, how we were producing strong stories almost every night in Kukës and at the border, and that I did not want to risk disappearing into Kosovo where it might take weeks to get a story out, and by then it might look more like history than news. I also admitted that I was nervous about the trip. He looked aghast, disbelieving, and hurt. That made it worse, as if I was taking a step back from the top table of news people who will not let a few risks stop them getting at the heart of the story. Elida, who was beautiful, intelligent and brave, eventually married a delightful news producer called Kerem Lawton. He was killed by shelling in 2001, in a village in Kosovo called Krivenik, close to the border with Macedonia. By then Elida was pregnant; Kerem was buried with a scan of his unborn daughter next to his heart.

Kurt Schork had been a friend and colleague since we first met in Iraqi Kurdistan after the 1991 Gulf war. He was living on boiled eggs, a vegetarian in a land of meat-eaters. Kurt and I saw in the New Year of 1992 together in a filthy hotel in Salahaddin, one of the Kurdish towns in northern Iraq, with more boiled eggs, and chicken, chickpeas, whisky and tea. We sat with an affable Kurdish politician called Hoshyar Zabari, who became Iraqi foreign minister in the new Iraq after the Americans and their allies invaded in 2003. Now the Kurds are about as close to independent as you can be without being in the United Nations, and they are among the masters in Iraq, and if he was alive Kurt would probably be spending a lot of time in Baghdad. Kurt was thirteen years older than me, already well into his forties, and had just taken up journalism after a couple of other brilliant careers. He had been a Rhodes Scholar at Oxford University with Bill Clinton, worked in politics with Michael Dukakis, the Massachusetts Democrat who ran for president, run New York City's bridges and tunnels, and made some money in business before he turned to the reporting trade that he had wanted to do all along. I was looking out for Kurt in Kurdistan, because a couple of months earlier I had seen a remarkable account of a massacre he had witnessed in Sulimaniya, of Iraqi prisoners of war by Kurdish peshmerga fighters. This was how he wrote about the killing in a book called *Crimes of War: What the Public Should Know*:

By the time I reached the main building at least seventy-five Iraqi soldiers had been herded into a large room. None was armed or resisting and many appeared to have been wounded in the fighting before it stopped. These prisoners were also shot and killed. Kurds with Kalashnikovs emptied magazine after magazine into what became a bloodsoaked pile of bodies. Some Kurdish non-combatants joined in the slaughter, using blocks of concrete to crush the heads of Iraqi soldiers who had not yet died of their wounds. Within thirty minutes, all the Iraqi soldiers at the location – probably about 125 – were dead.

I admired the fact that he was an eyewitness, and the spare language he used about the killing. When events are dramatic, it is best to use plain words and to let what happens speak for itself. In Bosnia, where he arrived a couple of weeks before me when the war started in the early summer of 1992, he was the most prominent foreign journalist, reporting on the war's brutalities and on the contradictions, absurdities and occasional successes of the international response to it. He campaigned for truth and his example made the rest of us better journalists. Once he asked Barry Frewer, the Canadian spokesman for the UN in Sarajevo, what sounded like an innocent, straightforward question: 'Would you say that Sarajevo is under siege?' Self-evidently it was. But Kurt had heard that the UN was trying to spin away from using the word. Frewer would not give a straight answer, and other journalists, like dogs smelling blood, harried the luckless man into saying things like, 'You call it a siege. We say they [the Serbs] are deployed in a tactically advantageous position.'

Outside the morning briefings, Kurt spent his time relentlessly chasing down stories around the battered city, and also pizzas, which as a vegetarian he could eat. He was balding, bespectacled and intense. That first summer in Sarajevo in 1992 bit deep into him, tying him to the war and to the place and to the fact that hundreds of thousands of innocent Europeans were dying in the worst bloodshed in their continent since 1945.

'War reporting is a privilege,' he once wrote. 'After three years, the grime and gore of combat, the dreadful logic of ethnic hatred are no longer abstractions for me. More important, every day, I see the grace and dignity of ordinary people trying to survive under extraordinary circumstances.'

After Kurt was killed the Bosnian government renamed the road from the airport to the town after him, appropriately since that was where journalists coming into Sarajevo ran the gauntlet of Serb snipers. Some of his ashes were buried in the Lion Cemetery, and his friends subscribed to a fountain that was put there in his memory.

I was horrified to hear that Kurt and Miguel were dead, but I was not surprised. They were men who were driven, in different ways, to report the news, and they went to very dangerous places very often. As far as I know Miguel and Kurt were not reckless on the day they were killed, at least not by the strange logic of war journalists, as Abed, Malek and I had not thought ourselves reckless in south Lebanon. By most other people's logic, it was highly dangerous to be in south Lebanon or Sierra Leone that particular week, but that was what we did and we thought that knowing what is happening in the worst places in the world was necessary. So the only thing any of us could have done, to stay true to our view of journalism, was to be there, to push a bit harder, to drive a few more miles down the road.

Like me, Miguel had been getting more cautious. The last time I saw him, not long before he was killed, was at the annual dinner of the Royal Television Society in London, where he was being named cameraman of the year. He had just been in Grozny, which he told me was the worst time of his career, with so much shelling it was often impossible to work. When Chechen fighters led him through the front line to get into Grozny, they went within a few yards of the Russian positions. Don't worry, they told him, the boys in the bunkers are more frightened than you are, and they'll never dare to fire. When another friend and colleague, the Reuters cameraman Mark Chisholm, arrived in Sierra Leone, Miguel made a point of telling him how dangerous the place was; and all the close calls made him say something Chisholm thought was strange: 'One of two things will happen on this story. One of us will get the big scoop of fighting pictures, or one of us will get killed.' Mark and Yannis Behrakis, a Reuters photographer, were with Kurt and Miguel and a group of Sierra Leonean soldiers when they were ambushed. After Kurt and Miguel and the soldiers were killed, Mark and Yannis, who were both wounded, escaped by crawling for hours through the undergrowth.

Until Abed, Miguel and Kurt were killed I still felt, some of the time, as indestructible as I had been in El Salvador eleven years earlier. After they died, I lost any idea of immortality. It was a youthful illusion, but I had hung on to it, and at the age of forty I realised properly that what I had learned from wars – that life is insecure, and time is short – applied to me and my friends as well, not just other people. I felt calm, but subconsciously I must have been reeling. Sitting on that wall after I did my standupper at the Fatima Gate, with the Israelis firing spasmodically over the heads of the crowd, was the beginning of something new. At last, I was ready to accept that time in war zones is a numbers game. The more you do it, the more likely you are to be wounded or to get killed. It is matter of statistics, not experience. If you are sitting in your car, as Abed was, and the crew of a tank you can't even see has you in its sights and decides to kill you, then you will die. Everyone who goes voluntarily into a war zone needs to know and understand that their adventure could kill them.

Back home in Jerusalem I had meetings with various Israeli generals about Abed's death. They said that the soldiers in the tank had thought that we were Hezbollah fighters – 'terrorists' – who were carrying an anti-tank weapon and were about to attack them. I tried to point out that if Hezbollah always started their operations by parking a Mercedes in full view of Israeli positions in broad daylight, then walking down a road waving at the Israelis on the other side of the border wire, Israel would never have had to end its occupation. Zvi Stauber, an adviser to the Israeli Prime Minister, told me that there were some young soldiers in the tank, not long out of school, who were terrified about what could happen to them. He wanted me to feel sorry for the men who killed Abed, and tried to kill Malek and me. At another meeting, an Israeli general tried to shout us down when Julia and I dared to try to discuss his version of what had happened. He was enraged that we were not going to nod, accept his explanation, shake his hand and let bygones be bygones. He said, barely able to contain his rage, that I did not realise what it was like to live under the constant threat of attack. Julia and I could see that they were not prepared to listen, and ended the meeting. Israel's refusal to address the killing of Abed in any serious way left all sorts of unanswered questions. If they thought that Malek and I were Hezbollah fighters when we left the car, about to attack, why not shoot us first? Why did they hit the car instead?

The BBC did its own investigation. It collected video from the Jerusalem-based camera teams who were on the Israeli side of the border wire. The pictures showed clearly that for around twenty-four hours the Israelis had been opening fire on cars that were moving on the Lebanese side. Several of them were moving away from the direction in which the Israelis were retreating. When I saw the pictures I couldn't help wondering what might have been said if the pictures had been of Serbian tanks doing something similar in Kosovo a year earlier. A vision of Madeleine Albright, who was then the US Secretary of State, presenting the pictures at a news conference ran through my mind. Amnesty International also investigated what happened. It said that at least four times on 22 and 23 May Israeli troops fired tank shells across the border at Lebanese civilians, killing four people, including Abed, and wounding several others.

Amnesty's report said that 'if these attacks were indeed wilfully directed at civilians, the Israeli army has committed war crimes and those responsible should be brought to justice . . . These killings happened after the withdrawal of the IDF and the SLA when there was no hostile military action and many Lebanese civilians were on the move celebrating the withdrawal and the return to their villages. These people all appear to have been targeted without warning.' The day before we were there, Amnesty found, some armed men, as well as hundreds of civilians, including many children, had been driving or walking along the road celebrating the Israeli withdrawal and the return of villagers to south Lebanon. Witnesses told them that a tank shell destroyed a Mercedes, killing a local man, 22-year-old Abd al-Karim Assaf from Mays al-Jabal, and wounding five others. Shortly afterwards another shell exploded near a pickup truck which was approaching the burning Mercedes, killing Ibrahim Maruni, a sixteen-year-old boy.

The video collected by the BBC in Jerusalem, filmed from kibbutz Manara, showed the attacks clearly. The pictures also show a group of Israeli civilians, including children, watching what was happening from the café at the kibbutz. Next to them, an Israeli officer is talking on the radio to the commander of the

265

tank. Invariably, when IDF soldiers believe that an attack is coming, they order Israeli civilians to take cover. Why didn't they this time, if they were certain we were going to try to kill them? Later on the same day another Lebanese man, Salman Rammal, was driving a bulldozer that was removing a roadblock which had been abandoned by Israel's mercenary force, the South Lebanon Army. Dozens of people were celebrating around him when he was killed by another tank shell.

When we stopped just before Abed was killed, I had seen the wreckage of a burnt-out car. It must have been the Mercedes of Abd al-Karim Assaf from Mays al-Jabal. Because the wreckage was cold, I assumed it was a sign that the war had moved down the road and was now somewhere else. We knew from the car radio that the Israelis had almost completed their withdrawal, so I estimated they were at least thirty minutes ahead of us. I think I was about right, but only as far as the Lebanese side of the wire was concerned. It did not occur to me that the Israelis would open fire across the border. The BBC investigators, who were former military people, found the spot where the Israeli tank had been positioned. It was only 1,200 metres from the place where we stopped to film.

The killing of Abed Takkoush by the IDF created a lot of bad publicity for Israel. Abed was popular and good at his job, and newspapers around the world ran the news of what had happened. Reporters who had worked with Abed had their own stories about him. In the *Washington Post*, for example, Doug Struck wrote about what happened: 'It was a simple assassination, a last-minute potshot by a gunner in defeat.' The IDF issued a statement with their side of the story. I thought it was full of inconsistencies. It said it had laid down 'interdictory fire at suspicious vehicles travelling in its direction'. But no vehicles were travelling in its direction. The tank was on a security road in Israel. The Lebanese civilian vehicles, including ours, were on a recognised road in Lebanon. The border wire was in between. The statement said that 'at 12:32 the tank crew observed a suspicious vehicle carrying individuals in civilian clothing and suspected that they were members of a terrorist Lebanese group carrying equipment and preparing for an anti-tank missile firing against IDF tanks'. My watch said the shooting happened at noon, give or take a couple of minutes. Their failure to get even the time right throws doubt on the accuracy of the IDF records and suggests more questions than it answers. Why were the IDF tank crew reporting our presence half an hour after they opened fire? If they could see that we were wearing civilian clothing, why couldn't they see our camera gear? And if they could see what I was wearing, surely they could see me waving my arms at the kibbutz on the Israeli side of the wire, wondering if any of my friends in Israel would be able to spot me through their lenses?

The fact is that we were not behaving like a squad of Hezbollah fighters. Over many years, and after hard lessons inflicted by the IDF, Hezbollah worked out how to fight an effective guerrilla war. They used cover and surprise and night attacks to great effect. It is simply not convincing to say we were suspicious and therefore legitimate targets.

All the evidence suggested in fact that the IDF tank crew did not think they were under attack from experienced Hezbollah guerrillas. I think it shows that they thought they were dealing with defenceless Lebanese civilians. Over twenty-five years, the IDF had shown that to protect their own people they were prepared to kill Lebanese civilians in disproportionate numbers. I saw it most vividly in Qana in south Lebanon on 18 July 1996, when Israel shelled a base of UN peacekeeping troops and killed 106 local people who had gone there because they thought it would be safer than their villages, which were also being shelled. A few weeks before the massacre, I had sat in the Ministry of Defence in Tel Aviv, in the office of Uri Lubrani, Israel's co-ordinator of policy in Lebanon. He boasted that Israel's intelligence was so good that it knew every house in south Lebanon and everyone who lived in them. Yet after Qana one of the explanations put forward by Israel for killing so many civilians was that its maps were wrong, an idea disputed by Timor Goksul, the political adviser to UNIFIL, the UN peacekeeping force. Echoing what Lubrani had said to me, Goksul told *Time* magazine that when Israeli troops were pulling out of parts of south Lebanon in 1985, 'We saw them videotaping every building and street' in Qana and other villages.

There were other inconsistencies in Israel's explanation. Until an amateur videotape proved otherwise, they denied that one of their drones, pilotless aircraft that can transmit live pictures, was in the area. And there was an air of callousness in the way that Israel blithely said that a regrettable mistake had been made. Ari Shavit, a columnist in Israel's leading liberal newspaper, *Ha'aretz*, picked up the mood. 'How easily we killed them [in Qana] without shedding a tear,' he wrote. 'We did not denounce the crime, did not arrange for a legal clarification, because this time we tried to deny the abominable horror and move on.' The Lebanese were not surprised that Israel valued the lives of its people above the lives of theirs; after all, they were enemies. But they were struck hard yet again by the way that Israel's allies, led by the United States, seemed to them to feel the same way. In the UN base in Qana on the day of the massacre, when the buildings were still on fire and troops were still picking up body parts, I asked an Irish officer what would have happened had the Lebanese shelled northern Israel and killed more than 100 Israeli civilians. He smiled grimly. 'President Clinton would be at the funeral, we'd be in our shelters and the Israelis would be in Beirut.'

Cold Turkey

Abed drove us down to Qana that day in 1996. Four years later the Israelis said about him too, in paragraph six of their statement on his killing, that 'a tragic mistake had been made'. I do not believe it was a mistake. I think the evidence the BBC and Amnesty collected shows clearly that on the day Abed was killed and the day before, Israel had been firing at civilian cars to try to close the road. They had been surprised by the thousands of civilians who had heard the news that the Israelis were leaving and who flooded into what was becoming Israel's former occupation zone. Some of them were locals, who had not been able until then to get to their home villages. But many others were sightseers, who wanted to check for themselves that the hated occupation was ending. The civilians were increasing the pressure on the SLA and the IDF, complicating things, and perhaps offering a chance for Hezbollah to move more freely. Israel wanted to keep them back, well away from their troops, until they were safely out of Lebanon. The evidence suggests that the tactic they chose was to attack a few vehicles to scare the Lebanese off the roads.

The death of Abed – and Kurt and Miguel's deaths as well – took a lot out of me. I stayed in Lebanon, doing more stories. Every time I slept I had drab, grey nightmares. In the one that came most, everyone I knew and loved died one after the other. In another I stood at a trap door and without feeling anything, killed everyone who came through it. A colleague saw me trying to behave as if nothing was happening, getting on with my job, being normal, on the outside anyway, and even cheerful. She took me aside and told me how she had been in a car in Central America that was shot up and the other passengers were killed. Afterwards she tried to get on with life, and would not accept that the experience had left a mark. By the time she worked out that something was wrong, it took a long time to fix. She told me very strongly not to fool myself that I could watch Abed being killed and then treat the experience like a bad day at the office. Before Abed's death, witnessing violence had never stopped me getting on with what I had to do. But now I could not sleep without bad dreams, and I could not walk down the road without flinching at loud noises and feeling that something terrible was about to happen. The BBC gave me the name of a counsellor in London. Paddington Station was covered with scaffolding when I got off the train from Heathrow airport. I found myself getting ready to dodge falling masonry, or tools that the builders might have dropped. In the taxi queue, I started thinking about what would happen if a bomb went off, looking for routes out of the blast area, wondering about first aid. Abed's death also kept replaying itself in my head.

Before he was killed, plenty of things I had seen had made me sad. Usually they were to do with the survivors of violence. Piles of dead bodies are tragic, but there is nothing to be done for them. Once there was a girl of about ten in the main hospital in Sarajevo who had been wounded by a shell. She had a nasty wound in her face, but she could walk and all she was worried about was consoling her mother, who was on a stretcher about to go into surgery. By the standards of the siege, they had a lucky escape. The mother was going to survive, was not even going to have an amputation. But the few paces the girl took across the hall to her mother, and the way she cradled her head, said so much about love and the spirit that humans have even at the worst of times that I have never forgotten them. But although that scene touched me deeply, it did not stop me functioning.

Neither, until Abed was killed, did more personal violence. In Albania in the spring of 1999 I was with a team that was robbed by masked and hooded men with Kalashnikovs. We were on the way out of Bayram Curi, which must be the most lawless town in Europe, where schoolboys drive round in stolen cars and everyone keeps a gun somewhere close. Its only hotel was called the Smell of the Mountains, though it smelled more of the communal latrines on each landing. The hotel's big selling point was that it was protected by Albanian special forces. The first night we stayed there a loud gunshot came from the lobby. One of the soldiers, on guard duty, had managed accidentally to shoot himself through the toe. It was not an impressive performance. Vaughan Smith and I barricaded the door of the room we were sharing with boxes of heavy camera gear and flak jackets.

A couple of days later we were ambushed on the way out of town. The masked men fired over the cars, and one of them stuck the barrel of his Kalashnikov into the car so close to my face that I could see the barrel was still smoking. Bayram Curi was so lawless that I thought that they could easily have shot us and forgotten about it by lunchtime. They took all Vaughan's camera gear (which was brand-new, as he had just replaced everything that had been stolen by the federal Yugoslav army in Montenegro while we were working together there the previous month). The flak jackets went too, and a big part of my roll of German marks. I managed to keep some of it hidden. A few minutes after they had sped off with our stuff in their vehicle, one of our drivers, a local man with criminal connections (there were no others in Bayram Curi) started waving the Kalashnikov he kept on the front seat, which he had theatrically cocked when the highwaymen attacked us, though I never thought he would use it as it was clear that he was in league with them. He shouted something about needing money for protecting us from an even worse fate, stopped the car, turned round and pointed the weapon at my chest. I realised he wanted anything that the robbers had left behind, including the remains of my cash. To make matters worse, while he raked in his loot he handed the gun, which was still cocked and ready to shoot, to his nephew, a boy of about ten, who was in the car too. He was talking about taking us back into Bayram Curi, at gunpoint, when a patrol of Albanian special forces came past. They scared off the villainous driver, turned round and drove back into Bayram Curi without us. Luckily we had another, more trustworthy driver, a man from Kukës, the local big town. His car had not been taken, he said, because the Bayram Curi boys knew that he would then be honour-bound to return with his brothers, his cousins and their guns. Afterwards I decided never to go to Bayram Curi again, but there were no other lasting effects.

The robbery was alarming when it happened, and shook me up for a day or two, but compared with the death of Abed it was a joke. The counsellor I saw in London told me that I had the symptoms of post-traumatic stress disorder. Even the feeling that something bad was always about to happen was part of it, something called hyper-vigilance. But so far all I had were symptoms. I did not have a full-blown case of PTSD. Everything that I had been experiencing, he said, was a normal reaction to extreme stress, a sort of mental bruise. As long as I faced up to what had happened, talked about it, and did not try to shove it to the back of my mind or, even worse, right out of it, then the nightmares and the other problems ought to go away in a month or six weeks. If they did not, I would have PTSD.

I started feeling better quite quickly. I was lucky because I had been forced to face up to what was happening very early on, and I saw an expert and started to work it out before too much damage was done. Seeing a counsellor, talking about what had happened, realising what I was suffering from, helped me a lot. The traditional way for journalists to deal with stress is to go to the bar to get drunk with people who had seen and done the same things. It is not a bad approach, and it worked for me for years. But sometimes it is not enough.

★

Everything was changing. A couple of weeks before Abed was killed, I had found out that I was going to be a father for the first time. I had also accepted a job as presenter of *Breakfast*, BBC1's early morning programme. As I stood watching Abed's car burn I found myself thinking that I had made the right decision to leave the Middle East. Malek and I survived and Abed did not; it was just chance, and could easily have been the other way round. When Malek and I got out, Abed stayed in the car because he was on the phone to his son. Until a couple of minutes before we pulled up I had been on the phone as well. Had I not finished my conversation, I might have been sitting in the car when the shell hit it. Finishing the phone call saved my life and meant that my unborn daughter had the chance of having a father.

I was filming a documentary at Petra, the ancient capital of the Nabateans in the Jordanian desert, when I agreed to present *Breakfast*. I stood looking up at the way that centuries of wind and sand had softened the carvings in the rock until they were polished and smooth, while the BBC voice at the other end explained how, after weeks of talking, they had improved the deal and now I had no reason to say no. It seemed crazy to turn down a job as a presenter on BBC1. So I said yes.

On the drive back to Jerusalem that night I sat in the back of the taxi and watched the desert and the Bedouins and the lights of the city getting closer and thought I did not want to leave any of it, but it seemed foolish to stay. I had been in Jerusalem for five years and on the road for nearly fifteen, and it was time to do something else. Reporting had become a huge comfort zone. The job was not stretching me any more. Presenting would, and it might open more doors than I was closing. I was flattered that they wanted me, and I had enjoyed presenting when I tried it out a couple of years earlier. Vanity was another factor. I was curious to know what it felt like to be recognised by more people, to be a face that spent hours on people's television sets and not just a few minutes in a news report. But even after I said yes I had some big doubts about whether I was doing the right thing, and in the four months or so that I had left before we had to go back to London, I kept trying mentally to write a letter to Tony Hall, the boss of BBC News, telling him why I couldn't present *Breakfast*.

But it kept coming down to the fact that I just did not want to leave what I was doing, and that did not seem like a good enough excuse. Leaving was the right thing to do, but I was addicted to the constant drama of life in the middle of the conflict between Israel and the Arabs, which was coming to a head again, and our life in Jerusalem was happy. President Clinton was orchestrating peace moves and I was desperate for them to work, not just because I wanted the people of the region to have better lives. That would have been a fine outcome, but what really bothered me was that I would not be there to do the story if it got violent again. In the summer of 2000, the Israeli papers carried grim predictions from the IDF about the chances of a guerrilla war in the West Bank. Palestinians, often calm on the outside, talked about the rage they felt inside. On another beautiful summer morning in Jerusalem I was getting ready to go to work, ironing a shirt, when I heard on the radio that the Camp David summit between Israel and the Palestinians had failed. In my head I had another go at writing the imaginary letter to Tony Hall. I had no idea what would happen next, but it did not feel good. I tried to think of ways that they would work it out so that they would keep on talking about peace. I looked on the bright side so hard that I ignored the signs of what was coming.

So we left Jerusalem, on 20 September 2000. The first week was fine. Being back in London was fun. We were looking for a house. Julia's pregnancy was going well and we had a lot of reasons to be happy. Then, on 28 September, Ariel Sharon, the juggernaut of the Israeli right wing, strode into the compound around the al-Aqsa mosque and the Dome of the Rock in Jerusalem, protected by one thousand Israeli policemen. A riot started, and people were getting killed. For the first few days, I hoped it would exhaust itself. I did not want a war when I was not there to cover it. I did not want the people I worked with in Jerusalem to have to do it without me. But the violence and the killing spread all over the West Bank and Gaza. Then, on the following Saturday, I was walking through Richmond to watch London Welsh play rugby when George Alagiah, who was presenting the evening news on the BBC, rang me to say it looked very serious. Had it been anyone other than George, I would have suspected he was rubbing my nose in it. He just thought I ought to know. It was every correspondent's nightmare. A huge story on my patch, and I wasn't there. In fact it wasn't my patch any more, but that didn't seem to matter much.

The thing about being an addict, or being in love, is that it is very painful when your drug, or your lover, is taken away. Over the eleven years since I had first been in a war zone, news reporting – especially in difficult or dangerous places – had become much more than a job. It was a passion, a big part of how I identified myself. I loved being on the circuit, knowing that if a big or violent story broke in the Middle East or anywhere else for that matter I had a good chance of going and that when I walked into the hotel where journalists were staying I would know at least half the people in the place. My appetite for risking my life had been diminishing for some time, as I was finding it harder to avoid making the connection that it meant that you had a chance of ending up dead. Still, I thought I had learned ways of cutting the risks and I told myself that even at the very beginning in El Salvador, when I was high on adrenaline, I was never stupid.

Now all of it was gone. I was in a pitiful condition in the first few months of the Palestinian uprising at the end of 2000, dog-tired from trying to adapt to the insane hours of morning television, high on self-pity, mad and getting madder watching other reporters doing what I thought was my story. I would get up at 3.30 in the morning, stand in the shower like a zombie until just before the car came at 4 to take me to work. If the programme was not leading on the Middle East, I was relieved. If it was, I would walk down from the newsroom to the studio raging, dreading having to do interviews with reporters fresh out of London who did not know much about the story, so frustrated I was, literally, kicking at the walls. The cleaners, who were about the only people around that early in the morning, ignored me.

Someone in *The Times* wrote an unkind but accurate piece about my deficiencies as a presenter. Sophie Raworth, who had to sit next to me on television every morning, is a very good pre-senter, and she was very tolerant, understood me far too well and did a lot to keep me from completely self-destructing on air. At times I felt like walking out of the studio. The worst single moment was when I woke in the afternoon from the unrestful sleep that morning TV presenters sometimes find themselves slid-ing into, feeling terrible and not knowing at first where I was, what time it was and whether I should be getting up to go to work or going off to find a late lunch. I turned on the radio to hear the familiar voice of the Palestinian negotiator, Saeb Erekat, shouting that the Israelis were using missiles fired from helicopters to attack them. Very soon afterwards it became common, not even newsworthy, but it was the first time that it was happening. Something snapped and I phoned Tony Hall, demanding to be sent back to Jerusalem, at least for a few days. And back I went, the next day. My brother Nicholas and his wife had gone to a lot of trouble to organise a welcome-home party which I kicked into touch, unceremoniously. But when I arrived in Jerusalem, and realised that other people were doing what I used to do more than adequately, and that of course I would be presenting *Breakfast* and not reporting the news, that it wasn't going to be as if I had never left, Jerusalem was the last place I wanted to be. I lay on my bed in my hotel room on the Saturday when we were supposed to have been celebrating our return home, exhausted as usual, with nothing to do because we were not on the air until Monday, feeling guilty, embarrassed and ridiculous.

Back in London, I still found it hard to have a job that was just a job and not an obsession. Foreign correspondents feel they are indispensable. They think that if they are not there to cover the news, the story will be incomplete and their newspaper or broadcast will not be as good without them. They get twitchy about being out of touch, or too far away from their patch. They are never off-duty. Presenting was different. When the programme was over, you were free to go until it was time to turn up again for your next shift. I found it very hard to go from indispensable to dispensable. But once my daughter Mattie was born in January 2001 I started to come to my senses. Julia was very ill after the birth and could have died. I realised that there were other things in life than getting on to aeroplanes to fly off to report the news. It was something I had never questioned from the moment I joined the BBC. But it was obvious. Gradually, I realised I was very lucky to be able to get home by about 10.30 in the morning to see my new daughter. And so what if I had to go to bed at 8 in the evening? By then I was exhausted anyway.

I started to enjoy working in the studio with Sophie. The BBC's body-language expert (yes, there is one), an enthusiastic American called Carla Hargis, helped a lot. She showed me better ways of picking up my cues, and how to sit and turn more easily so that I looked more natural on camera. I stopped missing being on the road. I started to like being a presenter and became quite good in the studio. But it is not easy to work the appalling hours of morning TV unless you're an insomniac, or have an American-style salary that is as insane as the hours you have to do, so after two years I gave it up.

Then my old life, my old addictions, started bubbling up again. At the beginning of 2003 I agreed to go to Baghdad to be the main TV correspondent in the coming war with Iraq. It was tempting. Since 1990 I had been to Iraq many times. Not many of those who were going to be at the war of 2003 had also seen the previous war and all the sanctions and bombings in between. I had. But everything had changed since I had sat in my room in Jordan in 1991, with an Iraqi visa in my passport, getting ready to go into Baghdad and writing some last letters to my parents and my girl-friend. Baghdad was going to be dangerous. Mattie, our daughter, had just had her second birthday and Julia was pregnant with a child who I knew already would be a son. What was I going to write for them if I didn't come back? Sorry, kids, but Daddy's career needed a shot in the arm so he thought he would go off to Baghdad and you're reading this because he got a shot in the head instead?

It was two years since I had stepped off the news conveyor belt and all my symptoms – for war reporting as well as post-traumatic stress – were long gone. I had just taken six months' unpaid leave to finish off a book, and to play with my daughter and cook meals for her. I had found that it was possible to live a very acceptable life not going from story to story and not going to wars. Besides, I had already done a war in Baghdad, at a time when it really mattered to my career and when nobody was relying on me. It seemed self-indulgent, excessive, to do another. The difference was not just my children. There were my dead friends and col-leagues – Abed Takkoush, dead in Lebanon. Kurt and Miguel in Sierra Leone, Rory Peck dead in Russia, Tihomir Tunuković in Bosnia, Julio Fuentes in Afghanistan . . . and all the others. It was a long list, of people who were as passionate about their jobs as I had been, who had once thought that they were indestructible, and even convinced others that they might be, and then found out too late that they were not.

I decided I didn't want to do the job. Turning down a story, especially one as big as the war in Baghdad, still felt very wrong. It went against every journalistic instinct I had, but they were being cancelled out by something that was much more powerful. It took a lot more agonising before I had the guts to ring the foreign editor Jonathan Baker to tell him. I felt physically sick before I made the call. I did not want to let them down, and I found it hard to accept that I was a different person. He was very decent about it, did not try to make me change my mind and when I put the phone down I still felt sick but I was relieved. It was the right decision, for me, at that moment. Before I had signed up for Baghdad I had been offered a very pleasant-sounding rear-echelon berth, with a lot of guaranteed air time, some desert camping, and very little chance of being shot at. Unfortunately that slot was now occupied, so Jonathan told me I was not going to be anywhere in the starting line-up. I could hardly argue, and didn't.

When the war started, it was not easy watching my colleague Rageh Omaar doing the job that I had been supposed to do. I did a few things in London, but I was not part of the war in the field. When ITN's Terry Lloyd was killed I did not think that I had been wiser to stay at home and that he had done the wrong thing by going. People need to do what is right for them at a particular time. I just felt depressed that another person I knew was dead. I had always respected Terry's work. We were good colleagues rather than big pals, and we had spent some evenings in the bar of the American Colony hotel in Jerusalem.

Since then, others I knew have been killed: Paul Moran, an Australian cameraman who was charitable enough to the Poms to send me a tape after we had worked together of Ian Botham's Ashes triumph, was killed by a suicide car bomb in northern Iraq in March 2003; Kaveh Golestan, BBC cameraman in Tehran, was killed by a mine, also in northern Iraq in April 2003; Mazen Dana, a Reuters cameraman I used to stand next to during afternoons of stone-throwing in Hebron on the West Bank in the 1990s, a big man you could rely on, who liked a joke, was shot by an American soldier outside Abu Ghraib in August 2003. Another cameraman, Paul Douglas of CBS News, who I knew from Sarajevo, was killed by a bomb along with his soundman James Brolan in Baghdad in May 2006, and the correspondent they were working with was badly hurt.

I wanted to go to Paul's funeral, but I could not face it. He was killed while I was in Beirut, where the BBC was opening a new office. Local television was there, and around fifty guests. I was asked to say a few words about Abed, to launch a new training scheme for local journalists that had been named after him. I had to cut short what I was saying when I broke down. I had felt very calm before I started. I had written about his death, and talked about it, in public, and on television, many times. I had also spoken, lots of times, about the ways it affected me, all without crying or even getting close to it. But being in Beirut, and seeing his youngest son Tariq in the audience, and Ahmed Itani who came to get Abed's body from the hospital at Tibnin, and remembering what it had been like to work with him, brought all of the emotion back. Part of it was the guilt I still have about not just surviving, but walking away without a scratch. Part of it was seeing Tariq, who was deprived of his father when he was barely a teenager because I had decided to stop to film, which gave the Israeli who killed him the chance, or excuse, to load a shell into the gun on his tank and fire it into the back of his Mercedes.

Cold Turkey

That night we had a big dinner at one of Beirut's excellent restaurants, and drinks in its bar, which has a roof and walls that slide open so the breeze from the sea and the city lights come to join in as well. Beirut was looking prosperous. The hotels were starting to fill up with Arabs from the Gulf with oil money to spend. They were hoping for the best summer since the 1970s, before the civil war.

I had no idea that only a little more than a month later I would be back in Beirut, to cover another major war with Israel.

10

Lebanon, 2006

Whoever built the Rest House in Tyre had big ideas for the future. It is in a beautiful spot, the first development on an unspoilt stretch of the Mediterranean at the southern end of Tyre, at one end of a great sweep of sand that runs along a bay at least ten miles wide. When I say unspoilt, I mean that this is a corner of the Mediterranean that has not been colonised by the tourist industry. In most other senses of the word, for thirty years war has been spoiling everything in south Lebanon, which is why the Rest House is not just the first, but its only beach playground. In the summer of 2006 the Rest House was a weird and screwed-up holiday camp, sucked into the strange parallel universe of the international news media, there for the new war, which was really a continuation of the old one.

The border with Israel was hidden from the Rest House by the headland at the other end of the bay, but you could hear and see quite a bit of what the Israelis were doing in the war, and what the Hezbollah fighters were doing to them. Israeli warplanes were in the sky most of the time, dropping bombs, and, occasionally, leaflets, which shimmered down to the ground, usually warning civilians to get out or get killed. Sometimes explosions came in from the villages a couple of times a minute for hours at a stretch. Much less often would come a different kind of bang, sonic booms caused by Hezbollah rockets as they went towards Israel. Four or five would be fired at a time, leaving streams of vapour, like a giant fork prodding the sky.

The BBC had a series of rooms in one of the wings of the Rest House, facing the sea. You could almost call them vacation cabanas, except for the sweat-sodden flak jackets drying in the sun outside them, and the four-wheel drives with 'TV' marked on them with tape. We plotted our day's work around a plastic beach table on a stretch of grass under a palm tree, and in the evenings drank beer around it after I had finished with the last feed of the day, usually a live one for the BBC's *Ten O'Clock News*, which went out at midnight local time. At the other end of the lawn, without beer but tolerant about ours, was the team from Hezbollah's television station, al-Manar, well-behaved, youngish men with beards, who spent every evening talking quietly and smoking fruit-scented tobacco from hubbly-bubbly water-pipes.

The Rest House sprawled along a beach that was still littered with white plastic sunbeds and coloured umbrellas. The strangest thing about it was that, while the war was going on around Tyre, the Rest House felt like a neutral zone, safe in its parallel media universe. It was an illusion. If Hezbollah's fighters had wanted to launch missiles from its shabby, parched grounds, they would not have hesitated, and neither would the Israelis, if they had a strong reason to bomb it. But since the boys from al-Manar, who presumably had connections with their colleagues who were firing the missiles, were happy to sit back smoking their shisha, the Rest House felt like a fine place to be.

Just down the way from us, next to a parade of closed-up

restaurants and shops that had once sold T-shirts and beach toys, were lines of generators and satellite trucks that beamed pictures out across the world. Sometimes loud music came out of the trucks, with bass notes that mingled with the booms rolling in off the hills. The pool deck had been taken as a live position, because it was a little raised up and it backed on to the beach and the escarpment that lay between Tyre and the Israeli border. Quite often, explosions rose up behind the reporters speaking live, and they would try to direct their camera to zoom in on the puffs of smoke, though it was hard to get the sound because of the noise made by more than a dozen people broadcasting simultaneously. Fox News set up their headquarters below the deck where the live shots were happening, in an empty sunken paddling pool. Down on the beach newsmen and women who had either spent the day at the live position, or outside the strange world of the Rest House with the wounded, displaced and distraught, or watching stinking, maggoty bodies being buried, would sit down under a palm tree, or take a dip in the Mediterranean.

I had the chance to check out my old addiction, my old love, during the summer's war. I am glad to say that the war drug, my fine old romance, has not put its hooks back in. I know that because I found myself struggling to do things that were once so routine that they would not have taken a second thought. While I was in Tyre it was too dangerous to go further south, into the border villages. I tried to illustrate the fact in a standupper by going to the southern side of town and explaining what was happening down the road, and why it was not a good idea to go any further. That was when I knew that I could not do the job the way that I used to, and did not want to either.

A few hundred yards from where the houses ended there was a big crater in the road, with the wreckage of a car half-buried in it. It would have made a nice, warlike background for what I was planning to say. But even on the edge of Tyre, I felt uncomfortable, and exposed. The whole time an Israeli pilotless drone was buzzing around the sky, watching, looking for targets, sending back information to its controllers in Israel, information I kept thinking was about us, how we might want to kill them, and how they'd better kill us first.

'Don't worry mate,' said Craig Summers, one of the BBC's security advisers, a big, sensible bloke, who had been doing the driving. 'It's fine here.' Somewhere in my brain I was gobsmacked that he thought I was in need of reassurance. Me? I was always the one who did the reassuring. But I must have looked twitchy, because instead of the war drug I seemed to be having a dose of the fear virus, which had never been a problem in the past. Hanging around next to that shell-hole did not seem at all fine to me, so we went back into town, the piece to camera undone. The theory was that if we drove slowly the Israeli drones or helicopters would see the TV markings on the roof of the car and leave us alone. But I kept thinking about the Israeli generals explaining after Abed was killed how their soldiers thought the camera and the tripod was some sort of weapon. Even when they accepted that they had killed the wrong man, and expressed regret at his family's loss, they never once said that they were wrong to take the shot. Their story was that we were terrorists, and even after they agreed that we were not, what mattered at the Ministry of Defence in Tel Aviv was that, however fleetingly or incorrectly, we had been terrorists in the minds of their soldiers.

We did the piece at a junction further into Tyre, less photogenic, and probably no more safe. I still didn't feel very good being there. While we were filming a big BMW came roaring up the empty road from the south. It was marked 'TV' and inside was a reporting team wearing flak jackets and looking tense. A big part of front-line reporting will always come down to the desire of the journalists to go further down the road, closer to where the story is, and closer to the places where it is easy to die. The grim, sweaty faces of the men in the BMW suggested that they had been far enough down the road, perhaps a bit too far, for one day. I looked at them and thought, that would have been me once.

Because of all the times I drove around south Lebanon with Abed Takkoush, I know the place well. I was only in Tyre for a short time, to get a feel for how it had changed. I spent most of my Lebanese war in Beirut, watching from a distance as the Israelis tried to use shock and awe, air strikes right out of the US Air Force's 2003 Iraq playbook, to try to destroy Hezbollah's stronghold in the southern suburbs of the city. They smashed the buildings but in Beirut Hezbollah, as an organisation, was barely scratched. After ten days or so of bombing, Hezbollah's public relations officer called our office to say that we would be allowed to visit the heart of the southern suburbs. I was working with Nik Millard, the cameraman I had been with in Goražde in Bosnia in 1992, and many other places after that. We had been to the edge of the suburbs, and seen some of the damage, but had never been deep into south Beirut, the narrow streets where Hezbollah had its offices which had taken the brunt of the Israeli attacks. The BBC was based in the centre of Beirut, which was untouched by the bombs.

Beirut is the Middle East's capital of elegance, where appearances count, even when there's a war on. In the press room at the Grand Serail, the imposing Ottoman building where the Lebanese government is run, one of the local TV reporters had chosen her outfit with care. She was dressed for war, but in a cute way. On top of a camouflage T-shirt she was wearing a tight brown shirt, which had epaulettes and a badge on the sleeve, military style but picked out in much more elegant spidery gold thread. Next to her a couple of middle-aged male technicians were not impressed, and went on playing cards, slapping each one down on the table. Outside, the shops and restaurants were closed, and the biggest explosions from the southern suburbs thundered around the empty streets, but as long as Israel continued to leave downtown Beirut alone, it was not dangerous. The suburbs were different.

Hezbollah had the whole of south Beirut under very tight control. Two-man teams, on motor scooters and usually armed only with walkie-talkies, were everywhere, looking out for strangers, checking anyone suspicious. The streets were almost empty, because most of the population of 500,000 people had fled, but the Hezbollah guys told anyone who was left to take cover if they heard Israeli drones or aircraft. One day we were checked by five separate patrols in fifteen minutes. Going to the most devastated part of south Beirut was another step towards danger. A lot of time had passed since Nik and I were in Goražde in 1992. We both had children; he had been to as many wars as me, and had his own near-death experiences, including one with a suicide bomber in Afghanistan only a couple of months before the Lebanon war. I don't think either of us doubted that we would go with Hezbollah into the middle of the ruins, but we both had our doubts about being there at all and wanted to get it over and done with as quickly as possible, before the Israelis decided to make the rubble bounce again. In the end, the story was pulling us in. Our fixer, a Lebanese journalist called Tima Khalil, at the same stage of the war-reporting cycle as Nik and I, decided to come too.

'Mate,' Nik said wearily, 'if you're at the party, you can't stay in the kitchen.'

It went fine. We got a strong story, it was nerve-wracking, but we were in and out in half an hour, and we all had a spring in our step when we got back to the office. We became regular visitors to the southern suburbs, trying to pick times of day – usually late afternoon – when Israel tended not to be doing any bombing. One afternoon I sat watching the comings and goings at a checkpoint as Tima pushed Hezbollah to let us through. The checkpoint was under an intact section of a flyover that bombs had taken a great bite out of about 100 yards away. One of the men, clean-shaven, looked as if he was in charge, giving orders to a colleague wearing webbing with ammunition pouches attached, and carrying a Kalashnikov. Other Hezbollah teams buzzed around, with their scooters and walkie-talkies. A row of shops was near them, most of them damaged by bombs, with smashed windows and bent shutters. Anyone could have walked straight in to the shops, and in most wars that I have been to plenty would have. But I did not see one looted shop anywhere in the southern suburbs.

An older man, with a maroon shirt and a pistol tucked into the waistband of his black trousers, came out of one of the partly destroyed buildings, and went over to talk with the men at the checkpoint. The Hezbollah men were very calm. A few minutes later there was a shift change. Another bearded man was dropped off from a motor scooter, took the webbing and the ammo pouches and the Kalashnikov from his colleague, who hopped on to the scooter and disappeared back up the road. A small black and white cat jumped on to an old sofa that they had arranged at the checkpoint, stretched, and settled itself down to sleep. The new man with the gun checked it, and looked sharp, keen and in control. The more time I spent in south Beirut the clearer it was that the bombs were not breaking Hezbollah.

On the last day of the war Hezbollah fired more rockets into Israel than on any other single day. Some of them came from places that Israel had bombed repeatedly. One of them was a complex of bunkers built into a bare hillside close to Naqura, on the coast very close to the western end of the border between Israel and Lebanon. A veteran official at UNIFIL, the UN force in south Lebanon, a local man who knew many Hezbollah fighters, told me that he had no idea that the bunkers were there until they started firing from them. 'How the hell did they build them without us or the Israelis seeing them?' he asked. 'They must have taken the concrete up a spoonful at a time.'

The war was fought live on television. Whenever the Israelis sent their thunderstom into the city, the first reaction of most journalists who happened to be in our building, where almost all the foreign broadcasters were based, was to rush to the window to see if there was any smoke rising. Actually, it was much easier to turn to one of the news channels, local ones as well as the international Arab giants, Al-Jazeera and Al-Arabiya. They all had cameras on a hill overlooking the southern suburbs, staffed twenty-four hours, and would cut to the live smoke and flame in seconds, at the press of a button. The BBC, CNN and Sky often did too.

The psychological effect of weapons, air strikes and rocket attacks is magnified by the fact that these days, you can experience the horror they produce in your sitting room, as it happens, or very soon afterwards even if you are thousands of miles from the war. Just one of Nik Millard's shots, a big close-up of the bandaged face of Huweida Khaled, an eight-year-old girl whose father and two brothers had been killed, hit one viewer, John Sentamu, the Anglican Archbishop of York, so hard he said it was like a bayonet in his heart. He cancelled his holiday, shaved his head as a symbol of atonement and spent a week fasting and praying, sleeping in a tent at his cathedral. Nik filmed Huweida in Beirut University Hospital. As usual some of the war's strongest pictures were coming from the weakest people, and as usual, to get the raw material for reporting a war, we fed on their misfortunes. Without them, we would not have had a story. Their worst days were our good days, as they always are in wars.

But should reporters stay away from the weak and vulnerable? Would it be more gutsy to stick with the fighting men, who know what they are getting into? The problem with that it is not how modern wars work. Soldiers still die, but wars now are more than ever about killing civilians. The historian Eric Hobsbawm wrote that civilians have suffered more since the end of the Cold War 'because most military operations since then have been conducted not by conscript armies, but by small bodies of regular or irregular troops, in many cases operating high-technology weapons and protected against the risk of casualties'. Hobsbawm pointed out that only 5 per cent of those who died in the First World War were civilians; in the Second World War it was 66 per cent. He estimated that '80 to 90 per cent of those affected by war today are civilians'. In the war in Lebanon in 2006, 1,109 civilians were killed, according to the government in Beirut. Hezbollah says that it lost 55 fighters (though Israel claims to have killed ten times as many). Israel lost 116 soldiers and 43 civilians, according to figures from the army and the police. The civilian deaths were reduced in Israel because half a million people could get out of range of Hezbollah's rockets by leaving their homes in the firing line in the north. Most of those who stayed had access to shelters. Nearly one million Lebanese, around a quarter of the population, were displaced by the war, but because Israel's reach was wider and its firepower vastly greater, getting out of the firing line was much harder.

It is vital for journalists to concentrate on what is happening to civilians. Both Israel and Hezbollah broke the laws of war repeatedly, according to Human Rights Watch. If we want to produce an accurate picture of modern war, journalists have to gather first-hand accounts of what the military forces of countries and groups like Hezbollah – so-called non-state actors – do to civilians.

When I started out as a reporter I was cynical about the importance of upholding the sort of principles of behaviour that are enshrined in international humanitarian law. I thought all that mattered were the realities of power, however unpleasant, and that the strong would always do what they wanted to the weak. My views changed because of all the years I have spent watching what happens when the weak are crushed by the strong. Even the strongest need to know that there are limits, and there should be costs attached to ignoring them. International humanitarian law is also an excellent template for journalists to use when they are trying to assess what is happening in a war. It provides a framework, and a checklist, that can turn impressionistic stories into forensic journalism.

Hezbollah's war would not have been possible without the financial and military support of Iran and Syria. Israel's war in Lebanon would not have been possible without military aid and diplomatic cover at the United Nations from the United States, which in turn had vital support in the Security Council from Britain. The viewers of our broadcasts in Britain, and in other countries, have the right to hear what is being done in their name, good or bad.

The war in Lebanon and northern Israel in the summer of 2006 was a classic modern conflict. On one side was a state, a major military power, and on the other a non-state actor, a guerrilla organisation. Civilians were first in the firing line. Almost everything that happened in Beirut, Israel, and within range of the journalists at the Tyre Rest House was carried live on television or replayed on videotape very soon after it took place. What happened on the battlefield was very important; but defeat and victory have been measured by people's perceptions, which were based on what people saw on television. The broadcasters are messengers, but they also have to be responsible enough to recognise that what they do affects those perceptions. Instant news reduces the time that leaders have, especially in Western-style democracies, to take decisions, and increases the pressures of running a war, which are already severe.

Non-stop information also makes managing the endgame very difficult. Israelis who told pollsters when the ceasefire came that they believed their country did not achieve its war aims did not do so because TV told them to say it, but because they saw on TV that Hezbollah was able to fire rockets into Israel until the end of the war, and then soldiers coming back from Lebanon told them what it was really like. For the same reason, Arabs now believe that Hezbollah's leader Hassan Nasrallah is the biggest hero their people have produced since Gamal Abdul Nasser faced down Britain, France and Israel over Suez in 1956.

It was the sixth major war between Israel and one of its Arab neighbours, and it shook the fragile way that power is shared in Lebanon, reviving old fears of a new civil war. Hezbollah gave Israel its biggest military test in more than thirty years; Israeli military and political leaders had a bad war. When it started they said their aim was to destroy Hezbollah's military power and to rescue the two soldiers whose capture by Hezbollah in a cross-border raid sparked it all off. Neither objective was achieved. Worse still, from Israel's point of view, is that what it calls the deterrent power of its army was damaged. By that they mean its ability to take on any combination of enemies and, in short order, beat them soundly. Many Israelis believed that the war threatened the existence of their state, because of Hezbollah's connections with Iran, their rival as the superpower of the region. Israel will not let that rest; throughout its history it has always taken action to restore the deterrent power of the IDF if it thinks it is waning, usually by rearming, retraining and then giving the army a chance to show what it can do. Since Hezbollah also has unfinished business with Israel, there's a strong chance that round two will happen sooner or later.

Every Middle East crisis is dangerous because they are all hardwired into each other, and they all feed back into the central conflict between Israel and the Palestinians. For millions of Arabs, Hezbollah was taking revenge for the humiliation and rage they feel about the fate of the Palestinians and the invasion of Iraq. Israelis who were feeling safer from suicide bombers as their separation barrier with the Palestinians was reaching completion have had a graphic lesson in what rockets can do, and so have Palestinian militants. Israel is keeping up severe military pressure in Gaza, where the Palestinians have crude rockets that are nothing like as powerful as Hezbollah's.

The pro-Western Sunni rulers of Saudi Arabia, Egypt and Jordan are nervous about the success of the Shias in Hezbollah, and the popularity of Hassan Nasrallah in their countries. Just before the ceasefire King Abdullah of Jordan, perhaps the best Arab friend that Western governments have, told the BBC that 'the endgame is very dim. I can't read the political map of the Middle East any more because I just see so many heavy clouds that are over our shoulders at this stage, and I really feel and fear for the future of the Middle East.' The Saudis were publicly very critical of Hezbollah's 'adventurism' at first. But as their people, Sunnis as well as the Shia minority, watched the war on television, outraged by Israel's actions and delighted by Hezbollah's, they were forced to rally behind them, accepting Nasrallah's view that Israeli soldiers have to leave Lebanon before anything else can happen.

Iran will be more than satisfied with the performance of Hezbollah, which it regards as a strategic weapon against Israel. Iran is sitting happily on a mountain of oil money, much more secure since 2001, as the Americans have obligingly removed its two biggest enemies, the Taliban in Afghanistan and Saddam Hussein in Iraq. Better still for Tehran, the new arrangements in Iraq have delivered power into the hands of the majority group, the Shias, Iran's co-religionists.

The Americans believed that everything that happened in Lebanon in the summer was part of their 'war on terror', and for Washington, it did not go well. There were surreal moments, not just the US Secretary of State's Condoleezza Rice's explanation that Washington opposed a simple ceasefire resolution at the United Nations because the war represented 'the birth pangs of a new Middle East'. At the US Embassy compound in Beirut, which is guarded by a private army of Lebanese security men, they laid out a small consignment of medical supplies – part, they said, of a much bigger shipment – and wrapped them in a couple of huge stars and stripes flags. The Ambassador was driven the short distance from his office in his armoured limousine – his close protection detail wanted to limit his exposure in the open air even inside his own embassy – and proudly allowed himself to be photographed next to the Bush administration's contribution to the alleviation of Lebanon's humanitarian crisis. His security people manned watchtowers in which they had set up heavy machine-guns. In the distance, smoke came from fires started by Israeli bombs in south Beirut. The Ambassador seemed surprised when he was asked whether there was any conflict between donating bandages and medical kits to Lebanon at the same time that Washington was expediting the delivery of satellite-guided bombs to Israel.

He may have not seen a conflict, but plenty of Arabs did, and concluded that if this was America's new Middle East, they would rather go without. America's unconditional support of Israel has taken it down to a new low point in Arab esteem, and once again its lack of diplomatic leverage in the Middle East has been demonstrated. Backing Israeli action against the Shiites of Hezbollah will also cause it more trouble in Shia communities in Iraq.

The war has left the outlook in the region more uncertain than ever. The gap between Israel, the American-led West and Arab and Islamic countries is widening, without a doubt. But they are being forced apart for reasons that are complicated and subtle as well as violent and dangerous. There are easy-to-propagate theories on either side about why it is happening. Israel, the Bush administration, Tony Blair and others believe that they are locked in a life-and-death struggle with Islamist extremism – and that Hezbollah and its co-sponsors in Iran and even secular Syria are right at the centre of it. Their Manichean view of the Middle East has its reflection inside what Mr Blair calls the 'arc of extremism', among those who believe that they are in a fight with new Western crusaders who must be confronted with violence.

If both sides are right about the view through the arrow-slits of their respective stockades, then the battle between capitalism and communism has been succeeded by another terrible struggle, and we all have to get ready for a very long war. But what if they are wrong? I came into journalism as the world that was created by 1945 was crumbling. Most of the reporting I have done over more than twenty years since then has been about what replaces the old order. By the end of the Cold War, both camps were realising that many of their assessments of the other side's strengths and intentions had been wrong; what had seemed to be defensive actions had been read by the other side as aggressive, creating misperceptions that deepened the conflict. The trouble then was caused by simple catchphrases, a failure to understand the motivations of the people on the other side of the divide, unreliable intelligence, and by those who had a stake in prolonging the confrontation. Is the same thing happening again? Are the current crop of leaders, in the mainly Christian West and the Arab and Islamic East, making the same mistakes? The ironic and tragic lesson of the Cold War is that leaders who have the erroneous belief that they are in an elemental struggle about the future can end up creating the nightmares from which they think they are protecting us.

I had been hoping not to go to any more wars. But since the middle of 2005 I have been the Middle East Editor of the BBC. My brief is to try to explain the big themes, and I travel to the Middle East very often. Unfortunately, you can't be a foreign correspondent in my part of the world, at this time in its history, without accepting a certain amount of risk. But what I am not any more is a front-line reporter, which is a worthwhile, vital but very different business from what I do now. For me, the risks of heading straight for the action are no longer worth it. Too many of the friends and colleagues I used to make those journeys with are dead. I am still a journalist but I do not plan to walk into any more besieged cities, or deal with drunken, trigger-happy soldiers at checkpoints, or lie in the snow listening to explosions and thinking that they are about to kill me. I don't think there will be any Mostars or Groznys, but journalism in the Middle East is not a 9-to-5 job. I used to go to the most dangerous parts of wars to be where things were happening, to do the story, to find out the truth, to live on the edge and because a lot of the time it was fun. I miss the camaraderie and the laughs, the sense of mission and the feeling of belonging to a small and exclusive society. A lot of the passion I used to have for news reporting has gone, left behind on the graves of my dead friends and of the thousands that I did not know whose deaths I reported. But I am still looking for the story, though in a different way, and I am wiser and happy that the old passion has been replaced by something better, which is the knowledge that I want to be part of my children's lives for a long time. In the end, you have to choose.

Acknowledgements

To all the friends and colleagues I have worked with on the road and in London.

To Jasmina Alibegovic, brave, gracious and funny throughout the siege of Sarajevo. To Jimmy Michel and Boaz Paldi, for introducing me to the land between the River Jordan and the Mediterranean. To Mohammed Darweesh and Saddoun al-Janabi in Baghdad.

To the editors who trusted me at important moments, especially John Mahoney, Chris Cramer, Richard Tait, Ian Hargreaves, Steve Selman, Kevin Bakhurst, Malcolm Downing, Jonathan Baker, Jon Williams, Paul Woolwich, Fran Unsworth and Helen Boaden.

To Jane Logan, Simon Wilson, Rubi Gat, Jeannie Assad and Keren Pakes, who read the chapter about Jerusalem and told me where I was going wrong. Any mistakes they failed to spot are my fault. That applies to the rest of the book too.

To the people in studio TC7 at Television Centre, especially in make-up and the green room, who put up with me for two years.

To Chuck Tayman, Nik Millard, Nick Marcus, Dan Butcher and the BBC Media Exchange for invaluable help with photographs and video images. Thanks to Tamzin Jaggers for tracking down the recordings my father made in Aberfan in 1966.

To my agent Julian Alexander and my editor at Simon & Schuster, Andrew Gordon, both patient men.

Information about news coverage in the Falkland Islands came from *Fog of War* by Derrick Mercer, Geoff Mungham and Kevin Williams (Heinemann, 1987).

The biggest thanks are to my brothers and sisters; my parents, who gave me everything; and to the loves of my life, Julia, Mattie and Boatie.

RÉPUBLIQUE ALGÉRIENNE
DÉMOCRATIQUE ET POPULAIRE
الجمهورية الجزائرية الديمقراطية الشعبية

VISA N° 2303/97
رقم التأشيرة

N° du PASSEPORT 74005840/
رقم الجواز

NOMBRE D'ENTREES UNE
عدد الدخول

DUREE de SEJOUR QUINZE JOUR
مدة الإقامة

MOTIF de SEJOUR JOURNALISME
سبب الإقامة

Date Limite d'Utilisation
انتهاء مدة الاستعمال
30 OCT 97

TAXE PERÇUE 2000A
ثمن التأشيرة

في
A Al...

Republika Bosna i Hercegovina
FEDERACIJA BOSNE I HERCEGOVINE
VLADA

PRESS

Ime/Name: JEREMY

Prezime/Surname: BOWEN

Zemlja/Country: ENGLESKA

Br.pasoša/Passport no. 327935

Agencija/Agency: BBC NEWS

22   VISAS

E 17 NOV. 1989
RIO. AEREA EL SALVADOR, C.A.

S 25 NOV. 1989
MIO. AEREA EL SALVADOR, C.A.

CONSULADO GENERAL
EL SALVADOR
EN
WASHINGTON, D.

VISA NO. 28
Turismo Gratuita

Buena para ingresar a la R
El Salvador por cualquier, v
necer en ella por

Válida por un periodo de

Fecha: NOV 1

الجمهورية اللبنانية
وزارة الداخلية
ترخيص لتغطية الانتخابات النيا

٢٥٤٦
الرقم المتسلسل

جيريمي بوين
الاسم والشهرة

BBC News
اسم المؤسسة

مراسل
الصفة

العقيد خليل ابي راشد

ISHTAR   ISHTAR

IRAQ 10   IRAQ 1
دينار   دينار